THE EXTRAORDINARY
ODYSSEY
OF A GREAT WRITER

At an age when most men are content
simply to remember the past, John Steinbeck set off on a remarkable journey
across America. Ultimately it took him
through almost forty states: from Long
Island to Maine, through the Middle West
to Chicago, onward by way of Minnesota,
North Dakota, Montana and Idaho to
Seattle, south to San Francisco and his
birthplace, Salinas, eastward to New Mexico, Arizona and Texas, on to New Orleans, Alabama, Virginia, Pennsylvania
and finally to New Jersey and New York.
His account of this extraordinary odyssey
is one of the most profound and revealing
documents of our time.

"A RELAXED, SAD, FUNNY AND
GLORIOUS TRIP. HIS BEST BOOK."

TULSA WORLD

"A New Vision

"One of the best books John Steinbeck has ever written. Perceptive, revealing and completely delightful . . . A vibrant, thoughtful and remarkably illuminating panorama of our land and its people. A book to savor slowly, to consider carefully and to enjoy thoroughly."

BOSTON HERALD

"Trenchant observations about life, glowing descriptions of nature, wonderful revealing scraps of conversation, penetrating insight into American mores, searching thoughts on loneliness, all recorded by a master of the writing craft."

CHICAGO TRIBUNE

"Unlike any other Steinbeck."

NEW YORK HERALD TRIBUNE

---

of America"

"He captured vividly the country's uprooted restlessness, the melodramatic contrasts of its scenery, the growing standardization, the enormous waste, the horror of racial tension. Intimate, wise, charming, and perceptive."

BOOK-OF-THE-MONTH CLUB NEWS

"A reflective, loving, gentle book, filled with wisdom."

OAKLAND TRIBUNE

"Delightful, leisurely reading, full of the sights and sounds of the land and rich with color and salty humor."

MIAMI HERALD

Books by John Steinbeck

Published by Bantam Books, Inc.

John Steinbeck

Travels with Charley

IN SEARCH OF AMERICA

BANTAM BOOKS · TORONTO · NEW YORK · LONDON

TRAVELS WITH CHARLEY

*A Bantam Book / published by arrangement with
The Viking Press, Inc.*

PRINTING HISTORY

Viking edition published July 1962

2nd printing ...... July 1962	7th printing . November 1962
3rd printing .... August 1962	8th printing . November 1962
4th printing .. October 1962	9th printing . December 1962
5th printing .. October 1962	10th printing . December 1962
6th printing . November 1962	11th printing ....January 1963

Book-of-the-Month Club selection August 1962

Portions of this book appeared serially in HOLIDAY
under the title "In Quest of America"

Bantam edition published July 1963

2nd printing ...... July 1963	11th printing ..... April 1964
3rd printing ...... July 1963	12th printing ...... June 1964
4th printing ...... July 1963	13th printing ...... July 1964
5th printing .... August 1963	14th printing .. October 1964
6th printing September 1963	15th printing .. February 1965
7th printing ....October 1963	16th printing....... July 1965
8th printing . November 1963	17th printing . November 1965
9th printing .. February 1964	18th printing .. February 1966
10th printing .... March 1964	19th printing ...... July 1966

20th printing
21st printing
22nd printing
23rd printing

*Bantam Books are published by Bantam Books, Inc., a subsidiary
of Grosset & Dunlap, Inc. Its trade-mark, consisting of the words
"Bantam Books" and the portrayal of a bantam, is registered in the
United States Patent Office and in other countries. Marca Registrada.
Bantam Books, Inc., 271 Madison Avenue, New York, N. Y. 10016.*

PRINTED IN THE UNITED STATES OF AMERICA

This book is dedicated to Harold Guinzburg with respect born of an association and affection that just growed.

—JOHN STEINBECK

PART ONE

WHEN I WAS VERY YOUNG AND THE URGE TO be someplace else was on me, I was assured by mature people that maturity would cure this itch. When years described me as mature, the remedy prescribed was middle age. In middle age I was assured that greater age would calm my fever and now that I am fifty-eight perhaps senility will do the job. Nothing has worked. Four hoarse blasts of a ship's whistle still raise the hair on my neck and set my feet to tapping. The sound of a jet, an engine warming up, even the clopping of shod hooves on pavement brings on the ancient shudder, the dry mouth and vacant eye, the hot palms and the churn of stomach high up under the rib cage. In other words, I don't improve; in further words, once a bum always a bum. I fear the disease is incurable. I set this matter down not to instruct others but to inform myself.

When the virus of restlessness begins to take possession of a wayward man, and the road away from Here seems broad and straight and sweet, the victim must first find in himself a good and sufficient reason for going. This to the practical bum is not difficult. He has a built-in garden of reasons to choose from. Next he must plan his trip in time and space, choose a direction and a destination. And last he must implement the journey. How to go, what to take, how long to stay. This part of the process is invariable and immortal. I set it down only so that newcomers to bumdom, like teen-agers in new-hatched sin, will not think they invented it.

Once a journey is designed, equipped, and put in process, a new factor enters and takes over. A trip, a safari, an exploration, is an entity, different from all other journeys. It has personality, temperament, individuality, uniqueness. A journey is a person in itself; no two are alike. And all plans, safeguards, policing, and coercion are fruitless. We find after years of struggle that we do not take a trip; a trip takes us. Tour masters, schedules, reservations, brass-bound and inevitable, dash themselves to wreckage on the personality of the trip. Only when this is recognized can the blown-in-the-glass bum relax and go along with it. Only then do the frustrations fall away. In this a journey is like marriage. The certain way to be wrong is to think you control it. I feel better now, having said this, although only those who have experienced it will understand it.

My plan was clear, concise, and reasonable, I think. For many years I have traveled in many parts of the world. In America I live in New York, or dip into Chicago or San Francisco. But New York is no more America than Paris is France or London is England. Thus I discovered that I did not know my own country. I, an American writer, writing about America, was working from memory, and the memory is at best a faulty, warpy reservoir. I had not heard the speech of America, smelled the grass and trees and sewage, seen its hills and water, its color and quality of light. I knew the changes only from books and newspapers. But more than this, I had not felt the country for twenty-five years. In short, I was writing of something I did not know about, and it seems to me that in a so-called writer this is criminal. My memories were distorted by twenty-five intervening years.

Once I traveled about in an old bakery wagon, double-doored rattler with a mattress on its floor. I stopped where people stopped or gathered, I listened and looked and felt, and in the process had a picture of my country the accuracy of which was impaired only by my own shortcomings.

So it was that I determined to look again, to try to rediscover this monster land. Otherwise, in writing, I could not tell the small diagnostic truths which are the foundations of the larger truth. One sharp difficulty presented itself. In the intervening twenty-five years my name had become reasonably well known. And it has been my experience that when people have heard of you, favorably or not, they change; they become, through shyness or the other qualities that publicity inspires, something they are not under ordinary circumstances. This being so, my trip demanded that I leave my name and my identity at home. I had to be peripatetic eyes and ears, a kind of moving gelatin plate. I could not sign hotel registers, meet people I knew, interview others, or even ask searching questions. Furthermore, two or more people disturb the ecologic complex of an area. I had to go alone and I had to be self-contained, a kind of casual turtle carrying his house on his back.

With all this in mind I wrote to the head office of a great corporation which manufactures trucks. I specified my purpose and my needs. I wanted a three-quarter-ton pick-up truck, capable of going anywhere under possibly rigorous conditions, and on this truck I wanted a little house built like the cabin of a small boat. A trailer is difficult to maneuver on mountain roads, is impossible and often illegal to park, and is subject to many restrictions. In due time, specifications came through, for a tough, fast, comfortable vehicle, mounting a camper top—a little house with double bed, a four-burner stove, a heater, refrigerator and lights operating on butane, a chemical toilet, closet space, storage space, windows screened against insects—exactly what I wanted. It was delivered in the summer to my little fishing place at Sag Harbor near the end of Long Island. Although I didn't want to start before Labor Day, when the nation settles back to normal living, I did want to get used to my turtle shell, to equip it and learn it. It arrived in August, a beautiful thing, powerful and yet lithe. It was almost as easy to handle as a passenger car. And because my planned trip had aroused some satiric remarks among my friends, I named it Rocinante, which you will remember was the name of Don Quixote's horse.

Since I made no secret of my project, a number of controversies arose among my friends and advisers. (A projected journey spawns advisers in schools.) I was told that since my photograph was as widely distributed as my publisher could make it, I would find it impossible to move about without being recognized. Let me say in advance that in over ten thousand miles, in thirty-four states, I was not recognized even once. I believe that people identify things only in context. Even those people who might have known me against a background I am supposed to have, in no case identified me in Rocinante.

I was advised that the name Rocinante painted on the side of my truck in sixteenth-century Spanish script would cause curiosity and inquiry in some places. I do not know how many people recognized the name, but surely no one ever asked about it.

Next, I was told that a stranger's purpose in moving about the country might cause inquiry or even suspicion. For this reason I racked a shotgun, two rifles, and a couple of fishing rods in my truck, for it is my experience that if a man is going hunting or fishing his purpose is understood and even applauded. Actually, my hunting days are over. I no longer kill or catch anything I cannot get into a frying pan; I am too old for sport killing. This stage setting turned out to be unnecessary.

It was said that my New York license plates would arouse interest and perhaps questions, since they were the only outward identifying marks I had. And so they did—perhaps twenty or thirty times in the whole trip. But such contacts followed an invariable pattern, somewhat as follows:

Local man: "New York, huh?"

Me: "Yep."

Local man: "I was there in nineteen thirty-eight —or was it thirty-nine? Alice, was it thirty-eight or thirty-nine we went to New York?"

Alice: "It was thirty-six. I remember because it was the year Alfred died."

Local man: "Anyway, I hated it. Wouldn't live there if you paid me."

There was some genuine worry about my traveling alone, open to attack, robbery, assault. It is well known that our roads are dangerous. And here I admit I had senseless qualms. It is some years since I have been alone, nameless, friendless, without any of the safety one gets from family, friends, and accomplices. There is no reality in the danger. It's just a very lonely, helpless feeling at first—a kind of desolate feeling. For this reason I took one companion on my journey—an old French gentleman poodle known as Charley. Actually his name is Charles le Chien. He was born in Bercy on the outskirts of Paris and trained in France, and while he knows a little poodle-English, he responds quickly only to commands in French. Otherwise he has to translate, and that slows him down. He is a very big poodle, of a color called *bleu,* and he is blue when he is clean. Charley is a born diplomat. He prefers negotiation to fighting, and properly so, since he is very bad at fighting. Only once in his ten years has he been in trouble—when he met a dog who refused to negotiate. Charley lost a piece of his right ear that time. But he is a good watch dog— has a roar like a lion, designed to conceal from night-wandering strangers the fact that he couldn't bite his way out of a *cornet de papier*. He is a good friend and traveling companion, and would rather travel about than anything he can imagine. If he occurs at length in this account, it is because he contributed much to the trip. A dog, particularly an exotic like Charley, is a bond between strangers. Many conversations en route began with "What degree of a dog is that?"

The techniques of opening conversation are universal. I knew long ago and rediscovered that the best way to attract attention, help, and conversation is to be lost. A man who seeing his mother starving to death on a path kicks her in the stomach to clear the way, will cheerfully devote several hours of his time giving wrong directions to a total stranger who claims to be lost.

UNDER THE BIG OAK TREES OF MY PLACE AT Sag Harbor sat Rocinante, handsome and self-contained, and neighbors came to visit, some neighbors we didn't even know we had. I saw in their eyes something I was to see over and over in every part of the nation—a burning desire to go, to move, to get under way, anyplace, away from any Here. They spoke quietly of how they wanted to go someday, to move about, free and unanchored, not toward something but away from something. I saw this look and heard this yearning everywhere in every state I visited. Nearly every American hungers to move. One small boy about thirteen years old came back every day. He stood apart shyly and looked at Rocinante; he peered in the door, even lay on the ground and studied the heavy-duty springs. He was a silent, ubiquitous small boy. He even came at night to stare at Rocinante. After a week he could stand it no longer. His words wrestled their way hell-bent through his shyness. He said, "If you'll take me with you, why, I'll do anything. I'll cook, I'll wash all the dishes, and do all the work and I'll take care of you."

Unfortunately for me I knew his longing. "I wish I could," I said. "But the school board and your parents and lots of others say I can't."

"I'll do anything," he said. And I believe he would. I don't think he ever gave up until I drove away without him. He had the dream I've had all my life, and there is no cure.

Equipping Rocinante was a long and pleasant process. I took far too many things, but I didn't know what I would find. Tools for emergency, tow lines, a small block and tackle, a trenching tool and crowbar, tools for making and fixing and improvising. Then there were emergency foods. I would be late in the northwest and caught by snow. I prepared for at least a week of emergency. Water was easy; Rocinante carried a thirty-gallon tank.

I thought I might do some writing along the way, perhaps essays, surely notes, certainly letters. I took paper, carbon, typewriter, pencils, notebooks, and not only those but dictionaries, a compact encyclopedia, and a dozen other reference books, heavy ones. I suppose our capacity for self-delusion is boundless. I knew very well that I rarely make notes, and if I do I either lose them or can't read them. I also knew from thirty years of my profession that I cannot write hot on an event. It has to ferment. I must do what a friend calls "mule it over" for a time before it goes down. And in spite of this self-knowledge I equipped Rocinante with enough writing material to take care of ten volumes. Also I laid in a hundred and fifty pounds of those books one hasn't got around to reading—and of course those are the books one isn't ever going to get around to reading. Canned goods, shotgun shells, rifle cartridges, tool boxes, and far too many clothes, blankets and pillows, and many too many shoes and boots, padded nylon sub-zero underwear, plastic dishes and cups and a plastic dishpan, a spare tank of bottled gas. The overloaded springs sighed and settled lower and lower. I judge now that I carried about four times too much of everything.

Now, Charley is a mind-reading dog. There have been many trips in his lifetime, and often he has to be left at home. He knows we are going long before the suitcases come out, and he paces and worries and whines and goes into a state of mild hysteria, old as he is. During the weeks of preparation he was underfoot the whole time and made a damned nuisance of himself. He took to hiding in the truck, creeping in and trying to make himself look small.

Labor Day approached, the day of truth when millions of kids would be back in school and tens of millions of parents would be off the highways. I was prepared to set out as soon after that as possible. And about that time hurricane Donna was reported tromping her way out of the Caribbean in our direction. On Long Island's tip, we have had enough of that to be highly respectful. With a hurricane approaching we prepare to stand a siege. Our little bay is fairly well protected, but not that well. As Donna crept toward us I filled the kerosene lamps, activated the hand pump to the well, and tied down everything movable. I have a twenty-two-foot cabin boat, the *Fayre Eleyne*. I battened her down and took her to the middle of the bay, put down a huge old-fashioned hook anchor and half-inch chain, and moored her with a long swing. With that rig she could ride a hundred-and-fifty-mile wind unless her bow pulled out.

Donna sneaked on. We brought out a battery radio for reports, since the power would go off if Donna struck. But there was one added worry—Rocinante, sitting among the trees. In a waking nightmare I saw a tree crash down on the truck and crush her like a bug. I placed her away from a possible direct fall, but that didn't mean that the whole top of a tree might not fly fifty feet through the air and smash her.

By early morning we knew by radio that we were going to get it, and by ten o'clock we heard that the eye would pass over us and that it would reach us at 1:07—some exact time like that. Our bay was quiet, without a ripple, but the water was still dark and the *Fayre Eleyne* rode daintily slack against her mooring.

Our bay is better protected than most, so that many small craft came cruising in for mooring. And I saw with fear that many of their owners didn't know how to moor. Finally two boats, pretty things, came in, one towing the other. A light anchor went down and they were left, the bow of one tethered to the stern of the other and both within the swing of the *Fayre Eleyne*. I took a megaphone to the end of my pier and tried to protest against this foolishness, but the owners either did not hear or did not know or did not care.

The wind struck on the moment we were told it would, and ripped the water like a black sheet. It hammered like a fist. The whole top of an oak tree crashed down, grazing the cottage where we watched. The next gust stove one of the big windows in. I forced it back and drove wedges in top and bottom with a hand ax. Electric power and telephones went out with the first blast, as we knew they must. And eight-foot tides were predicted. We watched the wind rip at earth and sea like a surging pack of terriers. The trees plunged and bent like grasses, and the whipped water raised a cream of foam. A boat broke loose and tobogganed up on the shore, and then another. Houses built in the benign spring and early summer took waves in their second-story windows. Our cottage is on a little hill thirty feet above sea level. But the rising tide washed over my high pier. As the wind changed direction I moved Rocinante to keep her always to leeward of our big oaks. The *Fayre Eleyne* rode gallantly, swinging like a weather vane away from the changing wind.

The boats which had been tethered one to the other had fouled up by now, the tow line under propeller and rudder and the two hulls bashing and scraping together. Another craft had dragged its anchor and gone ashore on a mud bank.

Charley dog has no nerves. Gunfire or thunder, explosions or high winds leave him utterly unconcerned. In the midst of the howling storm, he found a warm place under a table and went to sleep.

The wind stopped as suddenly as it had begun, and although the waves continued out of rhythm they were not wind-tattered, and the tide rose higher and higher. All the piers around our little bay had disappeared under water, and only their piles or hand rails showed. The silence was like a rushing sound. The radio told us we were in the eye of Donna, the still and frightening calm in the middle of the revolving storm. I don't know how long the calm lasted. It seemed a long time of waiting. And then the other side struck us, the wind from the opposite direction. The *Fayre Eleyne* swung sweetly around and put her bow into the wind. But the two lashed boats dragged anchor, swarmed down on *Fayre Eleyne,* and bracketed her. She was dragged fighting and protesting downwind and forced against a neighboring pier, and we could hear her hull crying against the oaken piles. The wind registered over ninety-five miles now.

I found myself running, fighting the wind around the head of the bay toward the pier where the boats were breaking up. I think my wife, for whom the *Fayre Eleyne* is named, ran after me, shouting orders for me to stop. The floor of the pier was four feet under water, but piles stuck up and offered hand-holds. I worked my way out little by little up to my breast pockets, the shore-driven wind slapping water in my mouth. My boat cried and whined against the piles, and plunged like a frightened calf. Then I jumped and fumbled my way aboard her. For the first time in my life I had a knife when I needed it. The bracketing wayward boats were pushing *Eleyne* against the pier. I cut anchor line and tow line and kicked them free, and they blew ashore on the mudbank. But *Eleyne*'s anchor chain was intact, and that great old mud hook was still down, a hundred pounds of iron with spear-shaped flukes wide as a shovel.

Eleyne's engine is not always obedient, but this day it started at a touch. I hung on, standing on the deck, reaching inboard for wheel and throttle and clutch with my left hand. And that boat tried to help—I suppose she was that scared. I edged her out and worked up the anchor chain with my right hand. Under ordinary conditions I can barely pull that anchor with both hands in a calm. But everything went right this time. I edged over the hook and it tipped up and freed its spades. Then I lifted it clear of the bottom and nosed into the wind and gave it throttle and we headed into that goddamn wind and gained on it. It was as though we pushed our way through thick porridge. A hundred yards offshore I let the hook go and it plunged down and grabbed bottom, and the *Fayre Eleyne* straightened and raised her bow and seemed to sigh with relief.

Well, there I was, a hundred yards offshore with Donna baying over me like a pack of white-whiskered hounds. No skiff could possibly weather it for a minute. I saw a piece of branch go skidding by and simply jumped in after it. There was no danger. If I could keep my head up I had to blow ashore, but I admit the half-Wellington rubber boots I wore got pretty heavy. It couldn't have been more than three minutes before I grounded and that other Fayre Eleyne and a neighbor pulled me out. It was only then that I began to shake all over, but looking out and seeing our little boat riding well and safely was nice. I must have strained something pulling that anchor with one hand, because I needed a little help home; a tumbler of whisky on the kitchen table was some help too. I've tried since to raise that anchor with one hand and I can't do it.

The wind died quickly and left us to wreckage— power lines down, and no telephone for a week. But Rocinante was not damaged at all.

PART TWO

IN LONG-RANGE PLANNING FOR A TRIP, I think there is a private conviction that it won't happen. As the day approached, my warm bed and comfortable house grew increasingly desirable and my dear wife incalculably precious. To give these up for three months for the terrors of the uncomfortable and unknown seemed crazy. I didn't want to go. Something had to happen to forbid my going, but it didn't. I could get sick, of course, but that was one of my main but secret reasons for going at all. During the previous winter I had become rather seriously ill with one of those carefully named difficulties which are the whispers of approaching age. When I came out of it I received the usual lecture about slowing up, losing weight, limiting the cholesterol intake. It happens to many men, and I think doctors have memorized the litany. It had happened to so many of my friends. The lecture ends, "Slow down. You're not as young as you once were." And I had seen so many begin to pack their lives in cotton wool, smother their impulses, hood their passions, and gradually retire from their manhood into a kind of spiritual and physical semi-invalidism. In this they are encouraged by wives and relatives, and it's such a sweet trap.

Who doesn't like to be a center for concern? A kind of second childhood falls on so many men. They trade their violence for the promise of a small increase of life span. In effect, the head of the house becomes the youngest child. And I have searched myself for this possibility with a kind of horror. For I have always lived violently, drunk hugely, eaten too much or not at all, slept around the clock or missed two nights of sleeping, worked too hard and too long in glory, or slobbed for a time in utter laziness. I've lifted, pulled, chopped, climbed, made love with joy and taken my hangovers as a consequence, not as a punishment. I did not want to surrender fierceness for a small gain in yardage. My wife married a man; I saw no reason why she should inherit a baby. I knew that ten or twelve thousand miles driving a truck, alone and unattended, over every kind of road, would be hard work, but to me it represented the antidote for the poison of the professional sick man. And in my own life I am not willing to trade quality for quantity. If this projected journey should prove too much then it was time to go anyway. I see too many men delay their exits with a sickly, slow reluctance to leave the stage. It's bad theater as well as bad living. I am very fortunate in having a wife who likes being a woman, which means that she likes men, not elderly babies. Although this last foundation for the journey was never discussed, I am sure she understood it.

The morning came, a bright one with the tawny look of autumn in the sunlight. My wife and I parted very quickly, since both of us hate good-bys, and neither one of us wanted to be left when the other had gone. She gunned her motor and exploded away for New York and I, with Charley beside me, drove Rocinante to the Shelter Island Ferry, and then to a second ferry to Greenport and a third from Orient Point to the coast of Connecticut, across Long Island Sound, for I wanted to avoid New York traffic and get well on my way. And I confess to a feeling of gray desolation.

On the ferry deck the sun was sharp and the coast of the mainland only an hour away. A lovely sloop stood away from us, her genoa set like a curving scarf, and all the coastal craft trudged up the Sound or wallowed heavily toward New York. Then a submarine slipped to the surface half a mile away, and the day lost part of its brightness. Farther away another dark creature slashed through the water, and another; of course they are based in New London, and this is their home. And perhaps they are keeping the world's peace with this venom. I wish I could like submarines, for then I might find them beautiful, but they are designed for destruction, and while they may explore and chart the sea bottom, and draw new trade lines under the Arctic ice, their main purpose is threat. And I remember too well crossing the Atlantic on a troop ship and knowing that somewhere on the way the dark things lurked searching for us with their single-stalk eyes. Somehow the light goes bleak for me when I see them and remember burned men pulled from the oil-slicked sea. And now submarines are armed with mass murder, our silly, only way of deterring mass murder.

Only a few people stood in the wind on the top deck of the clanking iron ferry boat. A young man in a trench coat, with cornsilk hair and delphinium eyes red-edged by the dull wind, turned to me and then pointed. "That's the new one," he said. "She can stay down three months."

"How can you tell them?"

"I know them. I'm on them."

"Atomic?"

"Not yet, but I've got an uncle on one, and maybe pretty soon."

"You're not in uniform."

"Just had a leave."

"Do you like to serve on them?"

"Sure I do. The pay's good and there's all kinds of—future."

"Would you like to be down three months?"

"You'd get used to it. The food's good and there's movies and—I'd like to go under the Pole, wouldn't you?"

"I guess I would."

"And there's movies and all kinds of—future."

"Where are you from?"

"From over there—New London—born there. My uncle's in the service and two cousins. I guess we're a kind of submarine family."

"They worry me."

"Oh, you'd get over that, sir. Pretty soon you wouldn't even think you were submerged—that is, if you haven't got something wrong with you. Ever had claustrophobia?"

"No."

"Well, then. You soon get used to it. Care to go below for a cup of coffee? There's plenty of time."

"Sure I would."

And could be he's right and I'm wrong. It's his world, not mine any more. There's no anger in his delphinium eyes and no fear and no hatred either, so maybe it's all right. It's just a job with good pay and a future. I must not put my memories and my fear on him. Maybe it won't be true again, but that's his lookout. It's his world now. Perhaps he understands things I will never learn.

We drank our coffee out of paper cups, and through the square ferry windows he pointed out the dry docks and the skeletons of new submarines. "Nice thing about it is if there's a storm you can submerge, and it's quiet. Sleep like a baby and all hell busting loose up above." He gave me directions for getting out of town, some of the few accurate ones I got on the whole trip.

"So long," I said. "I hope you have a good— future."

"It's not bad, you know. Good-by, sir."

And driving along a back Connecticut road, tree-bordered and gardened, I knew he had made me feel better and surer.

For weeks I had studied maps, large-scale and small, but maps are not reality at all—they can be tyrants. I know people who are so immersed in road maps that they never see the countryside they pass through, and others who, having traced a route, are held to it as though held by flanged wheels to rails. I pulled Rocinante into a small picnic area maintained by the state of Connecticut and got out my book of maps. And suddenly the United States became huge beyond belief and impossible ever to cross. I wondered how in hell I'd got myself mixed up in a project that couldn't be carried out. It was like starting to write a novel. When I face the desolate impossibility of writing five hundred pages a sick sense of failure falls on me and I know I can never do it. This happens every time. Then gradually I write one page and then another. One day's work is all I can permit myself to contemplate and I eliminate the possibility of ever finishing. So it was now, as I looked at the bright-colored projection of monster America. The leaves of the trees about the camp ground were thick and heavy, no longer growing but hanging limp and waiting for the first frost to whip them with color and the second to drive them to the earth and terminate their year.

Charley is a tall dog. As he sat in the seat beside me, his head was almost as high as mine. He put his nose close to my ear and said, "Ftt." He is the only dog I ever knew who could pronounce the consonant *F*. This is because his front teeth are crooked, a tragedy which keeps him out of dog shows; because his upper front teeth slightly engage his lower lip Charley can pronounce *F*. The word "Ftt" usually means he would like to salute a bush or a tree. I opened the cab door and let him out, and he went about his ceremony. He doesn't have to think about it to do it well. It is my experience that in some areas Charley is more intelligent than I am, but in others he is abysmally ignorant. He can't read, can't drive a car, and has no grasp of mathematics. But in his own field of endeavor, which he was now practicing, the slow, imperial smelling over and anointing of an area, he has no peer. Of course his horizons are limited, but how wide are mine?

We drove on in the autumn afternoon, heading north. Because I was self-contained, I thought it might be nice if I could invite people I met along the way to my home for a drink, but I had neglected to lay in liquor. But there are pretty little bottle stores on the back roads of this state. I knew there were some dry states but had forgotten which they were, and it was just as well to stock up. A small store was set well back from the road in a grove of sugar maples. It had a well-kept garden and flower boxes. The owner was a young-old man with a gray face, I suspect a teetotaller. He opened his order book and straightened the carbons with patient care. You never know what people will want to drink. I ordered bourbon, scotch, gin, vermouth, vodka, a medium good brandy, aged applejack, and a case of beer. It seemed to me that those might take care of most situations. It was a big order for a little store. The owner was impressed.

"Must be quite a party."

"No—it's just traveling supplies."

He helped me to carry the cartons out and I opened Rocinante's door.

"You going in that?"

"Sure."

"Where?"

"All over."

And then I saw what I was to see so many times on the journey—a look of longing. "Lord! I wish I could go."

"Don't you like it here?"

"Sure. It's all right, but I wish I could go."

"You don't even know where I'm going."

"I don't care. I'd like to go anywhere."

Eventually I had to come out of the tree-hidden roads and do my best to bypass the cities. Hartford and Providence and such are big cities, bustling with manufacturing, lousy with traffic. It takes far longer to go through cities than to drive several hundred miles. And in the intricate traffic pattern, as you try to find your way through, there's no possibility of seeing anything. But now I have been through hundreds of towns and cities in every climate and against every kind of scenery, and of course they are all different, and the people have points of difference, but in some ways they are alike. American cities are like badger holes, ringed with trash—all of them—surrounded by piles of wrecked and rusting automobiles, and almost smothered with rubbish. Everything we use comes in boxes, cartons, bins, the so-called packaging we love so much. The mountains of things we throw away are much greater than the things we use. In this, if in no other way, we can see the wild and reckless exuberance of our production, and waste seems to be the index. Driving along I thought how in France or Italy every item of these thrown-out things would have been saved and used for something. This is not said in criticism of one system or the other but I do wonder whether there will come a time when we can no longer afford our wastefulness—chemical wastes in the rivers, metal wastes everywhere, and atomic wastes buried deep in the earth or sunk in the sea. When an Indian village became too deep in its own filth, the inhabitants moved. And we have no place to which to move.

I had promised my youngest son to say good-by in passing his school at Deerfield, Massachusetts, but I got there too late to arouse him, so I drove up the mountain and found a dairy, bought some milk, and asked permission to camp under an apple tree. The dairy man had a Ph.D. in mathematics, and he must have had some training in philosophy. He liked what he was doing and he didn't want to be somewhere else—one of the very few contented people I met in my whole journey.

I prefer to draw a curtain over my visit to Eagle-brook school. It can be imagined what effect Rocinante had on two hundred teen-age prisoners of education just settling down to serve their winter sentence. They visited my truck in droves, as many as fifteen at a time in the little cabin. And they looked courteous curses at me because I could go and they could not. My own son will probably never forgive me. Soon after I drove off, I stopped to make sure there were no stowaways.

My route went north in Vermont and then east in New Hampshire in the White Mountains. The roadside stands were piled with golden pumpkins and russet squashes and baskets of red apples so crisp and sweet that they seemed to explode with juice when I bit into them. I bought apples and a gallon jug of fresh-pressed cider. I believe that everyone along the highways sells moccasins and deerskin gloves. And those who don't sell goat-milk candy. Until then, I had not seen the factory-outlet stores in the open country selling shoes and clothes. The villages are the prettiest, I guess, in the whole nation, neat and white-painted, and—not counting the motels and tourist courts—unchanged for a hundred years except for traffic and paved streets.

The climate changed quickly to cold and the trees burst into color, the reds and yellows you can't believe. It isn't only color but a glowing, as though the leaves gobbled the light of the autumn sun and then released it slowly. There's a quality of fire in these colors. I got high in the mountains before dusk. A sign beside a stream offered fresh eggs for sale, and I drove up a farm road and bought some eggs and asked permission to camp beside the stream and offered to pay.

The farmer was a spare man, with what we think of as a Yankee face and the flat vowels we consider Yankee pronunciation.

"No need to pay," he said. "The land's not working. But I would like to look at that rig you've got there."

I said, "Let me find a level place and put it in order, then come down for a cup of coffee—or something."

I backed and filled until I found a level place where I could hear the eager stream rattling; it was almost dark. Charley had said "Ftt" several times, meaning this time that he was hungry. I opened Rocinante's door, turned on the light, and found utter chaos inside. I have stowed a boat very often against roll and pitch, but the quick stops and starts of a truck are a different hazard. The floor was littered with books and papers. My typewriter roosted uncomfortably on a pile of plastic dishes, a rifle had fallen down and nudged itself against the stove, and one entire ream of paper, five hundred sheets, had drifted like snow to cover the whole place. I lighted the gas mantle lamp, stuffed the debris in a little closet, and put on water for coffee. In the morning I would have to reorganize my cargo. No one can tell how to do it. The technique must be learned the way I learned it, by failures. The moment it was dark it became bitterly cold, but the lamp and the gas burners of the stove warmed my little house cozily. Charley ate his supper, did his tour of duty, and retired into a carpeted corner under the table which was to be his for the next three months.

There are so many modern designs for easy living. On my boat I had discovered the aluminum, disposable cooking utensils, frying pans and deep dishes. You fry a fish and throw the pan overboard. I was well equipped with these things. I opened a can of corned-beef hash and patted it into a disposable dish and set it on an asbestos pad over a low flame, to heat very slowly. The coffee was barely ready when Charley let out his lion roar. I can't say how comforting it is to be told that someone is approaching in the dark. And if the approacher happened to have evil in his heart, that great voice would give him pause if he did not know Charley's basically pacific and diplomatic nature.

The farm owner knocked on my door and I invited him in.

"You've got it nice in here," he said. "Yes, sir, you've got it nice."

He slipped in the seat beside the table. This table can be lowered at night and the cushions can be converted to make a double bed. "Nice," he said again.

I poured him a cup of coffee. It seems to me that coffee smells even better when the frost is in. "A little something on the side?" I asked. "Something to give it authority?"

"No—this is fine. This is nice."

"Not a touch of applejack? I'm tired from driving, I'd like a spot myself."

He looked at me with the contained amusement that is considered taciturnity by non-Yankees. "Would you have one if I didn't?"

"No, I guess not."

"I wouldn't rob you then—just a spoonful."

So I poured each of us a good dollop of twenty-one-year-old applejack and slipped in on my side of the table. Charley moved over to make room and put his chin down on my feet.

There's a gentility on the road. A direct or personal question is out of bounds. But this is simple good manners anywhere in the world. He did not ask my name nor I his, but I had seen his quick eyes go to the firearms in their rubber slings, to the fishing rods pinioned against the wall.

Khrushchev was at the United Nations, one of the few reasons I would have liked to be in New York. I asked, "Have you listened to the radio today?"

"Five-o'clock report."

"What happened at the U.N.? I forgot to listen."

"You wouldn't believe it," he said. "Mr. K. took off his shoe and pounded the table."

"What for?"

"Didn't like what was being said."

"Seems a strange way to protest."

"Well, it got attention. That's about all the news talked about."

"They should give him a gavel so he could keep his shoes on."

"That's a good idea. Maybe it could be in the shape of a shoe so he wouldn't be embarrassed." He sipped the applejack with a deep appreciation. "That's pretty nice," he said.

"How do folks around here feel about all this talking back to the Russians?"

"I don't know about other people. But I think if you're talking back it's kind of like a rear-guard action. I'd like to see us do something so they had to talk back to us."

"You've got something there."

"Seems to me we're always defending ourselves."

I refilled the coffee cups and poured a little more applejack for both of us. "You think we should attack?"

"I think we should at least take the ball sometimes."

"I'm not taking a poll, but how does the election
seem to be going around here?"

"I wish I knew," he said. "People aren't talking.
I think this might be the secretest election we ever
had. People just won't put out an opinion."

"Could it be they haven't got one?"

"Maybe, or maybe they just don't want to tell. I
remember other elections when there would be
pretty peppery arguments. I haven't heard even
one."

And that's what I found all over the country—no
arguments, no discussion.

"Is it the same—other places?" He must have
seen my license plates, but he would not mention
that.

"That seems right to me. Do you think people are
scared to have an opinion?"

"Maybe some. But I know some that don't scare,
and they don't say, either."

"That's been my experience," I said. "But I
don't know, really."

"I don't either. Maybe it's all part of the same
thing. No thanks, no more. I can smell your supper's nearly ready. I'll step along."

"Part of what same thing?"

"Well, you take my grandfather and his father—
he was still alive until I was twelve. They knew
some things they were sure about. They were pretty
sure give a little line and then what *might* happen.
But now—what might happen?"

"I don't know."

"Nobody knows. What good's an opinion if you
don't know? My grandfather knew the number of

whiskers in the Almighty's beard. I don't even know what happened yesterday, let alone tomorrow. He knew what it was that makes a rock or a table. I don't even understand the formula that says nobody knows. We've got nothing to go on—got no way to think about things. I'll step along. Will I see you in the morning?"

"I don't know. I'm going to start early. I want to get clear across Maine to Deer Isle."

"Say, that's a pretty place isn't it?"

"I don't know yet. I haven't been there."

"Well, it's nice. You'll like it. Thanks for the—coffee. Good night."

Charley looked after him and sighed and went back to sleep. I ate my corned-beef hash, then made down my bed and dug out Shirer's *Rise and Fall of the Third Reich*. But I found I couldn't read, and when the light was off I couldn't sleep. The clattering stream on the rocks was a good reposeful sound, but the conversation of the farmer stayed with me —a thoughtful, articulate man he was. I couldn't hope to find many like him. And maybe he had put his finger on it. Humans had perhaps a million years to get used to fire as a thing and as an idea. Between the time a man got his fingers burned on a lightning-struck tree until another man carried some inside a cave and found it kept him warm, maybe a hundred thousand years, and from there to the blast furnaces of Detroit—how long?

And now a force was in hand how much more strong, and we hadn't had time to develop the means to think, for man has to have feelings and then words before he can come close to thought and, in the past at least, that has taken a long time.

Roosters were crowing before I went to sleep.

And I felt at last that my journey was started. I think I hadn't really believed in it before.

Charley likes to get up early, and he likes me to get up early too. And why shouldn't he? Right after his breakfast he goes back to sleep. Over the years he has developed a number of innocent-appearing ways to get me up. He can shake himself and his collar loud enough to wake the dead. If that doesn't work he gets a sneezing fit. But perhaps his most irritating method is to sit quietly beside the bed and stare into my face with a sweet and forgiving look on his face; I come out of deep sleep with the feeling of being looked at. But I have learned to keep my eyes tight shut. If I even blink he sneezes and stretches, and that night's sleep is over for me. Often the war of wills goes on for quite a time, I squinching my eyes shut and he forgiving me, but he nearly always wins. He liked traveling so much he wanted to get started early, and early for Charley is the first tempering of darkness with the dawn.

I soon discovered that if a wayfaring stranger wishes to eavesdrop on a local population the places for him to slip in and hold his peace are bars and churches. But some New England towns don't have bars, and church is only on Sunday. A good alternative is the roadside restaurant where men gather for breakfast before going to work or going hunting. To find these places inhabited, one must get up very early. And there is a drawback even to this. Early-rising men not only do not talk much to strangers, they barely talk to one another. Breakfast conversation is limited to a series of laconic grunts. The natural New England taciturnity reaches its glorious perfection at breakfast.

I fed Charley, gave him a limited promenade,

and hit the road. An icy mist covered the hills and froze on my windshield. I am not normally a breakfast eater, but here I had to be or I wouldn't see anybody unless I stopped for gas. At the first lighted roadside restaurant I pulled in and took my seat at a counter. The customers were folded over their coffee cups like ferns. A normal conversation is as follows:

WAITRESS: "Same?"
CUSTOMER: "Yep."
WAITRESS: "Cold enough for you?"
CUSTOMER: "Yep."
(Ten minutes.)
WAITRESS: "Refill?"
CUSTOMER: "Yep."

This is a really talkative customer. Some reduce it to "Burp" and others do not answer at all. An early morning waitress in New England leads a lonely life, but I soon learned that if I tried to inject life and gaiety into her job with a blithe remark she dropped her eyes and answered "Yep" or "Umph." Still, I did feel that there was some kind of communication, but I can't say what it was.

The best of learning came on the morning radio, which I learned to love. Every town of a few thousand people has its station, and it takes the place of the old local newspaper. Bargains and trades are announced, social doings, prices of commodities, messages. The records played are the same all over the country. If "Teen-Age Angel" is top of the list in Maine, it is top of the list in Montana. In the course of a day you may hear "Teen-Age Angel" thirty or forty times. But in addition to local news and chronicles, some foreign advertising creeps in. As I went farther and farther north and it got colder I was aware of more and more advertising for Florida real estate and, with the approach of the long and bitter winter, I could see why Florida is a golden word. As I went along I found that more and more people lusted toward Florida and that thousands had moved there and more thousands wanted to and would. The advertising, with a side look at Federal Communications, made few claims except for the fact that the land they were selling was in Florida. Some of them went out on a limb and promised that it was above tide level. But that didn't matter; the very name Florida carried the message of warmth and ease and comfort. It was irresistible.

I've lived in good climate, and it bores the hell out of me. I like weather rather than climate. In Cuernavaca, Mexico, where I once lived, and where the climate is as near to perfect as is conceivable, I have found that when people leave there they usually go to Alaska. I'd like to see how long an Aroostook County man can stand Florida. The trouble is that with his savings moved and invested there, he can't very well go back. His dice are rolled and can't be picked up again. But I do wonder if a down-Easter, sitting on a nylon-and-aluminum chair out on a changelessly green lawn slapping mosquitoes in the evening of a Florida October—I do wonder if the stab of memory doesn't strike him high in the stomach just below the ribs where it hurts. And in the humid ever-summer I dare his picturing mind not to go back to the shout of color, to the clean rasp of frosty air, to the smell of pine wood burning and the caressing warmth of kitchens. For how can one know color in perpetual green,

and what good is warmth without cold to give it
sweetness?

I drove as slowly as custom and the impatient
law permitted. That's the only way to see anything.
Every few miles the states provided places of rest
off the roads, sheltered places sometimes near dark
streams. There were painted oil drums for garbage,
and picnic tables, and sometimes fireplaces or bar-
becue pits. At intervals I drove Rocinante off the
road and let Charley out to smell over the register
of previous guests. Then I would heat my coffee
and sit comfortably on my back step and contemplate wood and water and the quick-rising mountains with crowns of conifers and the fir trees high
up, dusted with snow. Long ago at Easter I had a
looking-egg. Peering in a little porthole at the end,
I saw a lovely little farm, a kind of dream farm, and
on the farmhouse chimney a stork sitting on a nest.
I regarded this as a fairy-tale farm as surely imagined as gnomes sitting under toadstools. And then
in Denmark I saw that farm or its brother, and it
was true, just as it had been in the looking-egg.
And in Salinas, California, where I grew up, although we had some frost the climate was cool and
foggy. When we saw colored pictures of a Vermont
autumn forest it was another fairy thing and we
frankly didn't believe it. In school we memorized
"Snowbound" and little poems about Old Jack
Frost and his paintbrush, but the only thing Jack
Frost did for us was put a thin skin of ice on the
watering trough, and that rarely. To find not only
that this bedlam of color was true but that the pictures were pale and inaccurate translations, was to
me startling. I can't even imagine the forest colors
when I am not seeing them. I wondered whether

constant association could cause inattention, and asked a native New Hampshire woman about it. She said the autumn never failed to amaze her; to elate. "It is a glory," she said, "and can't be remembered, so that it always comes as a surprise."

In the stream beside the resting place I saw a trout rise from the dark water of a pool and make outflowing silver rings, and Charley saw it too and waded in and got wet, the fool. He never thinks of the future. I stepped into Rocinante to bring out my poor mite of garbage for the oil drum, two empty cans; I had eaten from one and Charley from the other. And among the books I had brought along, I saw a well-remembered cover and brought it out to the sunlight—a golden hand holding at once a serpent and a mirror with wings, and below in scriptlike letters "*The Spectator,* Edited by Henry Morley."

I seem to have had a fortunate childhood for a writer. My grandfather, Sam'l Hamilton, loved good writing, and he knew it too, and he had some bluestocking daughters, among them my mother. Thus it was that in Salinas, in the great dark walnut bookcase with the glass doors, there were strange and wonderful things to be found. My parents never offered them, and the glass doors obviously guarded them, and so I pilfered from that case. It was neither forbidden nor discouraged. I think today if we forbade our illiterate children to touch the wonderful things of our literature, perhaps they might steal them and find secret joy. Very early I conceived a love for Joseph Addison which I have never lost. He plays the instrument of language as Casals plays a cello. I do not know whether he influenced my prose style, but I could hope he

did. In the White Mountains in 1960, sitting in
the sun, I opened the well-remembered first volume, printed in 1883. I turned to Number 1 of *The
Spectator*—Thursday, March 1, 1711. It was
headed:

> *"Non fumum ex fulgore, sed ex fumo dare
>   lucem
> Cogitat, et speciosa dehinc miracula promat."*
>   —Horace.

I remember so well loving Addison's use of capital
letters for nouns. He writes under this date:

"I have observed that a Reader seldom peruses a
Book with Pleasure 'till he knows whether the
Writer of it be a black or fair Man, of a mild or
cholerick Disposition, Married or a Batchelor, with
other Particulars of the like Nature, that conduce
very much to the right Understanding of an Author.
To gratify this Curiosity, which is so natural to a
Reader, I design this Paper and my next, as Prefa-
tory Discourses to my following Writings and shall
give some Account in them of the several persons
that are engaged in this Work. As the chief trouble
of Compiling, Digesting and Correcting will fall to
my Share, I must do myself the Justice to open the
Work with my own History."

Sunday, January 29, 1961. Yes, Joseph Addison,
I hear and I will obey within Reason, for it appears
that the Curiosity you speak of has in no Way
abated. I have found many Readers more interested
in what I wear than in what I think, more avid to
know how I do it than in what I do. In regarding
my Work, some Readers profess greater Feeling for
what it makes than for what it says. Since a Sugges-

tion from the Master is a Command not unlike Holy Writ, I shall digress and comply at the same Time.

Among the generality of men I am tall—six feet even—although among the males of my family I am considered a dwarf. They range from six feet two inches to six feet five, and I know that both my sons, when they stretch their full height, will overtop me. I am very wide of shoulder and, in the condition I now find myself, narrow of hip. My legs are long in proportion to my trunk and are said to be shapely. My hair is a grizzled gray, my eyes blue and my cheeks ruddy, a complexion inherited from my Irish mother. My face has not ignored the passage of time, but recorded it with scars, lines, furrows, and erosions. I wear a beard and mustache but shave my cheeks; said beard, having a dark skunk stripe up the middle and white edges, commemorates certain relatives. I cultivate this beard not for the usual given reasons of skin trouble or pain of shaving, nor for the secret purpose of covering a weak chin, but as pure unblushing decoration, much as a peacock finds pleasure in his tail. And finally, in our time a beard is the one thing a woman cannot do better than a man, or if she can her success is assured only in a circus.

My costume for traveling was utilitarian if a trifle bizarre. Half-Wellington rubber boots with cork inner soles kept my feet warm and dry. Khaki cotton trousers, bought in an army-surplus store, covered my shanks, while my upper regions rejoiced in a hunting coat with corduroy cuffs and collar and a game pocket in the rear big enough to smuggle an Indian princess into a Y.M.C.A. My cap was one I have worn for many years, a blue serge British

naval cap with a short visor and on its peak the
royal lion and unicorn, as always fighting for the
crown of England. This cap is pretty ratty and salt-
crusted, but it was given me by the skipper of a
motor torpedo boat on which I sailed out of Dover
during the war—a gentle gentleman and a mur-
derer. After I left his command he attacked a German E-boat and held his fire trying to take it whole
since none had ever been captured, and in the
process he got himself sunk. I have worn his cap
ever since in his honor and in his memory. Besides,
I like it. It agrees with me. Down East this cap did
not draw a second glance, but when later, in Wisconsin, North Dakota, Montana, I had left the sea
far behind, I thought it drew attention, and I
bought what we used to call a stockman's hat, a
Stetson, not too wide of brim, a rich but conservative western hat of the kind my cow-harrying uncles
used to wear. Only when I came down to another
sea in Seattle did I reassume the naval cap.

Thus far with Addison's injunction, but my
Reader has me back in that New Hampshire picnic
place. As I sat there fingering the first volume of
The Spectator and considering how the mind usually does two things at once that it knows about and
probably several it doesn't, a luxurious car drove
in and a rather stout and bedizened woman released a rather stout and bedizened Pomeranian of
the female persuasion. I would not have known this
latter fact, but Charley knew. Emerging from behind the garbage can, he found her beautiful, his
French blood flared up, and he proceeded to gal-
lantries unmistakable even to the slack eyes of ma-
demoiselle's mistress. This creature let out a shriek
like a wounded rabbit, emerged from the car with

an explosive ooze, and would have snatched her darling to her bosom if she could have bent down that far. The best she could do was to fetch a slap at tall Charley's head. He quite naturally and casually took a nip at her hand before proceeding toward romance. Until that moment I never quite knew the meaning of the phrase "to make the welkin ring." In the first place I didn't know what a welkin was. I looked it up later. And that bull bitch of a woman sure as hell made it ring. I grabbed her hand and saw that the skin wasn't even broken, so I grabbed her dog, which promptly bit me good and drew blood before I could get the little monster by the throat and gently throttle it.

Charley regarded the whole scene as nonsense. He wet on the garbage can for the twentieth time and called it a day.

It took time to calm the lady. I brought out the bottle of brandy, which might have killed her, and she took a slug that should have killed her.

After all I've done for him you'd think Charley would have come to my aid, but he dislikes neurotics and he detests drunks. He climbed in Rocinante, crawled under the table, and went to sleep. Sic semper cum Frogs.

At last milady flailed away with her hand brake on, and the kind of a day I had built lay in ruins. Addison had crashed in flames, the trout no longer ringed the pool, and a cloud covered the sun and put a chill in the air. I found myself driving faster than I wanted to and it began to rain, a cold steel rain. I didn't give the lonely villages the attention they deserved, and before long I had crossed into Maine and continued eastward.

I wish any two states could get together on a

speed limit. Just about the time you get used to fifty miles an hour you cross a state line and it's sixty-five. I wonder why they can't settle down and agree. However, in one matter all states agree—each one admits it is the finest of all and announces that fact in huge letters as you cross the state line. Among nearly forty I didn't see a single state that hadn't a good word to say for itself. It seemed a little in-delicate. It might be better to let visitors find out for themselves. But maybe we wouldn't if it weren't drawn to our attention.

PREPARATION FOR THE WINTER IN NEW ENG-
land is drastic. The summer population must be
large and the roads and highways gorged with ref-
ugees from the sticky heat of Boston and New York.
Now the hot-dog stands, the ice-cream parlors, the
curiosity shops, deerskin-moccasin-and-glove places,
were all shuttered and closed, many of them with
cards saying "Open Next Summer." I can never get
used to the thousands of antique shops along the
roads, all bulging with authentic and attested trash
from an earlier time. I believe the population of
the thirteen colonies was less than four million
souls, and every one of them must have been frantically turning out tables, chairs, china, glass, candle
molds, and oddly shaped bits of iron, copper, and
brass for future sale to twentieth-century tourists.
There are enough antiques for sale along the roads
of New England alone to furnish the houses of a
population of fifty million. If I were a good busi-
nessman, and cared a tittle for my unborn great
grandchildren, which I do not, I would gather all
the junk and the wrecked automobiles, comb the
city dumps, and pile these gleanings in mountains
and spray the whole thing with that stuff the Navy
uses to mothball ships. At the end of a hundred
years my descendants would be permitted to open
this treasure trove and would be the antique kings
of the world. If the battered, cracked, and broken
stuff our ancestors tried to get rid of now brings so

much money, think what a 1954 Oldsmobile, or a 1960 toastmaster will bring—and a vintage Waring Mixor—Lord, the possibilities are endless! Things we have to pay to have hauled away could bring fortunes.

If I seem to be over-interested in junk, it is because I am, and I have a lot of it, too—half a garage full of bits and broken pieces. I use these things for repairing other things. Recently I stopped my car in front of the display yard of a junk dealer near Sag Harbor. As I was looking courteously at the stock, it suddenly occurred to me that I had more than he had. But it can be seen that I do have a genuine and almost miserly interest in worthless objects. My excuse is that in this era of planned obsolescence, when a thing breaks down I can usually find something in my collection to repair it— a toilet, or a motor, or a lawn mower. But I guess the truth is that I simply like junk.

Before I started my tour, I had known that at intervals of every few days I would have to stop at auto courts or motels, not so much to sleep but for the sake of hot, luxurious bathing. In Rocinante I heated water in a tea kettle and took sponge baths, but bathing in a bucket delivers little cleanliness and no pleasure whatever. A deep-dish sit-down in a tub with scalding water is a pure joy. Quite early on my trip, however, I invented a method for washing clothes which you will go a long way to better. It came about this way. I had a large plastic garbage bucket with cover and bail. Since the normal movement of the truck tipped it over, I tethered it by a length of strong elastic rope of cotton-covered rubber to the clothes pole in my little closet, where it could jiggle to its heart's content without spilling.

After a day of this, I opened it to dispose of the stuff at a roadside garbage can and found the most thoroughly mixed and kneaded garbage I have ever seen. I suppose all great inventions spring from some such experience. The next morning, I washed the plastic bucket, put in two shirts, underwear, and socks, added hot water and detergent, and hung it by its rubber rope to the clothes pole, where it jigged and danced crazily all day. That night I rinsed the clothes in a stream, and you've never seen clothes so clean. Inside Rocinante I strung a nylon line close to the window and hung the clothes to dry. From that time on, my clothing was washed on one day of driving and dried on the next. I even went overboard and washed sheets and pillow cases that way. So much for daintiness, but it didn't take care of hot baths.

Not far outside of Bangor I stopped at an auto court and rented a room. It wasn't expensive. The sign said "Greatly Reduced Winter Rates." It was immaculate; everything was done in plastics—the floors, the curtain, table tops of stainless burnless plastic, lamp shades of plastic. Only the bedding and the towels were of a natural material. I went to the small restaurant run in conjunction. It was all plastic too—the table linen, the butter dish. The sugar and crackers were wrapped in cellophane, the jelly in a small plastic coffin sealed with cellophane. It was early evening and I was the only customer. Even the waitress wore a sponge-off apron. She wasn't happy, but then she wasn't unhappy. She wasn't anything. But I don't believe anyone is a nothing. There has to be something inside, if only to keep the skin from collapsing. This vacant eye, listless hand, this damask cheek dusted like a doughnut with plastic powder, had to have a memory or a dream.

On a chance I asked, "How soon you going to Florida?"

"Nex' week," she said listlessly. Then something stirred in that aching void. "Say, how do you know I'm going?"

"Read your mind, I guess."

She looked at my beard. "You with a show?"

"No."

"Then how do you mean read my mind?"

"Maybe I guessed. Like it down there?"

"Oh, sure! I go every year. Lots of waitress jobs in the winter."

"What do you do down there, I mean for fun?"

"Oh, nothing. Just fool around."

"Do you fish or swim?"

"Not much. I just fool around. I don't like that sand, makes me itch."

"Make good money?"

"It's a cheap crowd."

"Cheap?"

"They rather spen' it on booze."

"Than what?"

"Than tips. Just the same here with the summer people. Cheap."

Strange how one person can saturate a room with vitality, with excitement. Then there are others, and this dame was one of them, who can drain off energy and joy, can suck pleasure dry and get no sustenance from it. Such people spread a grayness in the air about them. I'd been driving a long time, and perhaps my energy was low and my resistance down. She got me. I felt so blue and miserable I wanted to crawl into a plastic cover and die. What a date she must be, what a lover! I tried to imagine that last and couldn't. For a moment I considered giving her a five-dollar tip, but I knew what would happen. She wouldn't be glad. She'd just think I was crazy.

I went back to my clean little room. I don't ever drink alone. It's not much fun. And I don't think I will until I am an alcoholic. But this night I got a bottle of vodka from my stores and took it to my cell. In the bathroom two water tumblers were sealed in cellophane sacks with the words: "These glasses are sterilized for your protection." Across the toilet seat a strip of paper bore the message: "This seat has been sterilized with ultraviolet light for your protection." Everyone was protecting me and it was horrible. I tore the glasses from their covers. I violated the toilet-seat seal with my foot. I poured half a tumbler of vodka and drank it and then another. Then I lay deep in hot water in the tub and I was utterly miserable, and nothing was good anywhere.

Charley caught it from me, but he is a gallant dog. He came into the bathroom and that old fool played with the plastic bath mat like a puppy. What strength of character, what a friend! Then he rushed to the door and barked as though I were being invaded. And if it hadn't been for all that plastic he might have succeeded.

I remember an old Arab in North Africa, a man whose hands had never felt water. He gave me mint tea in a glass so coated with use that it was opaque, but he handed me companionship, and the tea was wonderful because of it. And without any protection my teeth didn't fall out, nor did running sores develop. I began to formulate a new law describing the relationship of protection to despondency. A sad soul can kill you quicker, far quicker, than a germ.

If Charley hadn't shaken and bounced and said "Ftt," I might have forgotten that every night he gets two dog biscuits and a walk to clear his head. I put on clean clothes and went out with him into the star-raddled night. And the Aurora Borealis was out. I've seen it only a few times in my life. It hung and moved with majesty in folds like an infinite traveler upstage in an infinite theater. In colors of rose and lavender and purple it moved and pulsed against the night, and the frost-sharpened stars shone through it. What a thing to see at a time when I needed it so badly! I wondered for a moment whether I should grab that waitress and kick her behind out to look at it, but I didn't dare. She could make eternity and infinity melt and run out through your fingers. The air had a sweet burn of frost, and Charley, moving ahead, saluted in detail a whole row of clipped privet, and he steamed as he went. When he came back, he was pleased and glad for me. I gave him three dog biscuits, rumpled up the sterile bed, and went out to sleep in Rocinante.

It is not unlike me that in heading toward the West I should travel east. That has always been my tendency. I was going to Deer Isle for a very good reason. My long-time friend and associate, Elizabeth Otis, has been going to Deer Isle every year. When she speaks of it, she gets an other-world look in her eyes and becomes completely inarticulate. When I planned my trip she said, "Of course you'll stop at Deer Isle."

"It's out of my way."

"Nonsense," she said in a tone I know very well. I gathered from her voice and manner that if I didn't go to Deer Isle I had better never show my face in New York again. She then telephoned Miss Eleanor Brace, with whom she always stays, and that was that. I was committed. All I knew about Deer Isle was that there was nothing you could say about it, but if I didn't go I was crazy. Also, Miss Brace was waiting for me.

I got thoroughly lost in Bangor, what with traffic and trucks, horns blaring and lights changing. I vaguely remembered that I should be on U.S. Highway 1, and I found it and drove ten miles in the wrong direction, back toward New York. I had been given written directions on how to go, detailed directions, but have you ever noticed that instructions from one who knows the country gets you more lost than you are, even when they are accurate? I also got lost in Ellsworth, which I am told is impossible. Then the roads narrowed and the lumber trucks roared past me. I was lost almost all day, even though I found Blue Hill and Sedgwick. Late in the despairing afternoon I stopped my truck and approached a majestic Maine state trooper. What a man he was, granite as any quarried about Portland, a perfect model for some future equestrian statue. I wonder if future heroes will be carved in marble jeeps or patrol cars?

"I seem to be lost, officer. I wonder if you could direct me?"

"Where is it you want to go?"

"I'm trying to get to Deer Isle."

He looked at me closely, and when he was satisfied that I wasn't joking he swung on his hips and pointed across a small stretch of open water, and he didn't bother to speak.

"Is that it?"

He nodded from up to down and left his head down.

"Well, how do I get there?"

I have always heard that Maine people are rather taciturn, but for this candidate for Mount Rushmore to point twice in an afternoon was to be unbearably talkative. He swung his chin in a small arc in the direction I had been traveling. If the afternoon had not been advancing I would have tried for another word from him even if doomed to failure. "Thank you," I said, and sounded to myself as though I rattled on forever.

First there was a very high iron bridge, as high-arched as a rainbow, and after a bit a low stone bridge built in the shape of an S-curve, and I was on Deer Isle. My written directions said that I must take every road branch that turned right, and the word "every" was underlined. I climbed a hill and turned right into pine woods on a smaller road, and turned right on a very narrow road and turned right again on wheel tracks on pine needles. It is so easy once you have been over it. I couldn't believe I would find the place, but in a hundred yards there was the great old house of Miss Eleanor Brace, and there she was to welcome me. I let Charley out, and suddenly an angry streak of gray burned across the clearing in the pines and bucketed into the house. That was George. He didn't welcome me and he particularly didn't welcome Charley. I never did rightly see George, but his sulking presence was everywhere. For George is an old gray cat who has accumulated a hatred of people and things so intense that even hidden upstairs he communicates his prayer that you will go away. If the bomb should fall and wipe out every living thing except Miss Brace, George would be happy. That's the way he would design a world if it were up to him. And he could never know that Charley's interest in him was purely courteous; if he did, he would be hurt in his misanthropy, for Charley has no interest in cats whatever, even for chasing purposes.

We didn't give George any trouble because for two nights we stayed in Rocinante, but I am told that when guests sleep in the house George goes into the pine woods and watches from afar, grumbling his dissatisfaction and pouring out his dislike. Miss Brace admits that for the purposes of a cat, whatever they are, George is worthless. He isn't good company, he is not sympathetic, and he has little aesthetic value.

"Perhaps he catches mice and rats," I suggested helpfully.

"Never," said Miss Brace. "Wouldn't think of it. And do you want to know something? George is a girl."

I had to restrain Charley because the unseen presence of George was everywhere. In a more enlightened day when witches and familiars were better understood, George would have found his, or rather her, end in a bonfire, because if ever there was a familiar, an envoy of the devil, a consorter with evil spirits, George is it.

One doesn't have to be sensitive to feel the strangeness of Deer Isle. And if people who have been going there for many years cannot describe it, what can I do after two days? It is an island that

nestles like a suckling against the breast of Maine,
but there are many of those. The sheltered darkling
water seems to suck up light, but I've seen that
before. The pine woods rustle and the wind cries
over open country that is like Dartmoor. Stonington, Deer Isle's chief town, does not look like an
American town at all in place or in architecture.
Its houses are layered down to the calm water of
the bay. This town very closely resembles Lyme
Regis on the coast of Dorset, and I would willingly
bet that its founding settlers came from Dorset or
Somerset or Cornwall. Maine speech is very like
that in West Country England, the double vowels
pronounced as they are in Anglo-Saxon, but the
resemblance is doubly strong on Deer Isle. And the
coastal people below the Bristol Channel are secret
people, and perhaps magic people. There's aught
behind their eyes, hidden away so deep that perhaps even they do not know they have it. And that
same thing is so in Deer Islers. To put it plainly,
this Isle is like Avalon; it must disappear when you
are not there. Or take for example the mystery of
the coon cats, huge tailless cats with gray coats
barred with black, which is why they are called
coon cats. They are wild; they live in the woods
and are very fierce. Once in a while a native brings
in a kitten and raises it, and it is a pleasure to him,
almost an honor, but coon cats are rarely even ap-
proximately tame. You take a chance of being
raked or bitten all the time. These cats are obviously of Manx origin, and even interbreeding with
tame cats they contribute taillessness. The story is
that the great ancestors of the coon cats were
brought by some ship's captain and that they soon
went wild. But I wonder where they get their size.

They are twice as big as any Manx cat I ever saw. Could it be that they bred with bobcat or lynx? I don't know. Nobody knows.

Down by the Stonington Harbor the summer boats were being pulled up for storage. And not only here but in other inlets nearby are very large lobster pounds crawling with those dark-shelled Maine lobsters from the dark water which are the best lobsters in the world. Miss Brace ordered up three, not more than a pound and a half, she said, and that night their excellence was demonstrated beyond a doubt. There are no lobsters like these— simply boiled, with no fancy sauces, only melted butter and lemon, they have no equals anywhere. Even shipped or flown alive away from their dark homes, they lose something.

At a wonderful store in Stonington, half hardware store and half ship's chandler, I bought a kerosene lamp with a tin reflector for Rocinante. I had the fear that I might somewhere run out of butane gas, and how would I read in bed then? I screwed the lamp bracket to the wall over my bed and trimmed the wick to make a golden butterfly of flame. And often on my trip I used it for warmth and color as well as light. It was exactly the same lamp that was in all the rooms at the ranch when I was a child. And no pleasanter light was ever designed, although old timers say that whale oil makes a nicer flame.

I have demonstrated that I can't describe Deer Isle. There is something about it that opens no door to words. But it stays with you afterward, and, more than that, things you didn't know you saw come back to you after you have left. One thing I remember very clearly. It might have been caused by the season with a quality of light, or the autumn clarity. Everything stood out separate from everything else, a rock, a rounded lump of sea-polished driftwood on a beach, a roof line. Each pine tree was itself and separate even if it was a part of a forest. Drawing a very long bow of relationships, could I say that the people have that same quality? Surely I never met such ardent individuals. I would hate to try to force them to do anything they didn't want to do. I heard many stories about the Isle—I remember it is Isle and not Island—and was given much taciturn advice. I will repeat only one admonishment from a native of Maine, and I will not put a name to that person for fear of reprisal.

"Don't ever ask directions of a Maine native," I was told.

"Why ever not?"

"Somehow we think it is funny to misdirect people and we don't smile when we do it, but we laugh inwardly. It is our nature."

I wonder if that is true. I could never test it, because through my own efforts I am lost most of the time without any help from anyone.

I have spoken with approval, even affection, of Rocinante but not of the pick-up truck on which the camper top rode. It was a new model, with a powerful V-6 engine. It had automatic transmission and an oversized generator to give me lights inside the cabin if I should need them. The cooling system was so loaded with antifreeze that it could have withstood polar weather. I believe that American-made automobiles for passengers are made to wear out so that they must be replaced. This is not so with the trucks. A trucker requires many more thousands of miles of good service than a passenger car owner. He is not to be dazzled with trimming or fins or doodads and he is not required by his status to buy a new model every year or so to maintain social face. Everything about my truck was made to last. Its frame was heavy, the metal rigid, the engine big and sturdy. Of course I treated it well in matters of oil changes and greasing, and I did not drive it to its limit or force it to do acrobatics required of sports cars. The cab was doublewalled, and a good heater had been installed. When I returned after more than ten thousand miles the engine was only well broken in. And it never failed or stuttered even once during the journey.

I moved up the coast of Maine, through Millbridge and Addison and Machias and Perry and South Robbinston, until there was no more coast. I never knew or had forgotten how much of Maine sticks up like a thumb into Canada with New Brunswick on the east. We know so little of our own geography. Why, Maine extends northward almost to the mouth of the St. Lawrence, and its upper border is perhaps a hundred miles north of Quebec. And another thing I had conveniently forgotten was how incredibly huge America is. As I drove north through the little towns and the increasing forest rolling away to the horizon, the season changed quickly and out of all proportion. Perhaps it was my getting away from the steadying hand of the sea, and also perhaps I was getting very far north. The houses had a snow-beaten look, and many were crushed and deserted, driven to earth by the winters. Except in the towns there was evidence of a population which had once lived here and farmed and had its being and had then been driven out. The forests were marching back, and where farm wagons once had been only the big logging trucks rumbled along. And the game had come back, too; deer strayed on the roads and there were marks of bear.

There are customs, attitudes, myths and directions and changes that seem to be part of the structure of America. And I propose to discuss them as they were first thrust on my attention. While these discussions go on you are to imagine me bowling along on some little road or pulled up behind a bridge, or cooking a big pot of lima beans and salt pork. And the first of these has to do with hunting. I could not have escaped hunting if I had wanted to, for open seasons spangle the autumn. We have inherited many attitudes from our recent ancestors who wrestled this continent as Jacob wrestled the angel, and the pioneers won. From them we take a belief that every American is a natural-born hunter. And every fall a great number of men set out to prove that without talent, training, knowledge, or practice they are dead shots with rifle or shotgun. The results are horrid. From the moment I left Sag Harbor the guns were booming at the migrating ducks, and as I drove in Maine the rifle shots in the forests would have frightened off any number of redcoats so long as they didn't know what was happening. This is bound to get me a bad name as a sportsman, but let me say at once that I have nothing against the killing of animals. Something has to kill them, I suppose. In my youth I often crawled miles on my belly through freezing wind for the pure glory of blasting a mudhen which even soaked in salt water made poor eating. I don't greatly care for venison or bear or moose or elk except for the livers. The recipes, the herbs, the wine, the preparation that goes into a good venison dish would make an old shoe a gourmet's delight. If I were hungry, I would happily hunt anything that runs or crawls or flies, even relatives, and tear them down with my teeth. But it isn't hunger that drives millions of armed American males to forests and hills every autumn, as the high incidence of heart failure among the hunters will prove. Somehow the hunting process has to do with masculinity, but I don't quite know how. I know there are any number of good and efficient hunters who know what they are doing; but many more are overweight gentlemen, primed with whisky and armed with high-powered rifles. They shoot at anything that moves or looks as though it might, and their success in killing one another may well prevent a population explosion. If the casualties were limited to their own kind there would be no problem, but the slaughter of cows, pigs, farmers, dogs, and highway signs makes autumn a dangerous season in which to travel. A farmer in upper New York State painted the word cow in big black letters on both sides of his white bossy, but the hunters shot it anyway. In Wisconsin, as I was driving through, a hunter shot his own guide between the shoulder blades. The coroner questioning this nimrod asked, "Did you think he was a deer?"

"Yes, sir, I did."

"But you weren't sure he was a deer."

"Well, no sir. I guess not."

With the rolling barrage going on in Maine, of course I was afraid for myself. Four automobiles were hit on opening day, but mainly I was afraid for Charley. I know that a poodle looks very like a buck deer to one of these hunters, and I had to find some way of protecting him. In Rocinante there was a box of red Kleenex that someone had given me as a present. I wrapped Charley's tail in red Kleenex and fastened it with rubber bands. Every morning I renewed his flag, and he wore it all the way west while bullets whined and whistled around us. This is not intended to be funny. The radios warned against carrying a white handkerchief. Too many hunters seeing a flash of white have taken it for the tail of a running deer and cured a head cold with a single shot.

But this legacy of the frontiersman is not a new thing. When I was a child on the ranch near Salinas, California, we had a Chinese cook who regularly made a modest good thing of it. On a ridge not far away, a sycamore log lay on its side supported by two of its broken branches. Lee's attention was drawn to this speckled fawn-colored chunk of wood by the bullet holes in it. He nailed a pair of horns to one end and then retired to his cabin until deer season was over. Then he harvested the lead from the old tree trunk. Some seasons he got fifty or sixty pounds of it. It wasn't a fortune but it was wages. After a couple of years, when the tree was completely shot away, Lee replaced it with four gunny sacks of sand and the same antlers. Then it was even easier to harvest his crop. If he had put out fifty of them it would have been a fortune, but Lee was a humble man who didn't care for mass production.

MAINE SEEMED TO STRETCH ON ENDLESSLY. I felt as Peary must have when he approached what he thought was the North Pole. But I wanted to see Aroostook County, the big northern county of Maine. There are three great potato-raising sections —Idaho, Suffolk County on Long Island, and Aroostook, Maine. Lots of people had talked of Aroostook County, but I had never met anyone who had actually been there. I had been told that the crop is harvested by Canucks from Canada who flood over the border at harvest time. My way went endlessly through forest country and past many lakes, not yet frozen. As often as I could I chose the small wood roads, and they are not conducive to speed. The temperature lifted and it rained endlessly and the forests wept. Charley never got dry, and smelled as though he were mildewed. The sky was the color of wet gray aluminum and there was no indication on the translucent shield where the sun might be, so I couldn't tell direction. On a curving road I might have been traveling east or south or west instead of the north I wanted. That old fake about the moss growing on the north sides of trees lied to me when I was a Boy Scout. Moss grows on the shady side, and that may be any side. I determined to buy a compass in the next town, but there wasn't any next town on the road I was traveling. The darkness crept down and the rain drummed on the steel roof of the cab and the windshield wipers sobbed their arcs. Tall dark trees lined the road, crowding the gravel. It seemed hours since I had passed a car or a house or a store, for this was the country gone back to forest. A desolate loneliness settled on me—almost a frightening loneliness. Charley, wet and shivering, curled up in his corner of the seat and offered no companionship. I pulled in behind the approach to a concrete bridge, but couldn't find a level place on the sloping roadside.

Even the cabin was dismal and damp. I turned the gas mantle high, lit the kerosene lamp, and lighted two burners of my stove to drive the loneliness away. The rain drummed on the metal roof. Nothing in my stock of foods looked edible. The darkness fell and the trees moved closer. Over the rain drums I seemed to hear voices, as though a crowd of people muttered and mumbled offstage. Charley was restless. He didn't bark an alarm, but he growled and whined uneasily, which is very unlike him, and he didn't eat his supper and he left his water dish untouched—and that by a dog who drinks his weight in water every day and needs to because of the outgo. I succumbed utterly to my desolation, made two peanut-butter sandwiches, and went to bed and wrote letters home, passing my loneliness around. Then the rain stopped falling and the trees dripped and I helped to spawn a school of secret dangers. Oh, we can populate the dark with horrors, even we who think ourselves informed and sure, believing nothing we cannot measure or weigh. I knew beyond all doubt that the dark things crowding in on me either did not exist or were not dangerous to me, and still I was afraid. I thought how terrible the nights must have been in a time when men knew the things were there and were deadly. But no, that's wrong. If I knew they were there, I would have weapons against them, charms, prayers, some kind of alliance with forces equally strong but on my side. Knowing they were not there made me defenseless against them and perhaps more afraid.

Long ago I owned a little ranch in the Santa Cruz mountains in California. In one place a forest of giant madrone trees joined their tops over a true tarn, a black, spring-fed lake. If there is such a thing as a haunted place, that one was haunted, made so by dim light strained through the leaves and various tricks of perspective. I had working for me a Filipino man, a hill man, short and dark and silent, of the Maori people perhaps. Once, thinking he must have come from a tribal system which recognizes the unseen as a part of reality, I asked this man if he was not afraid of the haunted place, particularly at night. He said he was not afraid because years before a witch doctor gave him a charm against evil spirits.

"Let me see that charm," I asked.

"It's words," he said. "It's a word charm."

"Can you say them to me?"

"Sure," he said and he droned, *"In nomine Patris et Fillii et Spiritus Sancti."*

"What does it mean?" I asked.

He raised his shoulders. "I don't know," he said. "It's a charm against evil spirits so I am not afraid of them."

I've dredged this conversation out of a strange-sounding Spanish but there is no doubt of his charm, and it worked for him.

Lying in my bed under the weeping night I did

my best to read to take my mind out of misery, but while my eyes moved on the lines I listened to the night. On the edge of sleep a new sound jerked me awake, the sound of footsteps, I thought, moving stealthily on gravel. On the bed beside me I had a flashlight two feet long, made for coon hunters. It throws a powerful beam at least a mile. I got up from bed and lifted my 30/30 carbine from the wall and listened again near the door of Rocinante —and I heard the steps come closer. Then Charley roared his warning and I opened the door and sprayed the road with light. It was a man in boots and a yellow oilskin. The light pinned him still.

"What do you want?" I called.

He must have been startled. It took him a moment to answer. "I want to go home. I live up the road."

And now I felt the whole silly thing, the ridiculous pattern that had piled up layer on layer. "Would you like a cup of coffee, or a drink?"

"No, it's late. If you'll take that light out of my face I'll get along."

I snapped off the light and he disappeared but his voice in passing said, "Come to think of it, what are you doing here?"

"Camping," I said, "just camped for the night." And I went to sleep the moment I hit the bed.

The sun was up when I awakened and the world was remade and shining. There are as many worlds as there are kinds of days, and as an opal changes its colors and its fire to match the nature of a day, so do I. The night fears and loneliness were so far gone that I could hardly remember them.

Even Rocinante, dirty and pine-needle-covered as she was, seemed to leap over the road with joy.

Now there were open fields among the lakes and forests, fields with the crumbly friable soil potatoes love. Trucks with flat beds loaded with empty potato barrels moved on the roads, and the mechanical potato digger turned up long windrows of pale-skinned tubers.

In Spanish there is a word for which I can't find a counterword in English. It is the verb *vacilar*, present participle *vacilando*. It does not mean vacillating at all. If one is vacilando, he is going somewhere but doesn't greatly care whether or not he gets there, although he has direction. My friend Jack Wagner has often, in Mexico, assumed this state of being. Let us say we wanted to walk in the streets of Mexico City but not at random. We would choose some article almost certain not to exist there and then diligently try to find it.

I wanted to go to the rooftree of Maine to start my trip before turning west. It seemed to give the journey a design, and everything in the world must have design or the human mind rejects it. But in addition it must have purpose or the human conscience shies away from it. Maine was my design, potatoes my purpose. If I had not seen a single potato my status as *vacilador* would not have been affected. As it turned out I saw almost more potatoes than I needed to see. I saw mountains of potatoes—oceans—more potatoes than you would think the world's population could consume in a hundred years.

I've seen many migrant crop-picking people about the country: Hindus, Filipinos, Mexicans, Okies away from their states. Here in Maine a great many were French Canadians who came over the border for the harvest season. It occurs to me that, just as the Carthaginians hired mercenaries to do their fighting for them, we Americans bring in mercenaries to do our hard and humble work. I hope we may not be overwhelmed one day by peoples not too proud or too lazy or too soft to bend to the earth and pick up the things we eat.

These Canucks were a hardy people. They traveled and camped by families and groups of families, perhaps even clans: men, women, boys, girls, and small children too. Only the nurslings did not work at picking up the potatoes and placing them in the barrels. Americans drove the trucks and used a windlass and a kind of davit to pull the filled barrels aboard. Then they drove away to deposit the crop in the potato barns with earth heaped high about their sides to prevent freezing.

My knowledge of Canuck French derives from motion pictures usually with Nelson Eddy and Jeanette MacDonald, and it consists largely of "By gar." It's odd, but I didn't hear a single one of the potato pickers say "By gar," and they must have seen the pictures and known what is right. The women and girls wore pants usually of corduroy and thick sweaters, and they covered their heads with bright-colored scarves to protect their hair from the dust that rises from the fields with the smallest wind. Most of these people traveled in big trucks covered with dark canvas tarpaulins, but there were some trailers and a few camper tops like Rocinante. At night some slept in the trucks and trailers, but also there were tents pitched in pleasant places, and the smells that came from their cooking fires indicated that they had not lost their French genius for making soup.

Fortunately the tents and trucks and two trailers

were settled on the edge of a clear and lovely lake. I parked Rocinante about ninety-five yards away but also on the lake's edge. Then I put on coffee to boil and brought out my garbage-bucket laundry, which had been jouncing for two days, and rinsed the detergent out at the edge of the lake. Attitudes toward strangers crop up mysteriously. I was down-wind from the camp and the odor of their soup drifted to me. Those people might have been murderers, sadists, brutes, ugly apish subhumans for all I knew, but I found myself thinking. "What charming people, what flair, how beautiful they are. How I wish I knew them." And all based on the delicious smell of soup.

In establishing contact with strange people, Charley is my ambassador. I release him, and he drifts toward the objective, or rather to whatever the objective may be preparing for dinner. I retrieve him so that he will not be a nuisance to my neighbors—*et voilà!* A child can do the same thing, but a dog is better.

The incident came off as smoothly as one might expect of a tested and well-rehearsed script. I sent out my ambassador and drank a cup of coffee while I gave him time to operate. Then I strolled to the camp to relieve my neighbors of the inconvenience of my miserable cur. They were nice-looking people, a dozen of them, not counting children, three of the girls pretty and given to giggling, two of the wives buxom and a third even buxomer with child, a patriarch, two brothers-in-law, and a couple of young men who were working toward being brothers-in-law. But the operating chieftain, with deference of course to the patriarch, was a fine-looking man of about thirty-five, broad-shouldered and lithe, with the cream-and-berries complexion of a girl and crisp black curling hair.

The dog had caused no trouble, he said. The truth was that they had remarked that he was a handsome dog. I of course found myself prejudiced in spite of his deficiencies, being his owner, but the dog had one advantage over most dogs. He was born and raised in France.

The group closed ranks. The three pretty girls giggled and were instantly smothered by the navy-blue eye of the chieftain, backed by a hiss from the patriarch.

Was that the truth? Where in France?

In Bercy, on the outskirts of Paris, did they know it?

No, unfortunately they had never been to the fatherland.

I hoped they might remedy that.

They should have known Charley for a French national by his manners. They had observed my *roulotte* with admiration.

It was simple but comfortable. If they found it convenient, I should be pleased to show it to them.

I was very kind. It would give them pleasure.

If the elevated tone indicates to you that it was carried on in French, you are wrong. The chieftain spoke a very pure and careful English. The one French word used was *roulotte*. The asides among themselves were in Canuck. My French is ridiculous, anyway. No, the elevated tone was a part and parcel of the pageantry of establishing a rapport. I gathered Charley to me. Might I expect them after their supper, which I smelled on the fire?

They would be honored.

I set my cabin in order, heated and ate a can of

chili con carne, made sure the beer was cold, and even picked a bouquet of autumn leaves and put them in a milk bottle on the table. The roll of paper cups laid in for just such an occasion had got squashed flat by a flying dictionary my first day out, but I made coasters from folded paper towels. It's amazing what trouble you will go to for a party. Then Charley barked them in and I was host in my own house. Six people can squeeze in behind my table, and they did. Two others beside me stood up, and the back door was wreathed with children's faces. They were very nice people but quite formal. I opened beer for the big ones and pop for the outsiders.

In due course these people told me quite a bit about themselves. They came over the border every year for the potato harvest. With everyone working, it made a nice little pool against the winter. Did they have any trouble with immigration people at the border? Well, no. The rules seemed to relax during the harvest season, and besides, the way was smoothed by a contractor to whom they paid a small percentage of their pay. But they didn't really pay him. He collected directly from the farmers. I've known quite a few migrant people over the years—Okies and Mexican wetbacks, and the Negroes who move into New Jersey and Long Island. And wherever I've seen them there has always been a contractor in the background to smooth the way for them for a consideration. Years ago the farmers tried to draw more labor than they needed so that they could lower wages. This seems to be no longer true, for government agencies channel only as many laborers as are needed, and some kind of minimum wage is maintained. In

other cases the migrants have been driven to movement and seasonal work by poverty and terrible
need.

Surely my guests for the evening were neither
mistreated nor driven. This clan, having put their
own small farm to bed for the winter in the Prov-
ince of Quebec, came over the line to make a small
nest egg. They even carried a little feeling of holiday with them almost like the hops- and strawberry-
pickers from London and the Midland cities of
England. These were a hardy and self-sufficient people, quite capable of taking care of themselves.

I opened more beer. After the night of desolate
loneliness I felt very good to be surrounded by
warm and friendly but cautious people. I tapped
an artesian well of good feeling and made a small
speech in my pidgin type of French. It began:
"Messy dam. *Je vous porte un cher souvenir de la
belle France—en particulier du Departement de
Charente.*"

They looked startled but interested. Then John
the chieftain slowly translated my speech into high-
school English and put it back into Canadian
French. "Charente?" he asked. "Why Charente?"
I leaned down and opened a compartment under
my sink and lifted out a bottle of very old and
reverend brandy brought along for weddings, frost
bite, and heart attacks. John studied the label with
the devout attention a good Christian might give to
the holy sacrament. And his words were reverent:
"Jesus Christ," he said. "I forgot. Charente—that's
where Cognac is." Then he read the purported year
of the bottle's nativity and softly repeated his first
words.

He passed the bottle to the patriarch in his corner, and the old man smiled so sweetly that for the first time I could see he lacked front teeth. The brother-in-law growled in his throat like a happy tomcat and the pregnant ladies twittered like *alouettes* singing to the sun. I handed John a corkscrew while I laid out the crystal—three plastic coffee cups, a jelly glass, a shaving mug, and several wide-mouthed pill bottles. I emptied their capsules into a saucepan and rinsed out the odor of wheat germ with water from the tap. The cognac was very, very good, and from the first muttered *"Santé"* and the first clicking sip you could feel the Brotherhood of Man growing until it filled Rocinante full—and the sisterhood also.

They refused seconds and I insisted. And the division of thirds was put on the basis that there wasn't enough to save. And with the few divided drops of that third there came into Rocinante a triumphant human magic that can bless a house, or a truck for that matter—nine people gathered in complete silence and the nine parts making a whole as surely as my arms and legs are part of me, separate and inseparable. Rocinante took on a glow it never quite lost.

Such a fabric cannot be prolonged and should not be. The patriarch gave some kind of signal. My guests squirmed out of their squeezed-up seats behind the table and the adieux, as they should be, were short and formal. Then they went into the night, their way home lighted by the chieftain John carrying a tin kerosene lantern. They walked in silence among sleepy stumbling children and I never saw them again. But I like them.

I didn't make down my bed because I wanted to start very early. I curled up behind the table and

slept a little while until in the dim false dawn
Charley looked into my face and said "Ftt." While
I heated my coffee, I made a little sign on card-
board and stuck it in the neck of the empty brandy
bottle, then passing the sleeping camp I stopped
and stood the bottle where they would see it. The
sign read: *"Enfant de France, Mort pour la Patrie."*
And I drove as quietly as I could, for on this day
I intended to drive a little west and then take the
long road south down the long reach of Maine.
There are times that one treasures for all one's life,
and such times are burned clearly and sharply on
the material of total recall. I felt very fortunate that
morning.

On such a trip as mine, so much there is to see
and to think about that event and thought set down
as they occurred would roil and stir like a slow-
cooking *minestrone*. There are map people whose
joy is to lavish more attention on the sheets of
colored paper than on the colored land rolling by.
I have listened to accounts by such travelers in
which every road number was remembered, every
mileage recalled, and every little countryside discovered. Another kind of traveler requires to know
in terms of maps exactly where he is pin-pointed
every moment, as though there were some kind of
safety in black and red lines, in dotted indications
and squirming blue of lakes and the shadings that
indicate mountains. It is not so with me. I was born
lost and take no pleasure in being found, nor much
identification from shapes which symbolize continents and states. Besides, roads change, increase,
are widened or abandoned so often in our country
that one must buy road maps like daily newspapers.
But since I know the passions of the mapifiers I

can report that I moved north in Maine roughly or parallel to U. S. Highway 1 through Houlton, Mars Hill, Presque Isle, Caribou, Van Buren, turned westward, still on U. S. 1, past Madawaska, Upper Frenchville, and Fort Kent, then went due south on State Highway 11 past Eagle Lake, Winterville, Portage, Squa Pan, Masardis, Knowles Corner, Patten, Sherman, Grindstone, and so to Millinocket.

I can report this because I have a map before me, but what I remember has no reference to the numbers and colored lines and squiggles. I have thrown this routing in as a sop and shall not make a habit of it. What I remember are the long avenues in the frost, the farms and houses braced against the winter, the flat, laconic Maine speech in crossroads stores where I stopped to buy supplies. The many deer that crossed the road on nimbling hooves and leaped like bounding rubber away from the passing Rocinante. The roaring lumber trucks. And always I remember that this huge area had once been much more settled and was now abandoned to the creeping forest, the animals, the lumber camps and the cold. The big towns are getting bigger and the villages smaller. The hamlet store, whether grocery, general, hardware, clothing, cannot compete with the supermarket and the chain organization. Our treasured and nostalgic picture of the village general store, the cracker-barrel store where an informed yeomanry gather to express opinions and formulate the national character, is very rapidly disappearing. People who once held family fortresses against wind and weather, against scourges of frost and drought and insect enemies, now cluster against the busy breast of the big town.

The new American finds his challenge and his love in traffic-choked streets, skies nested in smog, choking with the acids of industry, the screech of rubber and houses leashed in against one another while the townlets wither a time and die. And this, as I found, is as true in Texas as in Maine. Clarendon yields to Amarillo just as surely as Stacyville, Maine, bleeds its substance into Millinocket, where the logs are ground up, the air smells of chemicals, the rivers are choked and poisoned, and the streets swarm with this happy, hurrying breed. This is not offered in criticism but only as observation. And I am sure that, as all pendulums reverse their swing, so eventually will the swollen cities rupture like dehiscent wombs and disperse their children back to the countryside. This prophecy is underwritten by the tendency of the rich to do this already. Where the rich lead, the poor will follow, or try to.

Some years ago at Abercrombie and Fitch I bought a cattle caller, an automobile horn manipulated by a lever with which nearly all cow emotions can be imitated, from the sweet lowing of a romantic heifer to the growling roar of a bull in the prime and lust of his bullhood. I had this contraption on Rocinante, and it was most effective. When its call goes out, every bovine within hearing distance raises its head from grazing and moves toward the sound.

In the silver chill of the Maine afternoon, as I bucketed and lumbered over the pitted surface of a wood road, I saw four lady mooses moving with stately heaviness across my bow. As I came near they broke into a heavy-cushioned trot. On an impulse I pressed down the lever of the cattle caller and a bellow came out like that of a Miura bull as he poises before firing himself at the butterfly sweep of his first veronica. The ladies, who were on the point of disappearing into the forest, heard the sound, stopped, turned, and then came for me with gathering speed and with what looked to me like romance in their eyes—but four romances, each weighing well over a thousand pounds! And much as I favor love in all its aspects, I trod my accelerator and got the hell out of there fast. And I remembered a story of the great Fred Allen. His character was a Maine man telling of a moose hunt. "I sat on a log and blew my moose call and waited. Then suddenly I felt something like a warm bath mat on my neck and head. Well sir, it was a moosess licking me and there was a light of passion in her eyes."

"Did you shoot her?" he was asked.

"No, sir. I went away from there fast, but I have often thought that somewhere in Maine there's a moose with a broken heart."

Maine is just as long coming down as it is going up, maybe longer. I could and should have gone to Baxter State Park, but I didn't. I had dawdled too long and it was getting cold and I had visions of Napoleon at Moscow and the Germans at Stalingrad. So I retreated smartly—Brownville Junction, Milo, Dover-Foxcroft, Guilford, Bingham, Skowhegan, Mexico, Rumford, where I joined a road I had already traveled through the White Mountains. Perhaps this was weak of me, but I wanted to get on with it. The rivers were full of logs, bank to bank for miles, waiting their turn at the abbatoir to give their woody hearts so that the bulwarks of our civilization such as *Time* magazine and the *Daily News* can survive, to defend us against ignorance. The mill towns, with all respect, are knots of worms. You come out of serene country and suddenly you are tossed and battered by a howling hurricane of traffic. For a time you fight your way blindly in the mad crush of hurtling metal and then suddenly it dies away and you are in serene and quiet countryside again. And there is no margin or overlap. It is a mystery but a happy one.

In the short time since I had passed, the foliage of the White Mountains had changed and tattered. The leaves were falling, rolling in dusky clouds, and the conifers on the slopes were crusted with snow. I drove long and furiously, to Charley's great disgust. Any number of times he said "Ftt" to me and I ignored him, and barreled on across the upraised thumb of New Hampshire. I wanted a bath and a new bed and a drink and a little human commerce, and I thought to find it on the Connecticut River. It is very strange that when you set a goal for yourself, it is hard not to hold toward it even if it is inconvenient and not even desirable. The way was longer than I had thought and I was very tired. My years spoke for my attention with aching shoulders but I was aimed at the Connecticut River and I ignored the weariness, and this was utter nonsense. It was nearly dark when I found the place I wanted, not far from Lancaster, New Hampshire. The river was wide and pleasant, bordered with trees and edged with a pleasant meadow. And near the bank there stood what I was lusting for—a row of neat little white houses on the green meadow by the river, and a small, compactly housed office and lunch room with a sign on the roadside that bore the welcome words "Open" and "Vacancy." I swung Rocinante off the road and opened the cab door to let Charley out.

The afternoon light made mirrors of the windows of the office and lunch room. My whole body ached from the road as I opened the door and went in. Not a soul was there. The register was on the desk, stools at the lunch counter, pies and cakes under plastic covers; the refrigerator hummed; a few dirty dishes soaked in soapy water in the stainless-steel sink, and a faucet dripped slowly into it.

I banged the little bell on the desk, then called out, "Anybody here?" No answer, nothing. I sat down on a stool to await the return of the management. The numbered keys to the little white houses hung on a board. The daylight slipped away and the place darkened. I went outside to collect Charley and to verify my impression that the sign said "Open" and "Vacancy." By now it was getting dark. I brought out a flashlight and looked through the office for a note saying "Back in ten minutes," but there was none. I felt strangely like a Peeping Tom; I didn't belong there. Then I went outside and moved Rocinante out of the driveway, fed Charley, made some coffee, and waited.

It would have been simple to take a key, leave a note on the desk saying that I had done so, and open one of the little houses. It wasn't right. I couldn't do it. On the highway a few cars went by and crossed the bridge over the river, but none turned in. The windows of the office and grill flashed under approaching headlights and then blacked out again. I had planned to eat a light supper and then to fall dog-weary into bed. I made my bed, found I wasn't hungry after all, and lay down. But sleep would not come to me. I listened for the return of the management. At last I lighted my gas mantle and tried to read, but with listening I could not follow the words. At last I dozed, awakened in the dark, looked out—nothing, nobody. My little sleep was troubled and uneasy.

At dawn I arose and created a long, slow, time-wasting breakfast. The sun came up, searching out the windows. I walked down to the river to keep Charley company, returned, even shaved and took a sponge bath in a bucket. The sun was well up by now. I went to the office and entered. The refrigerator hummed, the faucet dripped into the cold soapy water of the sink. A new-born, heavy-winged fat fly crawled fretfully over a plastic pie cover. At nine-thirty I drove away and no one had come, nothing had moved. The sign still read "Open" and "Vacancy." I drove across the iron bridge, rattling the steel-tread plates. The empty place disturbed me deeply, and, come to think of it, it still does.

On the long journey doubts were often my companions. I've always admired those reporters who can descend on an area, talk to key people, ask key questions, take samplings of opinions, and then set down an orderly report very like a road map. I envy this technique and at the same time do not trust it as a mirror of reality. I feel that there are too many realities. What I set down here is true until someone else passes that way and rearranges the world in his own style. In literary criticism the critic has no choice but to make over the victim of his attention into something the size and shape of himself.

And in this report I do not fool myself into thinking I am dealing with constants. A long time ago I was in the ancient city of Prague and at the same time Joseph Alsop, the justly famous critic of places and events, was there. He talked to informed people, officials, ambassadors; he read reports, even the fine print and figures, while I in my slipshod manner roved about with actors, gypsies, vagabonds. Joe and I flew home to America in the same plane, and on the way he told me about Prague, and his Prague had no relation to the city I had seen and heard. It just wasn't the same place, and yet each of us was honest, neither one a liar, both pretty good observers by any standard, and we brought home two cities, two truths. For this reason I cannot commend this account as an America that you will find. So much there is to see, but our morning eyes describe a different world than do our afternoon eyes, and surely our wearied evening eyes can report only a weary evening world.

Sunday morning, in a Vermont town, my last day in New England, I shaved, dressed in a suit, polished my shoes, whited my sepulcher, and looked for a church to attend. Several I eliminated for reasons I do not now remember, but on seeing a John Knox church I drove into a side street and parked Rocinante out of sight, gave Charley his instructions about watching the truck, and took my way with dignity to a church of blindingly white ship lap. I took my seat in the rear of the spotless, polished place of worship. The prayers were to the point, directing the attention of the Almighty to certain weaknesses and undivine tendencies I know to be mine and could only suppose were shared by others gathered there.

The service did my heart and I hope my soul some good. It had been long since I had heard such an approach. It is our practice now, at least in the large cities, to find from our psychiatric priesthood that our sins aren't really sins at all but accidents that are set in motion by forces beyond our control. There was no such nonsense in this church. The minister, a man of iron with tool-steel eyes and a delivery like a pneumatic drill, opened up with prayer and reassured us that we were a pretty sorry lot. And he was right. We didn't amount to much to start with, and due to our own tawdry efforts we had been slipping ever since. Then, having softened us up, he went into a glorious sermon, a fire-and-brimstone sermon. Having proved that we, or perhaps only I, were no damn good, he painted with cool certainty what was likely to happen to us if we didn't make some basic reorganizations for which he didn't hold out much hope. He spoke of hell as an expert, not the mush-mush hell of these soft days, but a well-stoked, white-hot hell served by technicians of the first order. This reverend brought it to a point where we could understand it, a good hard coal fire, plenty of draft, and a squad of open-hearth devils who put their hearts into their work, and their work was me. I began to feel good all over. For some years now God has been a pal to us, practicing togetherness, and that causes the same emptiness a father does playing softball with his son. But this Vermont God cared enough about me to go to a lot of trouble kicking the hell out of me. He put my sins in a new perspective. Whereas they had been small and mean and nasty and best forgotten, this minister gave them some size and bloom and dignity. I hadn't been thinking very well of myself for some years, but if my sins had this dimension there was some pride left. I wasn't a naughty child but a first rate sinner, and I was going to catch it.

I felt so revived in spirit that I put five dollars in the plate, and afterward, in front of the church, shook hands warmly with the minister and as many of the congregation as I could. It gave me a lovely sense of evil-doing that lasted clear through till Tuesday. I even considered beating Charley to give him some satisfaction too, because Charley is only a little less sinful than I am. All across the country I went to church on Sundays, a different denomination every week, but nowhere did I find the quality of that Vermont preacher. He forged a religion designed to last, not predigested obsolescence.

I crossed into New York State at Rouses Point and stayed as near to Lake Ontario as I could because it was my intention to look at Niagara Falls, which I had never seen, and then to slip into Canada, from Hamilton to Windsor, keeping Lake Erie on the south, and to emerge at Detroit—a kind of end run, a small triumph over geography. We know, of course, that each of our states is an individual and proud of it. Not content with their names, they take descriptive titles also—the Empire State, the Garden State, the Granite State—titles proudly borne and little given to understatement. But now for the first time I became aware that each state had also its individual prose style, made sharply evident in its highway signs. Crossing state lines one is aware of this change of language. The New England states use a terse form of instruction, a tight-lipped, laconic style sheet, wasting no words and few letters. New York State shouts at you the whole time. Do this. Do that. Squeeze left. Squeeze right. Every few feet an imperious command. In Ohio the signs are more benign. They offer friendly advice, and are more like suggestions. Some states use a turgid style which can get you lost with the greatest ease. There are states which tell you what you may expect to find in the way of road conditions ahead, while others let you find out for yourself. Nearly all have abandoned the adverb for the adjective. Drive Slow. Drive Safe.

I am an avid reader of all signs, and I find that in the historical markers the prose of statehood reaches its glorious best, and most lyric. I have further established, at least to my own satisfaction, that those states with the shortest histories and the least world-shaking events have the most historical markers. Some Western states even find glory in half-forgotten murders and bank robberies. The towns not to be left behind proudly announce their celebrated sons, so the traveler is informed by signs and banners—Birthplace of Elvis Presley, of Cole Porter, of Alan P. Huggins. This is no new thing, of course. I seem to remember that small cities in ancient Greece quarreled bitterly over which was the birthplace of Homer. Within my memory an outraged home-town citizenry wanted Red Lewis back for tarring and feathering after he wrote *Main Street*. And today Sauk Centre celebrates itself for having produced him. We, as a nation, are as hungry for history as was England when Geoffrey of Monmouth concocted his History of British Kings, many of whom he manufactured to meet a growing demand. And as in states and communities, so in individual Americans this hunger for decent association with the past. Genealogists are worked to death winnowing the debris of ancestry for grains of greatness. Not long ago it was proved that Dwight D. Eisenhower was descended from the royal line of Britain, a proof if one were needed that everyone is descended from everyone. The then little town where I was born, which within my grandfather's memory was a blacksmith shop in a swamp, recalls with yearly pageantry a glowing past of Spanish dons and rose-eating senoritas who have in public memory wiped out the small, desolate tribe of grub- and grasshopper-eating Indians who were our true first settlers.

I find this interesting, but it does make for suspicion of history as a record of reality. I thought of these things as I read the historical markers across the country, thought how the myth wipes out the fact. On a very low level the following is the process of a myth. Visiting in the town where I was born, I talked with a very old man who had known me as a child. He remembered vividly seeing me, a peaked, shivering child walking past his house one freezing morning, my inadequate overcoat fastened across my little chest with horse-blanket pins. This in its small way is the very stuff of myths—the poor and suffering child who rises to glory, on a limited scale of course. Even though I didn't remember the episode, I knew it could not be true. My mother was a passionate sewer-on of buttons. A button off was more than sloppiness; it was a sin. If I had pinned my coat, my mother would have whaled me. The story could not be true, but this old gentleman so loved it that I could never convince him of its falsity, so I didn't try. If my home town wants me in horse-blanket pins, nothing I can do is likely to change it, particularly the truth.

It rained in New York State, the Empire State, rained cold and pitiless, as the highway-sign writers would put it. Indeed the dismal downpour made my intended visit to Niagara Falls seem redundant.

I was then hopelessly lost in the streets of a small but endless town in the neighborhood of Medina, I think. I pulled to the side of the street and got out my book of road maps. But to find where you are going, you must know where you are, and I didn't. The windows of the cab were tightly closed and opaque with streaming rain. My car radio played softly. Suddenly there was a knock on the window, the door was wrenched open, and a man slipped into the seat beside me. The man was quite red of face, quite whisky of breath. His trousers were held up by red braces over the long gray underwear that covered his chest.

"Turn that damn thing off," he said, and then turned off my radio himself. "My daughter saw you out the window," he continued. "Thought you was in trouble." He looked at my maps. "Throw those things away. Now, where is it you want to go?"

I don't know why it is a man can't answer such a question with the truth. The truth was that I had turned off the big highway 104 and into the smaller roads because the traffic was heavy and passing vehicles threw sheets of water on my windshield. I wanted to go to Niagara Falls. Why couldn't I have admitted it? I looked down at my map and said, "I'm trying to get to Erie, Pennsylvania."

"Good," he said. "Now, throw those maps away. Now you turn around, go two traffic lights, that'll bring you to Egg Street. Turn left there and about two hundred yards on Egg turn right at an angle. That's a twisty kind of street and you'll come to an overpass, but don't take it. You turn left there and it will curve around like this—see? Like this." His hand made a curving motion. "Now, when the curve straightens out you'll come to three branching roads. There's a big red house on the left-hand branch so you don't take that, you take the right-hand branch. Now, have you got that so far?"

"Sure," I said. "That's easy."

"Well repeat it back so I'll know you're going right."

I had stopped listening at the curving road. I said, "Maybe you better tell me again."

"I thought so. Turn around and go two traffic lights to Egg Street, turn left for two hundred yards and turn right at an angle on a twisty street till you come to an overpass but don't take it."

"That clears it up for me," I said quickly. "I sure do thank you for helping me out."

"Hell," he said, "I ain't even got you out of town yet."

Well, he got me out of town by a route which, if I could have remembered it, let alone followed it, would have made the path into the Labyrinth at Knossos seem like a throughway. When he was finally satisfied and thanked, he got out and slammed the door, but such is my social cowardice that I actually did turn around, knowing he would be watching out the window. I drove around two blocks and blundered my way back to 104, traffic or not.

NIAGARA FALLS IS VERY NICE. IT'S LIKE A large version of the old Bond sign on Times Square. I'm very glad I saw it, because from now on if I am asked whether I have seen Niagara Falls I can say yes, and be telling the truth for once.

When I told my adviser that I was going to Erie, Pennsylvania, I had no idea of going there, but as it turned out, I was. My intention was to creep across the neck of Ontario, bypassing not only Erie but Cleveland and Toledo.

I find out of long experience that I admire all nations and hate all governments, and nowhere is my natural anarchism more aroused than at national borders where patient and efficient public servants carry out their duties in matters of immigration and customs. I have never smuggled anything in my life. Why, then, do I feel an uneasy sense of guilt on approaching a customs barrier? I crossed a high toll bridge and negotiated a no man's land and came to the place where the Stars and Stripes stood shoulder to shoulder with the Union Jack. The Canadians were very kind. They asked where I was going and for how long, gave Rocinante a cursory inspection, and came at last to Charley.

"Do you have a certificate of rabies vaccination on the dog?"

"No, I haven't. You see he's an old dog. He was vaccinated long ago."

Another official came out. "We advise you not to cross the border with him, then."

"But I'm just crossing a small part of Canada and re-entering the U.S."

"We understand," they said kindly. "You can take him into Canada but the U.S. won't let him back."

"But technically I am still in the U.S. and there's no complaint."

"There will be if he crosses the line and tries to get back."

"Well, where can I get him vaccinated?"

They didn't know. I would have to retrace my way at least twenty miles, find a vet, have Charley vaccinated, and then return. I was crossing only to save a little time, and this would wipe out the time saved and much more.

"Please understand, it is your own government, not ours. We are simply advising you. It's the rule."

I guess this is why I hate governments, all governments. It is always the rule, the fine print, carried out by fine-print men. There's nothing to fight, no wall to hammer with frustrated fists. I highly approve of vaccination, feel it should be compulsory; rabies is a dreadful thing. And yet I found myself hating the rule and all governments that made rules. It was not the shots but the certificate that was important. And it is usually so with governments—not a fact but a small slip of paper. These were such nice men, friendly and helpful. It was a slow time at the border. They gave me a cup of tea and Charley half a dozen cookies. And they seemed genuinely sorry that I had to go to Erie, Pennsylvania, for the lack of a paper. And so I turned about and proceeded toward the Stars and Stripes and another government. Exiting I had not been required to stop, but now the barrier was down.

"Are you an American citizen?"

"Yes, sir, here's my passport."

"Do you have anything to declare?"

"I haven't been away."

"Have you a rabies vaccination certificate for your dog?"

"He hasn't been away either."

"But you are coming from Canada."

"I have not been in Canada."

I saw the steel come into eyes, the brows lower to a level of suspicion. Far from saving time, it looked as though I might lose much more than even Erie, Pennsylvania.

"Will you step into the office?"

This request had the effect on me a Gestapo knock on the door might have. It raises panic, anger, and guilty feelings whether or not I have done wrong. My voice took on the strident tone of virtuous outrage which automatically arouses suspicion.

"Please step into the office."

"I tell you I have not been in Canada. If you were watching, you would have seen that I turned back."

"Step this way, please, sir."

Then into the telephone: "New York license so-and-so. Yes. Pick-up truck with camper top. Yes—a dog." And to me: "What kind of dog is it?"

"Poodle."

"Poodle—I said poodle. Light brown."

"Blue," I said.

"Light brown. Okay. Thanks."

I do hope I did not sense a certain sadness at my innocence.

"They say you didn't cross the line."

"That's what I told you."

"May I see your passport?"

"Why? I haven't left the country. I'm not about to leave the country." But I handed over my passport just the same. He leafed through it, pausing at the entry-and-exit stamps of other journeys. He inspected my photograph, opened the yellow small-pox vaccination certificate stapled to the back cover. At the bottom of the last page he saw pencilled in a faint set of letters and figures. "What is this?"

"I don't know. Let me see. Oh, that! Why, it's a telephone number."

"What's it doing in your passport?"

"I guess I didn't have a slip of paper. I don't even remember whose number it is."

By now he had me on the run and he knew it. "Don't you know it is against the law to deface a passport?"

"I'll erase it."

"You should not write anything in your passport. That's the regulation."

"I won't ever do it again. I promise." And I wanted to promise him I wouldn't lie or steal or associate with persons of loose morals, or covet my neighbor's wife, or anything. He closed my passport firmly and handed it back to me. I'm sure he felt better having found that telephone number. Suppose after all his trouble he hadn't found me guilty of anything, and on a slow day.

"Thank you, sir," I said. "May I proceed now?"

He waved his hand kindly. "Go ahead," he said.

And that's why I went toward Erie, Pennsylvania, and it was Charley's fault. I crossed the high iron bridge and stopped to pay toll. The man leaned out the window. "Go on," he said, "it's on the house."

"How do you mean?"

"I seen you go through the other way a little while ago. I seen the dog. I knew you'd be back."

"Why didn't you tell me?"

"Nobody believes it. Go ahead. You get a free ride one way."

He wasn't government, you see. But government can make you feel so small and mean that it takes some doing to build back a sense of self-importance. Charley and I stayed at the grandest auto court we could find that night, a place only the rich could afford, a pleasure dome of ivory and apes and peacocks and moreover with a restaurant, and room service. I ordered ice and soda and made a scotch and soda and then another. Then I had a waiter in and bespoke soup and a steak and a pound of raw hamburger for Charley, and I overtipped mercilessly. Before I went to sleep I went over all the things I wished I had said to that immigration man, and some of them were incredibly clever and cutting.

From the beginning of my journey, I had avoided the great high-speed slashes of concrete and tar called "thruways," or "super-highways." Various states have different names for them, but I had dawdled in New England, the winter grew apace, and I had visions of being snowbound in North Dakota. I sought out U.S. 90, a wide gash of a super-highway, multiple-lane carrier of the nation's goods. Rocinante bucketed along. The minimum speed on this road was greater than any I had previously driven. I drove into a wind quartering in from my starboard bow and felt the buffeting, sometimes staggering blows of the gale I helped to make. I could hear the sough of it on the square surfaces of my camper top. Instructions screamed at me from the road once: "Do not stop! No stopping. Maintain speed." Trucks as long as freighters went roaring by, delivering a wind like the blow of a fist. These great roads are wonderful for moving goods but not for inspection of a countryside. You are bound to the wheel and your eyes to the car ahead and to the rear-view mirror for the car behind and the side mirror for the car or truck about to pass, and at the same time you must read all the signs for fear you may miss some instructions or orders. No roadside stands selling squash juice, no antique stores, no farm products or factory outlets. When we get these thruways across the whole country, as we will and must, it will be possible to drive from New York to California without seeing a single thing.

At intervals there are places of rest and recreation, food, fuel and oil, postcards, steam-table food, picnic tables, garbage cans all fresh and newly painted, rest rooms and lavatories so spotless, so incensed with deodorants and with detergents that it takes a time to get your sense of smell back. For deodorants are not quite correctly named; they substitute one smell for another, and the substitute must be much stronger and more penetrating than the odor it conquers. I had neglected my own country too long. Civilization had made great strides in my absence. I remember when a coin in a slot would get you a stick of gum or a candy bar, but in these dining palaces were vending machines where various coins could deliver handkerchiefs, comb-and-nail-file sets, hair conditioners and cosmetics, first-aid kits, minor drugs such as aspirin, mild physics, pills to keep you awake. I found myself entranced with these gadgets. Suppose you want a soft drink; you pick your kind—Sungrape or Cooly Cola—press a button, insert the coin, and stand back. A paper cup drops into place, the drink pours out and stops a quarter of an inch from the brim— a cold, refreshing drink guaranteed synthetic. Coffee is even more interesting, for when the hot black fluid has ceased, a squirt of milk comes down and an envelope of sugar drops beside the cup. But of all, the hot-soup machine is the triumph. Choose among ten—pea, chicken noodle, beef and veg., insert the coin. A rumbling hum comes from the giant and a sign lights up that reads "Heating." After a minute a red light flashes on and off until you open a little door and remove the paper cup of boiling-hot soup.

It is life at a peak of some kind of civilization. The restaurant accommodations, great scallops of counters with simulated leather stools, are as spotless as and not unlike the lavatories. Everything that can be captured and held down is sealed in clear plastic. The food is oven-fresh, spotless and tasteless; untouched by human hands. I remembered with an ache certain dishes in France and Italy touched by innumerable human hands.

These centers for rest, food, and replenishment are kept beautiful with lawns and flowers. At the front, nearest the highway, are parking places for passenger automobiles together with regiments of gasoline pumps. At the rear the trucks draw up, and there they have their services—the huge overland caravans. Being technically a truck, Rocinante took her place in the rear, and I soon made acquaintance with the truckers. They are a breed set apart from the life around them, the long-distance truckers. In some town or city somewhere their wives and children live while the husbands traverse the nation carrying every kind of food and product and machine. They are clannish and they stick together, speaking a specialized language. And although I was a small craft among monsters of transportation they were kind to me and helpful.

I learned that in the truck parks there are showers and soap and towels—that I could park and sleep the night if I wished. The men had little commerce with local people, but being avid radio listeners they could report news and politics from all parts of the nation. The food and fuel centers on the parkways or thruways are leased by the various states, but on other highways private enterprise has truckers' stations that offer discounts on fuel, beds, baths, and places to sit and shoot the breeze. But being a specialized group, leading special lives, associating only with their own kind, they would have made it possible for me to cross the country without talking to a local town-bound man. For the truckers cruise over the surface of the nation without being a part of it. Of course in the towns where their families live they have whatever roots are possible—clubs, dances, love affairs, and murders.

I liked the truckers very much, as I always like specialists. By listening to them talk I accumulated a vocabulary of the road, of tires and springs, of overweight. The truckers over long distances have stations along their routes where they know the service men and the waitresses behind the counters, and where occasionally they meet their opposite numbers in other trucks. The great get-together symbol is the cup of coffee. I found I often stopped for coffee, not because I wanted it but for a rest and a change from the unrolling highway. It takes strength and control and attention to drive a truck long distances, no matter how much the effort is made easier by air brakes and power-assisted steering. It would be interesting to know and easy to establish with modern testing methods how much energy in foot pounds is expended in driving a truck for six hours. Once Ed Ricketts and I, collecting marine animals, turning over rocks in an area, tried to estimate how much weight we lifted in an average collecting day. The stones we turned over were not large—weighing from three to fifty pounds. We estimated that on a rich day, when we had little sense of energy expended, each of us had lifted four to ten tons of rock. Consider then the small, unnoticed turning of the steering wheel, perhaps the exertion of only one pound for each motion, the varying pressure of foot on accelerator, not more than half a pound perhaps but an enormous total over a period of six hours. Then there are the muscles of shoulders and neck, constantly if unconsciously flexed for emergency, the eyes darting from road to rear-view mirror, the thousand decisions so deep that the conscious mind is not aware of them. The output of energy, nervous and muscular, is enormous. Thus the coffee break is a rest in many senses.

Quite often I sat with these men and listened to their talk and now and then asked questions. I soon learned not to expect knowledge of the country they passed through. Except for the truck stops, they had no contact with it. It was driven home to me how like sailors they were. I remember when I first went to sea being astonished that the men who sailed over the world and touched the ports to the strange and exotic had little contact with that world. Some of the truckers on long hauls traveled in pairs and took their turns. The one off duty slept or read paperbacks. But on the roads their interests were engines, and weather, and maintaining the speed that makes a predictable schedule possible. Some of them were on regular runs back and forth while others moved over single operations. It is a whole pattern of life, little known to the settled people along the routes of the great trucks. I learned only enough about these men to be sure I would like to know much more.

If one has driven a car over many years, as I have,

nearly all reactions have become automatic. One does not think about what to do. Nearly all the driving technique is deeply buried in a machine-like unconscious. This being so, a large area of the conscious mind is left free for thinking. And what do people think of when they drive? On short trips perhaps of arrival at a destination or memory of events at the place of departure. But there is left, particularly on very long trips, a large area for day-dreaming or even, God help us, for thought. No one can know what another does in that area. I myself have planned houses I will never build, have made gardens I will never plant, have designed a method for pumping the soft silt and decayed shells from the bottom of my bay up to my point of land at Sag Harbor, of leeching out the salt, thus making a rich and productive soil. I don't know whether or not I will do this, but driving along I have planned it in detail even to the kind of pump, the leeching bins, the tests to determine disappearance of salinity. Driving, I have created turtle traps in my mind, have written long, detailed letters never to be put to paper, much less sent. When the radio was on, music has stimulated memory of times and places, complete with characters and stage sets, memories so exact that every word of dialogue is recreated. And I have projected future scenes, just as complete and convincing—scenes that will never take place. I've written short stories in my mind, chuckling at my own humor, saddened or stimulated by structure or content.

I can only suspect that the lonely man peoples his driving dreams with friends, that the loveless man surrounds himself with lovely loving women, and that children climb through the dreaming of the childless driver. And how about the areas of regrets? If only I had done so-and-so, or had not said such-and-such—my God, the damn thing might not have happened. Finding this potential in my own mind, I can suspect it in others, but I will never know, for no one ever tells. And this is why, on my journey which was designed for observation, I stayed as much as possible on secondary roads where there was much to see and hear and smell, and avoided the great wide traffic slashes which promote the self by fostering daydreams. I drove this wide, eventless way called U.S. 90 which bypassed Buffalo and Erie to Madison, Ohio, and then found the equally wide and fast U.S. 20 past Cleveland and Toledo, and so into Michigan.

On these roads out of the manufacturing centers there moved many mobile homes, pulled by specially designed trucks, and since these mobile homes comprise one of my generalities, I may as well get to them now. Early in my travels I had become aware of these new things under the sun, of their great numbers, and since they occur in increasing numbers all over the nation, observation of them and perhaps some speculation is in order. They are not trailers to be pulled by one's own car but shining cars long as pullmans. From the beginning of my travels I had noticed the sale lots where they were sold and traded, but then I began to be aware of the parks where they sit down in uneasy permanence. In Maine I took to stopping the night in these parks, talking to the managers and to the dwellers in this new kind of housing, for they gather in groups of like to like.

They are wonderfully built homes, aluminum skins, double-walled, with insulation, and often paneled with veneer of hardwood. Sometimes as much as forty feet long, they have two to five rooms, and are complete with air-conditioners, toilets, baths, and invariably television. The parks where they sit are sometimes landscaped and equipped with every facility. I talked with the park men, who were enthusiastic. A mobile home is drawn to the trailer park and installed on a ramp, a heavy rubber sewer pipe is bolted underneath, water and electric power connected, the television antenna raised, and the family is in residence. Several park managers agreed that last year one in four new housing units in the whole country was a mobile home. The park men charge a small ground rent plus fees for water and electricity. Telephones are connected in nearly all of them simply by plugging in a jack. Sometimes the park has a general store for supplies, but if not the supermarkets which dot the countryside are available. Parking difficulties in the towns have caused these markets to move to the open country where they are immune from town taxes. This is also true of the trailer parks. The fact that these homes can be moved does not mean that they do move. Sometimes their owners stay for years in one place, plant gardens, build little walls of cinder blocks, put out awnings and garden furniture. It is a whole way of life that was new to me. These homes are never cheap and often are quite expensive and lavish. I have seen some that cost $20,000 and contained all the thousand appliances we live by—dishwashers, automatic clothes washers and driers, refrigerators and deep freezes.

The owners were not only willing but glad and proud to show their homes to me. The rooms, while small, were well proportioned. Every conceivable unit was built in. Wide windows, some even called picture windows, destroyed any sense of being closed in; the bedrooms and beds were spacious and the storage space unbelievable. It seemed to me a revolution in living and on a rapid increase. Why did a family choose to live in such a home? Well, it was comfortable, compact, easy to keep clean, easy to heat.

In Maine: "I'm tired of living in a cold barn with the wind whistling through, tired of the torment of little taxes and payments for this and that. It's warm and cozy and in the summer the air-conditioner keeps us cool."

"What is the usual income bracket of the mobiles?"

"That is variable but a goodly number are in the ten-thousand- to twenty-thousand-dollar class."

"Has job uncertainty anything to do with the rapid increase of these units?"

"Well perhaps there may be some of that. Who knows what is in store tomorrow? Mechanics, plant engineers, architects, accountants, and even here and there a doctor or a dentist live in the mobile. If a plant or a factory closes down, you're not trapped with property you can't sell. Suppose the husband has a job and is buying a house and there's a layoff. The value goes out of his house. But if he has a mobile home he rents a trucking service and moves on and he hasn't lost anything. He may never have to do it, but the fact that he can is a comfort to him."

"How are they purchased?"

"On time, just like an automobile. It's like paying rent."

And then I discovered the greatest selling appeal of all—one that crawls through nearly all American life. Improvements are made on these mobile homes every year. If you are doing well you turn yours in on a new model just as you do with an automobile if you can possibly afford to. There's status to that. And the turn-in value is higher than that of automobiles because there's a ready market for used homes. And after a few years the once expensive home may have a poorer family. They are easy to maintain, need no paint since they are usually of aluminum, and are not tied to fluctuating land values.

"How about schools?"

The school buses pick the children up right at the park and bring them back. The family car takes the head of the house to work and the family to a drive-in movie at night. It's a healthy life out in the country air. The payments, even if high and festooned with interest, are no worse than renting an apartment and fighting the owner for heat. And where could you rent such a comfortable ground-floor apartment with a place for your car outside the door? Where else could the kids have a dog? Nearly every mobile home has a dog, as Charley discovered to his delight. Twice I was invited to dinner in a mobile home and several times watched a football game on television. A manager told me that one of the first considerations in his business was to find and buy a place where television reception is good. Since I did not require any facilities, sewer, water, or electricity, the price to me for stopping the night was one dollar.

The first impression forced on me was that permanence is neither achieved nor desired by mobile people. They do not buy for the generations, but only until a new model they can afford comes out. The mobile units are by no means limited to the park communities. Hundreds of them will be found sitting beside a farm house, and this was explained to me. There was a time when, on the occasion of a son's marriage and the addition of a wife and later of children to the farm, it was customary to add a wing or at least a lean-to on the home place. Now in many cases a mobile unit takes the place of additional building. A farmer from whom I bought eggs and home-smoked bacon told me of the advantages. Each family has a privacy it never had before. The old folks are not irritated by crying babies. The mother-in-law problem is abated because the new daughter has a privacy she never had and a place of her own in which to build the structure of a family. When they move away, and nearly all Americans move away, or want to, they do not leave unused and therefore useless rooms. Relations between the generations are greatly improved. The son is a guest when he visits the parents' house, and the parents are guests in the son's house.

Then there are the loners, and I have talked with them also. Driving along, you see high on a hill a single mobile home placed to command a great view. Others nestle under trees fringing a river or a lake. These loners have rented a tiny piece of land from the owner. They need only enough for the unit and the right of passage to get to it. Sometimes the loner digs a well and a cesspool, and plants a small garden, but others transport their water in fifty-gallon oil drums. Enormous ingenuity is apparent with some of the loners in placing the water supply higher than the unit and connecting it with plastic pipe so that a gravity flow is insured.

One of the dinners that I shared in a mobile home was cooked in an immaculate kitchen, walled in plastic tile, with stainless-steel sinks and ovens and stoves flush with the wall. The fuel is butane or some other bottled gas which can be picked up anywhere. We ate in a dining alcove paneled in mahogany veneer. I've never had a better or a more comfortable dinner. I had brought a bottle of whisky as my contribution, and afterward we sat in deep comfortable chairs cushioned in foam rubber. This family liked the way they lived and wouldn't think of going back to the old way. The husband worked as a garage mechanic about four miles away and made good pay. Two children walked to the highway every morning and were picked up by a yellow school bus.

Sipping a highball after dinner, hearing the rushing of water in the electric dishwasher in the kitchen, I brought up a question that had puzzled me. These were good, thoughtful, intelligent people. I said, "One of our most treasured feelings concerns roots, growing up rooted in some soil or some community." How did they feel about raising their children without roots? Was it good or bad? Would they miss it or not?

The father, a good-looking, fair-skinned man with dark eyes, answered me. "How many people today have what you are talking about? What roots are there in an apartment twelve floors up? What roots are in a housing development of hundreds and thousands of small dwellings almost exactly alike? My father came from Italy," he said. "He grew up in Tuscany in a house where his family had lived maybe a thousand years. That's roots for you, no running water, no toilet, and they cooked with charcoal or vine clippings. They had just two rooms, a kitchen and a bedroom where everybody slept, grandpa, father and all the kids, no place to read, no place to be alone, and never had had. Was that better? I bet if you gave my old man the choice he'd cut his roots and live like this." He waved his hands at the comfortable room. "Fact is, he cut his roots away and came to America. Then he lived in a tenement in New York—just one room, walk-up, cold water and no heat. That's where I was born and I lived in the streets as a kid until my old man got a job upstate in New York in the grape country. You see, he knew about vines, that's about all he knew. Now you take my wife. She's Irish descent. Her people had roots too."

"In a peat bog," the wife said. "And lived on potatoes." She gazed fondly through the door at her fine kitchen.

"Don't you miss some kind of permanence?"

"Who's got permanence? Factory closes down, you move on. Good times and things opening up, you move on where it's better. You got roots you sit and starve. You take the pioneers in the history books. They were movers. Take up land, sell it, move on. I read in a book how Lincoln's family came to Illinois on a raft. They had some barrels of whisky for a bank account. How many kids in America stay in the place where they were born, if they can get out?"

"You've thought about it a lot."

"Don't have to think about it. There it is. I've got a good trade. Long as there's automobiles I can get work, but suppose the place I work goes broke. I got to move where there's a job. I get to my job

in three minutes. You want I should drive twenty
miles because I got roots?"

Later they showed me magazines designed exclusively for mobile dwellers, stories and poems and
hints for successful mobile living. How to stop a
leak. How to choose a place for sun or coolness.
And there were advertisements for gadgets, fascinat-
ing things, for cooking, cleaning, washing clothes,
furniture and beds and cribs. Also there were full-
page pictures of new models, each one grander and
more shiny than the next.

"There's thousands of them," said the father,
"and there's going to be millions."

"Joe's quite a dreamer," the wife said. "He's always figuring something out. Tell him your ideas,
Joe."

"Maybe he wouldn't be interested."

"Sure I would."

"Well, it's not a dream like she said, it's for real,
and I'm going to do it pretty soon now. Take a
little capital, but it would pay off. I been looking
around the used lots for the unit I want at the
price I want to pay. Going to rip out the guts and
set it up for a repair shop. I got enough tools nearly
already, and I'll stock little things like windshield
wipers and fan belts and cylinder rings and inner
tubes, stuff like that. You take these courts are
getting bigger and bigger. Some of the mobile people got two cars. I'll rent me a hundred feet of
ground right near and I'll be in business. There's
one thing you can say about cars, there's nearly
always something wrong with them that's got to be
fixed. And I'll have my house, this here one right
beside my shop. That way I would have a bell and
give twenty-four-hour service."

"Sounds like a good deal," I said. And it does.

"Best thing about it," Joe went on, "if business fell off, why, I'd just move on where it was good."

His wife said, "Joe's got it all worked out on paper where everything's going to go, every wrench and drill, even an electric welder. Joe's a wonderful welder."

I said, "I take back what I said, Joe. I guess you've got your roots in a grease pit."

"You could do worse. I even worked that out. And you know, when the kids grow up, we could even work our way south in the winter and north in the summer."

"Joe does good work," said his wife. "He's got his own steady customers where he works. Some men come fifty miles to get Joe to work on their cars because he does good work."

"I'm a real good mechanic," said Joe.

Driving the big highway near Toledo I had a conversation with Charley on the subject of roots. He listened but he didn't reply. In the pattern-thinking about roots I and most other people have left two things out of consideration. Could it be that Americans are a restless people, a mobile people, never satisfied with where they are as a matter of selection? The pioneers, the immigrants who peopled the continent, were the restless ones in Europe. The steady rooted ones stayed home and are still there. But every one of us, except the Negroes forced here as slaves, are descended from the restless ones, the wayward ones who were not content to stay at home. Wouldn't it be unusual if we had not inherited this tendency? And the fact is that we have. But that's the short view. What are roots and how long have we had them? If our species has existed for a couple of million years, what is its history? Our remote ancestors followed the game, moved with the food supply, and fled from evil weather, from ice and the changing seasons. Then after millennia beyond thinking they domesticated some animals so that they lived with their food supply. Then of necessity they followed the grass that fed their flocks in endless wanderings. Only when agriculture came into practice—and that's not very long ago in terms of the whole history—did a place achieve meaning and value and permanence. But land is a tangible, and tangibles have a way of getting into few hands. Thus it was that one man wanted ownership of land and at the same time wanted servitude because someone had to work it. Roots were in ownership of land, in tangible and immovable possessions. In this view we are a restless species with a very short history of roots, and those not widely distributed. Perhaps we have overrated roots as a psychic need. Maybe the greater the urge, the deeper and more ancient is the need, the will, the hunger to be somewhere else.

Charley had no answer to my premise. Also, he was a mess. I had promised myself to keep him combed and clipped and beautiful, and I hadn't done it. His fur was balled and dirty. Poodles do not shed any more than sheep do. At night, when I had planned this virtuous grooming, I was always too busy with something else. Also I discovered a dangerous allergy I didn't know he had. One night I had pulled up at a trucker's park where huge cattle trucks put up and cleaned their beds; around the park there was a mountain of manure and a fog of flies. Although Rocinante was screened the flies got in in their millions and hid in corners and would not be dislodged. For the first time I got out the bug bomb and sprayed heavily, and Charley broke into a sneezing attack so violent and prolonged that I had finally to carry him out in my arms. In the morning the cab was full of sleepy flies and I sprayed it and Charley had another attack. After that, whenever flying visitors invaded I had to close Charley out and air out the house or cab after the pests were dead. I never saw such a severe allergy.

Since I hadn't seen the Middle West for a long time many impressions crowded in on me as I drove through Ohio and Michigan and Illinois. The first was the enormous increase in population. Villages had become towns and towns had grown to cities. The roads squirmed with traffic; the cities were so dense with people that all attention had to be devoted to not hitting anyone or not being hit. The next impression was of an electric energy, a force, almost a fluid of energy so powerful as to be stunning in its impact. No matter what the direction, whether for good or for bad, the vitality was everywhere. I don't think for a second that the people I had seen and talked to in New England were either unfriendly or discourteous, but they spoke tersely and usually waited for the newcomer to open communication. Almost on crossing the Ohio line it seemed to me that people were more open and more outgoing. The waitress in a roadside stand said good morning before I had a chance to, discussed breakfast as though she liked the idea, spoke with enthusiasm about the weather, sometimes even offered some information about herself without my delving. Strangers talked freely to one another without caution. I had forgotten how rich and beautiful is the countryside—the deep topsoil, the wealth of great trees, the lake country of Michigan handsome as a well-made woman, and dressed and jeweled. It seemed to me that the earth was generous and outgoing here in the heartland, and perhaps the people took a cue from it.

One of my purposes was to listen, to hear speech, accent, speech rhythms, overtones and emphasis. For speech is so much more than words and sentences. I did listen everywhere. It seemed to me that regional speech is in the process of disappearing, not gone but going. Forty years of radio and twenty years of television must have this impact. Communications must destroy localness, by a slow, inevitable process. I can remember a time when I could almost pinpoint a man's place of origin by his speech. That is growing more difficult now and will in some foreseeable future become impossible. It is a rare house or building that is not rigged with spiky combers of the air. Radio and television speech becomes standardized, perhaps better English than we have ever used. Just as our bread, mixed and baked, packaged and sold without benefit of accident or human frailty, is uniformly good and uniformly tasteless, so will our speech become one speech.

I who love words and the endless possibility of words am saddened by this inevitability. For with local accent will disappear local tempo. The idioms, the figures of speech that make language rich and full of the poetry of place and time must go. And in their place will be a national speech, wrapped and packaged, standard and tasteless. Localness is not gone but it is going. In the many years since I have listened to the land the change is very great. Traveling west along the northern routes I did not hear a truly local speech until I reached Montana. That is one of the reasons I fell in love again with Montana. The West Coast went back to packaged English. The Southwest kept a grasp but a slipping grasp on localness. Of course the deep south holds on by main strength to its regional expressions, just as it holds and treasures some other anachronisms, but no region can hold out for long against the highway, the high-tension line, and the national television. What I am mourning is perhaps not worth saving, but I regret its loss nevertheless.

Even while I protest the assembly-line production of our food, our songs, our language, and eventually our souls, I know that it was a rare home that baked good bread in the old days. Mother's cooking was with rare exceptions poor, that good unpasteurized milk touched only by flies and bits of manure crawled with bacteria, the healthy old-time life was riddled with aches, sudden death from unknown causes, and that sweet local speech I mourn was the child of illiteracy and ignorance. It is the nature of a man as he grows older, a small bridge in time, to protest against change, particularly change for the better. But it is true that we have exchanged corpulence for starvation, and either one will kill us. The lines of change are down. We, or at least I, can have no conception of human life and human thought in a hundred years or fifty years. Perhaps my greatest wisdom is the knowledge that I do not know. The sad ones are those who waste their energy in trying to hold it back, for they can only feel bitterness in loss and no joy in gain.

As I passed through or near the great hives of production—Youngstown, Cleveland, Akron, Toledo, Pontiac, Flint, and later South Bend and Gary—my eyes and mind were battered by the fantastic hugeness and energy of production, a complication that resembles chaos and cannot be. So might one look down on an ant hill and see no method or direction or purpose in the darting hurrying inhabitants. What was so wonderful was that I could come again to a quiet country road, tree-bordered, with fenced fields and cows, could pull up Rocinante beside a lake of clear, clean water and see high overhead the arrows of southing ducks and geese. There Charley could with his delicate exploring nose read his own particular literature on bushes and tree trunks and leave his message there, perhaps as important in endless time as these pen scratches I put down on perishable paper. There in the quiet, with the wind flicking tree branches and distorting the water's mirror, I cooked improbable dinners in my disposable aluminum pans, made coffee so rich and sturdy it would float a nail, and, sitting on my own back doorsteps, could finally come to think about what I had seen and try to arrange some pattern of thought to accommodate the teeming crowds of my seeing and hearing.

I'll tell you what it was like. Go to the Ufizzi in Florence, the Louvre in Paris, and you are so crushed with the numbers, once the might of greatness, that you go away distressed, with a feeling like constipation. And then when you are alone and remembering, the canvases sort themselves out; some are eliminated by your taste or your limitations, but others stand up clear and clean. Then you can go back to look at one thing untroubled by the shouts of the multitude. After confusion I can go into the Prado in Madrid and pass unseeing the thousand pictures shouting for my attention and I can visit a friend—a not large Greco, *San Pablo con un Libro*. St. Paul has just closed the book. His finger marks the last page read and on his face are the wonder and will to understand after the book is closed. Maybe understanding is possible only after. Years ago when I used to work in the woods it was said of lumber men that they did their logging in the whorehouse and their sex in the woods. So I have to find my way through the exploding production lines of the Middle West while sitting alone beside a lake in northern Michigan.

As I sat secure in the silence, a jeep scuffed to a stop on the road and good Charley left his work and roared. A young man in boots, corduroys, and a red and black checked mackinaw climbed out and strode near. He spoke in the harsh unfriendly tone a man uses when he doesn't much like what he has to do.

"Don't you know this land is posted? This is private property."

Normally his tone would have sparked a tinder in me. I would have flared an ugliness of anger and he would then have been able to evict me with pleasure and good conscience. We might even have edged into a quarrel with passion and violence. That would be only normal, except that the beauty and the quiet made me slow to respond with resentment, and in my hesitation I lost it. I said, "I knew it must be private. I was about to look for someone to ask permission or maybe pay to rest here."

"The owner don't want campers. They leave papers around and build fires."

"I don't blame him. I know the mess they make."

"See that sign on that tree? No trespassing, hunting, fishing, camping."

"Well," I said, "that sounds as if it means business. If it's your job to throw me off, you've got to throw me off. I'll go peacefully. But I've just made a pot of coffee. Do you think your boss would mind if I finished it? Would he mind if I offered you a cup? Then you could kick me off quicker."

The young man grinned. "What the hell," he said. "You don't build no fires and you don't throw out no trash."

"I'm doing worse than that. I'm trying to bribe you with a cup of coffee. It's worse than that, too. I'm suggesting a dollop of Old Granddad in the coffee."

He laughed then. "What the hell!" he said. "Let me get my jeep off the road."

Well, the whole pattern was broken. He squatted crosslegged in the pine needles on the ground and sipped his coffee. Charley sniffed close and let himself be touched, and that's a rare thing for Charley. He does not permit strangers to touch him, just happens to be somewhere else. But this young man's fingers found the place behind the ears Charley delights to have rubbed, and he sighed contentedly and sat down.

"What you doing—going hunting? I see your guns in the truck."

"Just driving through. You know how you see a place and it's just right, and you're just tired enough, I guess you can't help stopping."

"Yeah," he said. "I know what you mean. You got a nice outfit."

"I like it and Charley likes it."

"Charley? Never heard of a dog named Charley. Hello, Charley."

"I wouldn't want to get you in trouble with your boss. Think I ought to drag ass now?"

"What the hell?" he said. "He ain't here. I'm in charge. You ain't doing no harm."

"I'm trespassing."

"Know something? Fella camped here, kind of a nut. So I came to kick him off. He said something funny. He says, 'Trespassing ain't a crime and ain't a misdemeanor.' He says it's a tort. Now what the hell does that mean? He was a kind of a nut."

"Search me," I said, "I'm not a nut. Let me warm up your coffee." I warmed it two ways.

"You make swell coffee," said my host.

"Before it gets too dark I've got to find a place to park. Know any place up the road where they'll let me stay the night?"

"If you pull over that way behind those pine trees nobody could see you from the road."

"But I'd be committing a tort."

"Yeah. I wish to Christ I knew what that meant."

He drove ahead of me in the jeep and helped me find a level place in the pine grove. And after dark he came into Rocinante and admired her facilities and we drank some whisky together and had a nice visit and told each other a few lies. I showed him some fancy jigs and poppers I'd bought at Abercrombie and Fitch, and gave him one, and I gave him some paperback thrillers I'd finished with, all loaded with sex and sadism, and also a copy of *Field and Stream*. In return he invited me to stay as long

as I wished and said that he'd come by tomorrow
and we'd do a little fishing, and I accepted for one
day at least. It's nice to have friends, and besides I
wanted a little time to think about the things I'd
seen, the huge factories and plants and the scurry
and production.

The guardian of the lake was a lonely man, the
more so because he had a wife. He showed me her
picture in a plastic shield in his wallet, a prettyish
blonde girl trying her best to live up to the pictures
in the magazines, a girl of products, home perma-
nents, shampoos, rinses, skin conditioners. She
hated being out in what she called the Sticks,
longed for the great and gracious life in Toledo or
South Bend. Her only company was found in the
shiny pages of *Charm* and *Glamour*. Eventually she
would sulk her way to success. Her husband would
get a job in some great clanging organism of
progress, and they would live happily ever after. All
this came through in small, oblique spurts in his
conversation. She knew exactly what she wanted
and he didn't, but his want would ache in him all
his life. After he drove away in his jeep I lived his
life for him and it put a mist of despair on me. He
wanted his pretty little wife and he wanted something else and he couldn't have both.

Charley had a dream so violent that he awakened
me. His legs jerked in the motions of running and
he made little yipping cries. Perhaps he dreamed
he chased some gigantic rabbit and couldn't quite
catch it. Or maybe in his dream something chased
him. On the second supposition I put out my hand
and awakened him, but the dream must have been
strong. He muttered to himself and complained

and drank half a bowl of water before he went back to sleep.

The guardian came back soon after sun-up. He brought a rod and I got out my own and rigged a spinning reel, and had to find my glasses to tie on the bright painted popper. The monofilament line is transparent, said to be invisible to fish, and is completely invisible to me without my glasses.

I said, "You know, I don't have a fishing license."

"What the hell," he said, "we probably won't catch anything anyway."

And he was right, we didn't.

We walked and cast and walked and did everything we knew to interest bass or pike. My friend kept saying, "They're right down there if we can just get the message through." But we never did. If they were down there, they still are. A remarkable amount of my fishing is like that, but I like it just the same. My wants are simple. I have no desire to latch onto a monster symbol of fate and prove my manhood in titanic piscine war. But sometimes I do like a couple of cooperative fish of frying size. At noon I refused an invitation to come to dinner and meet the wife. I was growing increasingly anxious to meet my own wife, so I hurried on.

There was a time not too long ago when a man put out to sea and ceased to exist for two or three years or forever. And when the covered wagons set out to cross the continent, friends and relations remaining at home might never hear from the wanderers again. Life went on, problems were settled, decisions were taken. Even I can remember when a telegram meant just one thing—a death in the family. In one short lifetime the telephone has changed all that. If in this wandering narrative I seem to have cut the cords of family joys and sorrows, of Junior's current delinquency and junior Junior's new tooth, of business triumph and agony, it is not so. Three times a week from some bar, supermarket, or tire-and-tool cluttered service station, I put calls through to New York and reestablished my identity in time and space. For three or four minutes I had a name, and the duties and joys and frustrations a man carries with him like a comet's tail. It was like dodging back and forth from one dimension to another, a silent explosion of breaking through a sound barrier, a curious experience, like a quick dip into a known but alien water.

It was established that my wife was to fly out to meet me in Chicago for a short break in my journey. In two hours, in theory at least, she would slice through a segment of the earth it had taken me weeks to clamber over. I became impatient, stuck to the huge toll road that strings the northern border of Indiana, bypassed Elkhart and South Bend and Gary. The nature of the road describes the nature of the travel. The straightness of the way, the swish of traffic, the unbroken speed are hypnotic, and while the miles peel off an imperceptible exhaustion sets in. Day and night are one. The setting sun is neither an invitation nor a command to stop, for the traffic rolls constantly.

Late in the night I pulled into a rest area, had a hamburger at the great lunch counter that never closes, and walked Charley on the close-clipped grass. I slept an hour but awakened long before daylight. I had brought city suits and shirts and shoes, but had forgotten to bring a suitcase to transport them from truck to hotel room. Indeed, I don't know where I could have stored a suitcase. In a garbage can under an arc light I found a clean corrugated paper carton and packed my city clothes. I wrapped my clean white shirts in road maps and tied the carton with fishing line.

Knowing my tendency to panic in the roar and crush of traffic, I started into Chicago long before daylight. I wanted to end up at the Ambassador East, where I had reservations, and, true to form, ended up lost. Finally, in a burst of invention, I hired an all-night taxi to lead me, and sure enough I had passed very near my hotel. If the doorman and bellhops found my means of traveling unusual, they gave no sign. I handed out my suits on hangers, my shoes in the game pocket of a hunting coat, and my shirts in their neat wrapping of New England road maps. Rocinante was whisked away to a garage for storage. Charley had to go to a kennel to be stored, bathed, and Hollanderized. Even at his age he is a vain dog and loves to be beautified, but when he found he was to be left and in Chicago, his ordinary aplomb broke down and he cried out in rage and despair. I closed my ears and went away quickly to my hotel.

I think I am well and favorably known at the Ambassador East, but this need not apply when I arrive in wrinkled hunting clothes, unshaven and lightly crusted with the dirt of travel and bleary-eyed from driving most of the night. Certainly I had a reservation, but my room might not be vacated until noon. The hotel's position was explained to me carefully. I understood it and forgave the management. My own position was that I would like a bath and a bed, but since that was impossible I would simply pile up in a chair in the lobby and go to sleep until my room was ready.

I saw in the desk man's eyes his sense of uneasiness. Even I knew I would be no ornament to this elegant and expensive pleasure dome. He signaled an assistant manager, perhaps by telepathy, and all together we worked out a solution. A gentleman had just checked out to catch an early airplane. His room was not cleaned and prepared, but I was welcome to use it until mine was ready. Thus the problem was solved by intelligence and patience, and each got what he wanted—I had my chance at a hot bath and a sleep, and the hotel was spared the mischance of having me in the lobby.

The room had not been touched since its former occupant had left. I sank into a comfortable chair to pull off my boots and even got one of them off before I began to notice things and then more things and more. In a surprisingly short time I forgot the bath and the sleep and found myself deeply involved with Lonesome Harry.

An animal resting or passing by leaves crushed grass, footprints, and perhaps droppings, but a human occupying a room for one night prints his character, his biography, his recent history, and sometimes his future plans and hopes. I further believe that personality seeps into walls and is slowly released. This might well be an explanation of ghosts and such manifestations. Although my conclusions may be wrong, I seem to be sensitive to the spoor of the human. Also, I am not shy about admitting that I am an incorrigible Peeping Tom. I have never passed an unshaded window without looking in, have never closed my ears to a conversation that was none of my business. I can justify or even dignify this by protesting that in my trade I must know about people, but I suspect that I am simply curious.

As I sat in this unmade room, Lonesome Harry began to take shape and dimension. I could feel that recently departed guest in the bits and pieces of himself he had left behind. Of course Charley, even with his imperfect nose, would have known more. But Charley was in a kennel preparing to be clipped. Even so, Harry is as real to me as anyone I ever met, and more real than many. He is not unique, in fact is a member of a fairly large group. Therefore he becomes of interest in any investigation of America. Before I begin to patch him together, lest a number of men grow nervous, let me declare that his name is not Harry. He lives in Westport, Connecticut. This information comes from the laundry strips from several shirts. A man usually lives where he has his shirts laundered. I only suspect that he commutes to work in New York. His trip to Chicago was primarily a business trip with some traditional pleasures thrown in. I know his name because he signed it a number of times on hotel stationery, each signature with a slightly different slant. This seems to indicate that he is not entirely sure of himself in the business world, but there were other signs of that.

He had started a letter to his wife which also ended in the wastebasket. "Darling: Everything is going OK. Tried to call your aunt but no answer. I wish you were here with me. This is a lonesome town. You forgot to put in my cuff links. I bought a cheap pair at Marshall Field. I'm writing this while I wait for C.E. to call. Hope he brings the cont . . ."

It's just as well that Darling didn't drop in to make Chicago less lonesome for Harry. His guest was not C.E. with a contract. She was a brunette and wore very pale lipstick—cigarette butts in the ash tray and the edge of a highball glass. They drank Jack Daniel's, a whole bottle—the empty bottle, six soda bottles, and a tub that had held ice cubes. She used a heavy perfume and did not stay the night—the second pillow used but not slept on, also no lipstick on discarded tissues. I like to think her name was Lucille—I don't know why. Maybe because it was and is. She was a nervous friend—smoked Harry's recessed, filtered cigarettes but stubbed each one out only one-third smoked and lighted another, and she didn't put them out, she crushed them, frayed the ends. Lucille wore one of those little smidgins of hats held on by inturned combs. One of the combs broke loose. That and a bobby pin beside the bed told me Lucille is a brunette. I don't know whether or not Lucille is professional, but at least she is practiced. There is a fine businesslike quality about her. She didn't leave too many things around, as an amateur might. Also she didn't get drunk. Her glass was empty but the vase of red roses—courtesy of the management—smelled of Jack Daniel's, and it didn't do them any good.

I wonder what Harry and Lucille talked about. I wonder whether she made him less lonesome. Somehow I doubt it. I think both of them were doing what was expected of them. Harry shouldn't have slugged his drinks. His stomach isn't up to it—Tums wrappers in the wastebasket. I guess his business is a sensitive one and hard on the stomach. Lonesome Harry must have finished the bottle after

Lucille left. He had a hangover—two foil tubes of Bromo Seltzer in the bathroom.

Three things haunted me about Lonesome Harry. First, I don't think he had any fun; second, I think he was really lonesome, maybe in a chronic state; and third, he didn't do a single thing that couldn't be predicted—didn't break a glass or a mirror, committed no outrages, left no physical evidence of joy. I had been hobbling around with one boot off finding out about Harry. I even looked under the bed and in the closet. He hadn't even forgotten a tie. I felt sad about Harry.

PART THREE

CHICAGO WAS A BREAK IN MY JOURNEY, A resumption of my name, identity, and happy marital status. My wife flew in from the East for her brief visit. I was delighted at the change, back to my known and trusted life—but here I run into a literary difficulty.

Chicago broke my continuity. This is permissible in life but not in writing. So I leave Chicago out, because it is off the line, out of drawing. In my travels, it was pleasant and good; in writing, it would contribute only a disunity.

When that time was over and the good-bys said, I had to go through the same lost loneliness all over again, and it was no less painful than at first. There seemed to be no cure for loneliness save only being alone.

Charley was torn three ways—with anger at me for leaving him, with gladness at the sight of Rocinante, and with pure pride in his appearance. For when Charley is groomed and clipped and washed he is as pleased with himself as is a man with a good tailor or a woman newly patinaed by a beauty parlor, all of whom can believe they are like that clear through. Charley's combed columns of legs were noble things, his cap of silver blue fur was rakish, and he carried the pompon of his tail like the baton of a bandmaster. A wealth of combed and clipped mustache gave him the appearance and attitude of a French rake of the nineteenth century, and incidentally concealed his crooked front teeth. I happen to know what he looks like without the tailoring. One summer when his fur grew matted and mildewed I clipped him to the skin. Under those sturdy towers of legs are spindly shanks, thin and not too straight; with his chest ruff removed one can see the sagging stomach of the middle-aged. But if Charley was aware of his deep-down inadequacy, he gave no sign. If manners maketh man, then manner and grooming maketh poodle. He sat straight and nobly in the seat of Rocinante and he gave me to understand that while forgiveness was not impossible, I would have to work for it.

He is a fraud and I know it. Once when our boys were little and in summer camp we paid them the deadly parents' visit. When we were about to depart, a lady parent told us she had to leave quickly to keep her child from going into hysterics. And with brave but trembling lips she fled blindly, masking her feeling to save her child. The boy watched her go and then with infinite relief went back to his gang and his business, knowing that he too had played the game. And I know for a fact that five minutes after I had left Charley he had found new friends and had made his arrangements for his comfort. But one thing Charley did not fake. He was delighted to be traveling again, and for a few days he was an ornament to the trip.

ILLINOIS DID A FAIR AUTUMN DAY FOR US, crisp and clean. We moved quickly northward, heading for Wisconsin through a noble land of good fields and magnificent trees, a gentleman's countryside, neat and white-fenced and I would guess subsidized by outside income. It did not seem to me to have the thrust of land that supports itself and its owner. Rather it was like a beautiful woman who requires the support and help of many faceless ones just to keep going. But this fact does not make her less lovely—if you can afford her.

It is possible, even probable, to be told a truth about a place, to accept it, to know it and at the same time not to know anything about it. I had never been to Wisconsin, but all my life I had heard about it, had eaten its cheeses, some of them as good as any in the world. And I must have seen pictures. Everyone must have. Why then was I unprepared for the beauty of this region, for its variety of field and hill, forest, lake? I think now I must have considered it one big level cow pasture because of the state's enormous yield of milk products. I never saw a country that changed so rapidly, and because I had not expected it everything I saw brought a delight. I don't know how it is in other seasons, the summers may reek and rock with heat, the winters may groan with dismal cold, but when I saw it for the first and only time in early October, the air was rich with butter-colored sunlight, not fuzzy but crisp and clear so that every frost-gay tree was set off, the rising hills were not compounded, but alone and separate. There was a penetration of the light into solid substance so that I seemed to see into things, deep in, and I've seen that kind of light elsewhere only in Greece. I remembered now that I had been told Wisconsin is a lovely state, but the telling had not prepared me. It was a magic day. The land dripped with richness, the fat cows and pigs gleaming against green, and, in the smaller holdings, corn standing in little tents as corn should, and pumpkins all about.

I don't know whether or not Wisconsin has a cheese-tasting festival, but I who am a lover of cheese believe it should. Cheese was everywhere, cheese centers, cheese cooperatives, cheese stores and stands, perhaps even cheese ice cream. I can believe anything, since I saw a score of signs advertising Swiss Cheese Candy. It is sad that I didn't stop to sample Swiss Cheese Candy. Now I can't persuade anyone that it exists, that I did not make it up.

Beside the road I saw a very large establishment, the greatest distributor of sea shells in the world—and this in Wisconsin, which hasn't known a sea since pre-Cambrian times. But Wisconsin is loaded with surprises. I had heard of the Wisconsin Dells but was not prepared for the weird country sculptured by the Ice Age, a strange, gleaming country of water and carved rock, black and green. To awaken here might make one believe it a dream of some other planet, for it has a non-earthly quality, or else the engraved record of a time when the world was much younger and much different. Clinging to the sides of the dreamlike waterways was the litter of our times, the motels, the hot-dog stands, the merchants of the cheap and mediocre and tawdry so loved by summer tourists, but these incrustations were closed and boarded against the winter and, even open, I doubt that they could dispel the enchantment of the Wisconsin Dells.

I stopped that night on a hilltop that was a truckers' place but of a special kind. Here the gigantic cattle trucks rested and scraped out the residue left by their recent cargoes. There were mountains of manure and over them mushroom clouds of flies. Charley moved about smiling and sniffing ecstatically like an American woman in a French perfume shop. I can't bring myself to criticize his taste. Some people like one thing and some another. The odors were rich and earthy, but not disgusting.

As the evening deepened, I walked with Charley among his mountains of delight to the brow of the hill and looked down on the little valley below. It was a disturbing sight. I thought too much driving had distorted my vision or addled my judgment, for the dark earth below seemed to move and pulse and breathe. It was not water but it rippled like a black liquid. I walked quickly down the hill to iron out the distortion. The valley floor was carpeted with turkeys, it seemed like millions of them, so densely packed that they covered the earth. It was a great relief. Of course, this was a reservoir for Thanksgiving.

To mill so close together is in the nature of turkeys in the evening. I remembered how on the ranch in my youth the turkeys gathered and roosted in clots in the cypress trees, out of reach of wildcats and coyotes, the only indication I know of that turkeys have any intelligence at all. To know them is not to admire them, for they are vain and hysterical. They gather in vulnerable groups and then panic at rumors. They are subject to all the sicknesses of other fowl, together with some they have invented. Turkeys seem to be manic-depressive types, gobbling with blushing wattles, spread tails, and scraping wings in amorous bravado at one moment and huddled in craven cowardice the next. It is hard to see how they can be related to their wild, clever, suspicious cousins. But here in their thousands they carpeted the earth waiting to lie on their backs on the platters of America.

I know it is a shame that I had never seen the noble twin cities of St. Paul and Minneapolis, but how much greater a disgrace that I still haven't, although I went through them. As I approached, a great surf of traffic engulfed me, waves of station wagons, rip tides of roaring trucks. I wonder why it is that when I plan a route too carefully it goes to pieces, whereas if I blunder along in blissful ignorance aimed in a fancied direction I get through with no trouble. In the early morning I had studied maps, drawn a careful line along the way I wished to go. I still have that arrogant plan—into St. Paul on Highway 10, then gently across the Mississippi. The S-curve in the Mississippi here would give me three crossings of the river. After this pleasant jaunt I meant to go through Golden Valley, drawn by its name. That seems simple enough, and perhaps it can be done, but not by me.

First the traffic struck me like a tidal wave and carried me along, a bit of shiny flotsam bounded in front by a gasoline truck half a block long. Behind me was an enormous cement mixer on wheels, its big howitzer revolving as it proceeded. On my right was what I judged to be an atomic cannon. As usual I panicked and got lost. Like a weakening swimmer I edged to the right into a pleasant street only to be stopped by a policeman, who informed me that trucks and such vermin were not permitted there. He thrust me back into the ravening stream.

I drove for hours, never able to take my eyes from the surrounding mammoths. I must have crossed the river but I couldn't see it. I never did see it. I never saw St. Paul or Minneapolis. All I saw was a river of trucks; all I heard was a roar of motors. The air saturated with Diesel fumes burned in my lungs. Charley got a coughing fit and I couldn't take time to pat him on the back. At a red light I saw that I was on an Evacuation Route. It took some time for that to penetrate. My head was spinning. I had lost all sense of direction. But the signs —"Evacuation Route"—continued. Of course, it is the planned escape route from the bomb that hasn't been dropped. Here in the middle of the Middle West an escape route, a road designed by fear. In my mind I could see it because I have seen people running away—the roads clogged to a standstill and the stampede over the cliff of our own designing. And suddenly I thought of that valley of the turkeys and wondered how I could have the gall to think turkeys stupid. Indeed, they have an advantage over us. They're good to eat.

It took me nearly four hours to get through the Twin Cities. I've heard that some parts of them are beautiful. And I never found Golden Valley. Charley was no help. He wasn't involved with a race that could build a thing it had to escape from. He didn't want to go to the moon just to get the hell away from it all. Confronted with our stupidities, Charley accepts them for what they are—stupidities.

Sometime in these bedlam hours I must have crossed the river again because I had got back on U.S. 10 and was moving north on the east side of the Mississippi. The country opened out and I stopped at a roadside restaurant, exhausted. It was a German restaurant complete with sausages, sauerkraut, and beer steins hanging in rows over the bar, shining but unused. I was the only customer at that time of day. The waitress was no Brunhild but a lean, dark-faced little thing, either a young and troubled girl or a very spry old woman, I couldn't tell which. I ordered bratwurst and sauerkraut and distinctly saw the cook unwrap a sausage from a cellophane slip cover and drop it in boiling water. The beer came in a can. The bratwurst was terrible and the kraut an insulting watery mess.

"I wonder if you can help me?" I asked the young-ancient waitress.

"What's your trouble?"

"I guess I'm a little lost."

"How do you mean lost?" she said.

The cook leaned through his window and rested bare elbows on the serving counter.

"I want to go to Sauk Centre and I don't seem to be getting there."

"Where'd you come from?"

"Minneapolis."

"Then what you doing this side of the river?"

"Well, I seem to have got lost in Minneapolis, too."

She looked at the cook. "He got lost in Minneapolis," she said.

"Nobody can get lost in Minneapolis," the cook said. "I was born there and I know."

The waitress said, "I come from St. Cloud and I can't get lost in Minneapolis."

"I guess I brought some new talent to it. But I want to go to Sauk Centre."

The cook said, "If he can stay on a road he can't get lost. You're on Fifty-two. Cross over at St. Cloud and stay on Fifty-two."

"Is Sauk Centre on Fifty-two?"

"Ain't no place else. You must be a stranger around here, getting lost in Minneapolis. I couldn't get lost blindfolded."

I said a little snappishly, "Could you get lost in Albany or San Francisco?"

"I never been there but I bet I wouldn't get lost."

"I been to Duluth," the waitress said. "And Christmas I'm going to Sioux Falls. I got a aunt there."

"Ain't you got relatives in Sauk Centre?" the cook asked.

"Sure, but that's not so far away—like he says San Francisco. My brother's in the Navy. He's in San Diego. You got relations in Sauk Centre?"

"No, I just want to see it. Sinclair Lewis came from there."

"Oh! Yeah. They got a sign up. I guess quite a few folks come to see it. It does the town some good."

"He's the first man who told me about this part of the country."

"Who is?"

"Sinclair Lewis."

"Oh! Yeah. You know him?"

"No, I just read him."

I'm sure she was going to say "Who?" but I stopped her. "You say I cross at St. Cloud and stay on Fifty-two?"

The cook said, "I don't think what's-his-name is there any more."

"I know. He's dead."

"You don't say."

THERE WAS A SIGN IN SAUK CENTRE ALL right: "Birthplace of Sinclair Lewis."

For some reason I went through there fast and turned north on 71 to Wadena and it got dark and I pounded on to Detroit Lakes. There was a face before me, a lean and shriveled face like an apple too long in the barrel, a lonely face and sick with loneliness.

I didn't know him well, never knew him in the boisterous days when he was called Red. Toward the end of his life he called me several times in New York and we would have lunch at the Algonquin. I called him Mr. Lewis—still do in my mind. He didn't drink any more and took no pleasure in his food, but now and then his eyes would glitter with steel.

I had read *Main Street* when I was in high school, and I remember the violent hatred it aroused in the countryside of his nativity.

Did he go back?

Just went through now and again. The only good writer was a dead writer. Then he couldn't surprise anyone any more, couldn't hurt anyone any more. And the last time I saw him he seemed to have shriveled even more. He said, "I'm cold. I seem to be always cold. I'm going to Italy."

And he did, and he died there, and I don't know whether or not it's true but I've heard he died alone. And now he's good for the town. Brings in some tourists. He's a good writer now.

If there had been room in Rocinante I would have packed the W.P.A. Guides to the States, all forty-eight volumes of them. I have all of them, and some are very rare. If I remember correctly, North Dakota printed only eight hundred copies and South Dakota about five hundred. The complete set comprises the most comprehensive account of the United States ever got together, and nothing since has even approached it. It was compiled during the depression by the best writers in America, who were, if that is possible, more depressed than any other group while maintaining their inalienable instinct for eating. But these books were detested by Mr. Roosevelt's opposition. If W.P.A. workers leaned on their shovels, the writers leaned on their pens. The result was that in some states the plates were broken up after a few copies were printed, and that is a shame because they were reservoirs of organized, documented, and well-written information, geological, historical, and economic. If I had carried my guides along, for example, I would have looked up Detroit Lakes, Minnesota, where I stopped, and would have known why it is called Detroit Lakes, who named it, when, and why. I stopped near there late at night and so did Charley, and I don't know any more about it than he does.

The next day a long-cultivated ambition was to blossom and fruit.

Curious how a place unvisited can take such hold on the mind so that the very name sets up a ringing. To me such a place was Fargo, North Dakota. Perhaps its first impact is in the name Wells-Fargo, but my interest certainly goes beyond that. If you will take a map of the United States and fold it in the middle, eastern edge against western, and crease it sharply, right in the crease will be Fargo. On double-page maps sometimes Fargo gets lost in the binding. That may not be a very scientific method for finding the east-west middle of the country, but it will do. But beyond this, Fargo to me is brother to the fabulous places of the earth, kin to those magically remote spots mentioned by Herodotus and Marco Polo and Mandeville. From my earliest memory, if it was a cold day, Fargo was the coldest place on the continent. If heat was the subject, then at that time the papers listed Fargo as hotter than any place else, or wetter or drier, or deeper in snow. That's my impression, anyway. But I know that a dozen or half a hundred towns will rise up in injured wrath to denounce me with claims and figures for having much more dreadful weather than Fargo. I apologize to them in advance. As a sop to hurt feelings, I must admit that when I passed through Moorhead, Minnesota, and rattled across the Red River into Fargo on the other side, it was a golden autumn day, the town as traffic-troubled, as neon-plastered, as cluttered and milling with activity as any other up-and-coming town of forty-six thousand souls. The countryside was no different from Minnesota over the river. I drove through the town as usual, seeing little but the truck ahead of me and the Thunderbird in my rear-view mirror. It's bad to have one's myth shaken up like that. Would Samarkand or Cathay or Cipango have suffered the same fate if visited? As soon as I had cleared the outskirts, the broken-metal-and-glass outer ring, and moved through Mapleton I found a

pleasant place to stop on the Maple River not far
from Alice—what a wonderful name for a town,
Alice. It had 162 inhabitants in 1950 and 124 at the
last census—and so much for the population explosion at Alice. Anyway, on the Maple River I drew
into a little copse, of sycamores I think, that over-
hung the stream, and paused to lick my mytho-
logical wounds. And I found with joy that the fact
of Fargo had in no way disturbed my mind's picture of it. I could still think of Fargo as I always
had—blizzard-riven, heat-blasted, dust-raddled. I
am happy to report that in the war between reality
and romance, reality is not the stronger.

Although it was only mid-morning, I cooked a
sumptuous dinner for myself, but I don't remember what it was. And Charley, who still had vestiges
of his Chicago grooming, waded in the water and
became his old dirty self again.

After the comfort and the company of Chicago I
had had to learn to be alone again. It takes a little
time. But there on the Maple River, not far from
Alice, the gift of it was coming back. Charley had
forgiven me in a nauseatingly superior way, but
now he had settled down to business also. The pull-
out place beside the water was pleasant. I brought
out my garbage-can washing machine and rinsed
clothes that had been jiggling in detergent for two
days. And then, because a pleasant breeze was
blowing, I spread my sheets to dry on some low
bushes. I don't know what kind of bushes they
were, but the leaves had a rich smell like sandal-
wood, and there's nothing I like better than scented
sheets. And I made some notes on a sheet of yellow
paper on the nature and quality of being alone.
These notes would in the normal course of events

have been lost as notes are always lost, but these particular notes turned up long afterward wrapped around a bottle of ketchup and secured with a rubber band. The first note says: "Relationship Time to Aloneness." And I remember about that. Having a companion fixes you in time and that the present, but when the quality of aloneness settles down, past, present, and future all flow together. A memory, a present event, and a forecast all equally present.

The second note lies obscurely under a streak of ketchup, or catsup, but the third is electric. It says: "Reversion to pleasure-pain basis," and this is from some observation of another time.

A number of years ago I had some experience with being alone. For two succeeding years I was alone each winter for eight months at a stretch in the Sierra Nevada mountains on Lake Tahoe. I was a caretaker on a summer estate during the winter months when it was snowed in. And I made some observations then. As the time went on I found that my reactions thickened. Ordinarily I am a whistler. I stopped whistling. I stopped conversing with my dogs, and I believe that subtleties of feeling began to disappear until finally I was on a pleasure-pain basis. Then it occurred to me that the delicate shades of feeling, of reaction, are the result of communication, and without such communication they tend to disappear. A man with nothing to say has no words. Can its reverse be true—a man who has no one to say anything to has no words as he has no need for words? Now and then there appear accounts of babies raised by animals—wolves and such. It is usually reported that the youngster crawls on all fours, makes those sounds learned from his foster parents, and perhaps even thinks like a wolf. Only through imitation do we develop toward originality. Take Charley, for example. He has always associated with the learned, the gentle, the literate, and the reasonable both in France and in America. And Charley is no more like a dog dog than he is like a cat. His perceptions are sharp and delicate and he is a mind-reader. I don't know that he can read the thoughts of other dogs, but he can read mine. Before a plan is half formed in my mind, Charley knows about it, and he also knows whether he is to be included in it. There's no question about this. I know too well his look of despair and disapproval when I have just thought that he must be left at home. And so much for the three notes below the red stain on the ketchup bottle.

Soon Charley moved downstream and found some discarded bags of garbage, which he went through with discrimination. He nosed over an empty bean can, sniffed in its opening, and rejected it. Then he took up the paper bag in his teeth and gently shook it so that more treasures rolled out, among them a balled-up piece of heavy white paper.

I opened it and smoothed the angry creases from its surface. It was a court order addressed to Jack So-and-so, informing him that if he didn't pay his back alimony he would be in contempt and punishable. The court sat in an eastern state, and this was North Dakota. Some poor guy on the lam. He shouldn't have left this spoor around, in case anyone was looking for him. I snapped my Zippo lighter and burned the evidence with full knowledge that I compounded the contempt. Good Lord, the trails we leave! Suppose someone, finding the ketchup bottle, tried to reconstruct me from my notes. I helped Charley sort over the garbage, but there was no other written material, only the containers of prepared foods. The man was no cook. He lived out of cans, but then perhaps his former wife did also.

It was only shortly after noon but I was so relaxed and comfortable that I hated to move. "Should we stay the night, Charley?" He inspected me and wagged his tail as a professor wags a pencil—once to the left, once to the right, and return to center. I sat on the bank, took off socks and boots, and dipped my feet in water so cold it burned until the freezing went deep and deadened feeling. My mother believed that cold water on the feet forced the blood to your head so that you thought better. "Time for examination, *mon vieux Chamal*," I said aloud, "which is another way of saying I feel comfortingly lazy. I came out on this trip to try to learn something of America. Am I learning anything? If I am, I don't know what it is. So far can I go back with a bag full of conclusions, a cluster of answers to riddles? I doubt it, but maybe. When I go to Europe, when I am asked what America is like, what will I say? I don't know. Well, using your olfactory method of investigation, what have you learned, my friend?"

Two complete wags. At least he didn't leave the question open.

"Does all America so far smell alike? Or are there sectional smells?" Charley began to turn around and around to the left, and then he reversed and turned eight times to the right before he finally settled and put his nose on his paws and his head within reach of my hand. He has a hard time getting down. When he was young a car hit him and broke his hip. He wore a cast for a long time. Now in his golden age his hip troubles him when he is tired. After too long a run he limps on his right hind leg. But because of his long turning before lying down, we sometimes call him a whirl poodle —much to our shame. If my mother's rule was right I was thinking pretty well. But she also said, "Cold feet—warm heart." And that's a different matter.

I had parked well away from the road and from any traffic for my time of rest and recount. I am serious about this. I did not put aside my sloth for the sake of a few amusing anecdotes. I came with the wish to learn what America is like. And I wasn't sure I was learning anything. I found I was talking aloud to Charley. He likes the idea but the practice makes him sleepy.

"Just for ducks, let's try a little of what my boys would call this generality jazz. Under heads and subheads. Let's take food as we have found it. It is more than possible that in the cities we have passed through, traffic-harried, there are good and distinguished restaurants with menus of delight. But in the eating places along the roads the food has been clean, tasteless, colorless, and of a complete sameness. It is almost as though the customers had no interest in what they ate as long as it had no character to embarrass them. This is true of all but the breakfasts, which are uniformly wonderful if you stick to bacon and eggs and pan-fried potatoes. At the roadsides I never had a really good dinner or a really bad breakfast. The bacon or sausage was good and packaged at the factory, the eggs fresh or kept fresh by refrigeration, and refrigeration was universal." I might even say roadside America is the paradise of breakfast except for one thing. Now and then I would see a sign that said "home-made sausage" or "home-smoked bacons and hams" or "new-laid eggs" and I would stop and lay in supplies. Then, cooking my own breakfast and making my own coffee, I found that the difference was instantly apparent. A freshly laid egg does not taste remotely like the pale, battery-produced refrigerated egg. The sausage would be sweet and sharp and pungent with spices, and my coffee a wine-dark happiness. Can I then say that the America I saw has put cleanliness first, at the expense of taste? And—since all our perceptive nerve trunks including that of taste are not only perfectible but also capable of trauma—that the sense of taste tends to disappear and that strong, pungent, or exotic flavors arouse suspicion and dislike and so are eliminated?

"Let's go a little farther into other fields, Charley. Let's take the books, magazines, and papers we have seen displayed where we have stopped. The dominant publication has been the comic book. There have been local papers and I've bought and read them. There have been racks of paperbacks with some great and good titles but overwhelmingly outnumbered by the volumes of sex, sadism, and homicide. The big-city papers cast their shadows over large areas around them, the *New York Times* as far as the Great Lakes, the *Chicago Tribune* all the way here to North Dakota. Here, Charley, I give you a warning, should you be drawn to generalities. If this people has so atrophied its taste buds as to find tasteless food not only acceptable but desirable, what of the emotional life of the nation? Do they find their emotional fare so bland that it must be spiced with sex and sadism through the medium of the paperback? And if this is so, why are there no condiments save ketchup and mustard to enhance their foods?

"We've listened to local radio all across the country. And apart from a few reportings of football games, the mental fare has been as generalized, as packaged, and as undistinguished as the food." I stirred Charley with my foot to keep him awake.

I had been keen to hear what people thought politically. Those whom I had met did not talk about the subject, didn't seem to want to talk about it. It seemed to me partly caution and partly a lack of interest, but strong opinions were just not stated. One storekeeper did admit to me that he had to do business with both sides and could not permit himself the luxury of an opinion. He was a graying man in a little gray store, a crossroads place where I stopped for a box of dog biscuits and a can of pipe tobacco. This man, this store might have been anywhere in the nation, but actually it was back in Minnesota. The man had a kind of gray wistful twinkle in his eyes as though he remembered humor when it was not against the law, so that I dared go out on a limb. I said, "It looks then as though the natural contentiousness of people had died. But I don't believe that. It'll just take another channel. Can you think, sir, of what that channel might be?"

"You mean where will they bust out?"

"Where do they bust out?"

I was not wrong, the twinkle was there, the precious, humorous twinkle. "Well, sir," he said, "we've got a murder now and then, or we can read about them. Then we've got the World Series. You can raise a wind any time over the Pirates or the Yankees, but I guess the best of all is we've got the Russians."

"Feelings pretty strong there?"

"Oh, sure! Hardly a day goes by somebody doesn't take a belt at the Russians." For some reason he was getting a little easier, even permitted himself a chuckle that could have turned to throat-clearing if he saw a bad reaction from me.

I asked, "Anybody know any Russians around here?"

And now he went all out and laughed. "Course not. That's why they're valuable. Nobody can find fault with you if you take out after the Russians."

"Because we're not doing business with them?"

He picked up a cheese knife from the counter and carefully ran his thumb along the edge and laid the knife down. "Maybe that's it. By George, maybe that's it. We're not doing business."

"You think then we might be using the Russians as an outlet for something else, for other things."

"I didn't think that at all, sir, but I bet I'm going to. Why, I remember when people took everything out on Mr. Roosevelt. Andy Larsen got red in the face about Roosevelt one time when his hens got the croup. Yes, sir," he said with growing enthusiasm, "those Russians got quite a load to carry. Man has a fight with his wife, he belts the Russians."

"Maybe everybody needs Russians. I'll bet even in Russia they need Russians. Maybe they call it Americans."

He cut a sliver of cheese from a wheel and held it out to me on the knife blade. "You've give me something to think about in a sneaking kind of way."

"I thought you gave it to me."

"How?"

"About business and opinions."

"Well, maybe so. Know what I'm going to do? Next time Andy Larsen comes in red in the face, I'm going to see if the Russians are bothering his hens. It was a great loss to Andy when Mr. Roosevelt died."

Now I don't say that an awful lot of people have this man's sense of things. Maybe they don't, but maybe they do—also in their privacy or in nonbusiness areas.

Charley raised his head and roared a warning without bothering to get to his feet. Then I heard a motor approaching, and trying to get up found my feet were long gone in sleep in the cold water. I couldn't feel them at all. While I rubbed and massaged them and they awakened to painful pins and needles, a vintage sedan pulling a short coupled trailer like a box turtle lumbered down from the road and took a position on the water about fifty yards away. I felt annoyance at this invasion of my privacy, but Charley was delighted. He moved on stiff legs with little delicate mincing steps to investigate the newcomer and in the manner of dogs and people did not look directly at the object of his interest. If I seem to be ridiculing Charley, look you at what I was doing in the next half hour and also what my neighbor was doing. Each of us went about our business, with slow deliberateness, each being very careful not to stare at the other and at the same time sneaking glances, appraising, evaluating. I saw a man, not young, not old, but with a jaunty springy step. He was dressed in olive-drab trousers and a leather jacket, and he wore a cowboy hat but with a flat crown and the brim curled and held to a peak by the chin strap. He had a classic profile, and even in the distance I could see that he wore a beard that tied into his side-burns and so found his hair. My own beard is restricted to my chin. The air had grown quickly chill. And I don't know whether my head was cold or that I didn't want to remain uncovered in the presence of a stranger. At any rate, I put on my old naval cap, made a pot of coffee, and sat on my back steps glancing with great interest at everything except my neighbor, who swept out his trailer and threw out a dishpan of soapy water while he pointedly unwatched me. Charley's interest was captured and held by various growlings and barkings that came from inside the trailer.

There must be in everyone a sense of proper and civil timing, for I had just resolved to speak to my neighbor, in fact had just stood up to move toward him, when he strolled toward me. He too had felt that the period of waiting was over. He moved with a strange gait reminiscent to me of something I couldn't place. There was a seedy grandeur about the man. In the time of chivalric myth this would be the beggar who turns out to be a king's son. As he came near I stood up from my iron back stoop to greet him.

He did not give me a sweeping bow, but I had the impression that he might have—either that or a full regimental salute.

"Good afternoon," he said. "I see you are of the profession."

I guess my mouth fell open. It's years since I have heard the term. "Well, no. No, I'm not."

Now it was his turn to look puzzled. "Not? But—my dear chap, if you're not, how do you know the expression?"

"I guess I've been on the fringes."

"Ah! Fringes. Of course. Backstage no doubt—direction, stage manager?"

"Flops," I said. "Would you like a cup of coffee?"

"Delighted." He never let down. That's one nice thing about those of the profession—they rarely do. He folded himself on the divan seat behind my table with a grace I never achieved in all my traveling. And I set out two plastic mugs and two glasses, poured coffee, and set a bottle of whisky within easy reach. It seemed to me a mist of tears came into his eyes, but it might be that they were in mine.

"Flops," he said. "Who hasn't known them hasn't played."

"Shall I pour for you?"

"Please do—no, no water." He cleared his palate with black coffee and then munched delicately on the whisky while his eye swept my abode. "Nice place you have here, very nice."

"Tell me, please, what made you think I was in the theater?"

He chuckled dryly. "Very simple, Watson. You know I've played that. Both parts. Well, first I saw your poodle, and then I observed your beard. Then on approaching I saw that you wore a naval cap with the British Royal Arms."

"Was that what broadened your *a*'s?"

"That might be, old chap. That certainly might be. I fall into such things, hardly knowing I'm doing it." Now, close up, I saw that he was not young.

His movements were pure youth but there was that about his skin texture and the edges of his lips that was middle-aged or past it. And his eyes, large warm brown irises set on whites that were turning yellow, corroborated this.

"Your health," I said. We emptied our plastic glasses, chased with coffee, and I refilled.

"If it isn't too personal or too painful—what did you do in the theater?"

"I wrote a couple of plays."

"Produced?"

"Yes. They flopped."

"Would I know your name?"

"I doubt it. Nobody else did."

He sighed. "It's a hard business. But if you're hooked, you're hooked. I was hooked by my grand-daddy and my daddy set the hook."

"Both actors?"

"And my mother and grandmother."

"Lord. That *is* show business. Are you"—I searched for the old word—"resting now?"

"Not at all. I'm playing."

"What, for God's sake, and where?"

"Wherever I can trap an audience. Schools, churches, service clubs. I bring culture, give read-ings. I guess you can hear my partner over there complaining. He's very good too. Part Airedale and part coyote. Steals the show when he feels like it."

I began to feel delighted with this man. "I didn't know such things went on."

"They don't, some of the time."

"Been at it long?"

"Three years less two months."

"All over the country?"

"Wherever two or three are gathered together.

I hadn't worked for over a year—just tramped the agencies and casting calls and lived up my benefits. With me there's no question of doing something else. It's all I know—all I ever have known. Once long ago there was a community of theater people on Nantucket island. My daddy bought a nice lot there and put up a frame house. Well, I sold that and bought my outfit there and I've been moving ever since, and I like it. I don't think I'll ever go back to the grind. Of course, if there should be a part—but hell, who'd remember me for a part—any part?"

"You're striking close to home there."

"Yes, it's a hard business."

"I hope you won't think I'm inquisitive even if I am. I'd like to know how you go about it. What happens? How do people treat you?"

"They treat me very well. And I don't know how I go about it. Sometimes I even have to rent a hall and advertise, sometimes I speak to the principal of the high school."

"But aren't people scared of gypsies, vagabonds, and actors?"

"I guess they are at first. At the beginning they take me for a kind of harmless freak. But I'm honest and I don't charge much, and after a little the material takes over and gets into them. You see, I respect the material. That makes the difference. I'm not a charlatan, I'm an actor—good or bad, an actor." His color had deepened with whisky and vehemence, and perhaps at being able to talk to someone with a little likeness of experience. I poured more into his glass this time and watched with pleasure his enjoyment of it. He drank and sighed. "Don't get something like this very often," he said. "I hope I haven't given you the impression that I'm rolling in receipts. Sometimes it's a little rough."

"Go on about it. Tell more."

"Where was I?"

"You were saying you respected your material and that you were an actor."

"Oh, yes. Well, there's one more thing. You know when show people come into what they call the sticks, they have a contempt for the yokels. It took me a little time, but when I learned that there aren't any yokels I began to get on fine. I learned respect for my audience. They feel that and they work with me, and not against me. Once you respect them, they can understand anything you can tell them."

"Tell about your material. What do you use?"

He looked down at his hands and I saw that they were well-kept and very white, as though he wore gloves most of the time. "I hope you won't think I'm stealing material," he said. "I admire the delivery of Sir John Gielgud. I heard him do his monologue of Shakespeare—*The Ages of Man.* And then I bought a record of it to study. What he can do with words, with tones, and inflections!"

"You use that?"

"Yes, but I don't steal it. I tell about hearing Sir John, and what it did to me, and then I say I'm going to try to give an impression of how he did it."

"Clever."

"Well, it does help, because it gives authority to the performance, and Shakespeare doesn't need billing, and that way I'm not stealing his material. It's like I'm celebrating him, which I do."

"How do they respond?"

"Well, I guess I'm pretty much at home with it now, because I can watch the words sink in, and they forget about me and their eyes kind of turn inward and I'm not a freak to them any more. Well —what do you think?"

"I think Gielgud would be pleased."

"Oh! I wrote to him and told him what I was doing and how I was doing it, a long letter." He brought a lumpy wallet from his hip pocket and extracted a carefully folded piece of aluminum foil, opened it, and with careful fingers unfolded a small sheet of notepaper with the name engraved at the top. The message was typed. It said, "Dear . . . : Thank you for your kind and interesting letter. I would not be an actor if I were not aware of the sincere flattery implied in your work. Good luck and God bless you. John Gielgud."

I sighed, and I watched his reverent fingers fold the note and close it in its armor of foil and put it away. "I never show that to anyone to get a show," he said. "I wouldn't think of doing that."

And I'm sure he wouldn't.

He whirled his plastic glass in his hand and regarded the rinse of whisky left in it, a gesture often designed to draw emptiness to the attention of a host. I uncorked the bottle.

"No," he said. "No more for me. I learned long ago that the most important and valuable of acting techniques is the exit."

"But I'd like to ask more questions."

"All the more reason for the exit." He drained the last drop. "Keep them asking," he said, "and exit clean and sharp. Thank you and good afternoon."

I watched him swing lightly toward his trailer

and I knew I would be haunted by one question. I called out,—"Wait a moment."

He paused and turned back to me.

"What does the dog do?"

"Oh, a couple of silly tricks," he said. "He keeps the performance simple. He picks it up when it goes stale." And he continued on to his home.

So it went on—a profession older than writing and one that will probably survive when the written word has disappeared. And all the sterile wonders of movies and television and radio will fail to wipe it out—a living man in communication with a living audience. But how did he live? Who were his companions? What was his hidden life? He was right. His exit whetted the questions.

THE NIGHT WAS LOADED WITH OMENS. THE grieving sky turned the little water to a dangerous metal and then the wind got up—not the gusty, rabbity wind of the seacoasts I know but a great bursting sweep of wind with nothing to inhibit it for a thousand miles in any direction. Because it was a wind strange to me, and therefore mysterious, it set up mysterious responses in me. In terms of reason, it was strange only because I found it so. But a goodly part of our experience which we find inexplicable must be like that. To my certain knowledge, many people conceal experiences for fear of ridicule. How many people have seen or heard or felt something which so outraged their sense of what should be that the whole thing was brushed quickly away like dirt under a rug?

For myself, I try to keep the line open even for things I can't understand or explain, but it is difficult in this frightened time. At this moment in North Dakota I had a reluctance to drive on that amounted to fear. At the same time, Charley wanted to go—in fact, made such a commotion about going that I tried to reason with him.

"Listen to me, dog. I have a strong impulse to stay amounting to celestial command. If I should overcome it and go and a great snow should close in on us, I would recognize it as a warning disregarded. If we stay and a big snow should come I would be certain I had a pipeline to prophecy."

Charley sneezed and paced restlessly. "All right, *mon cur*, let's take your side of it. You want to go on. Suppose we do, and in the night a tree should crash down right where we are presently standing. It would be you who have the attention of the gods. And there is always that chance. I could tell you many stories about faithful animals who saved their masters, but I think you are just bored and I'm not going to flatter you." Charley leveled at me his most cynical eye. I think he is neither a romantic nor a mystic. "I know what you mean. If we go, and no tree crashes down, or stay and no snow falls —what then? I'll tell you what then. We forget the whole episode and the field of prophecy is in no way injured. I vote to stay. You vote to go. But being nearer the pinnacle of creation than you, and also president, I cast the deciding vote."

We stayed and it didn't snow and no tree fell, so naturally we forgot the whole thing and are wide open for more mystic feelings when they come. And in the early morning swept clean of clouds and telescopically clear, we crunched around on the thick white ground cover of frost and got under way. The caravan of the arts was dark but the dog barked as we ground up to the highway.

Someone must have told me about the Missouri River at Bismarck, North Dakota, or I must have read about it. In either case, I hadn't paid attention. I came on it in amazement. Here is where the map should fold. Here is the boundary between east and west. On the Bismarck side it is eastern landscape, eastern grass, with the look and smell of eastern America. Across the Missouri on the Mandan side, it is pure west, with brown grass and water scorings and small outcrops. The two sides of the river might well be a thousand miles apart. As I was not prepared for the Missouri boundary, so I was not prepared for the Bad Lands. They deserve this name. They are like the work of an evil child. Such a place the Fallen Angels might have built as a spite to Heaven, dry and sharp, desolate and dangerous, and for me filled with foreboding. A sense comes from it that it does not like or welcome humans. But humans being what they are, and I being human, I turned off the highway on a shaley road and headed in among the buttes, but with a shyness as though I crashed a party. The road surface tore viciously at my tires and made Rocinante's overloaded springs cry with anguish. What a place for a colony of troglodytes, or better, of trolls. And here's an odd thing. Just as I felt unwanted in this land, so do I feel a reluctance in writing about it.

Presently I saw a man leaning on a two-strand barbed-wire fence, the wires fixed not to posts but to crooked tree limbs stuck in the ground. The man wore a dark hat, and jeans and long jacket washed palest blue with lighter places at knees and elbows. His pale eyes were frosted with sun glare and his lips scaly as snakeskin. A .22 rifle leaned against the fence beside him and on the ground lay a little heap of fur and feathers—rabbits and small birds. I pulled up to speak to him, saw his eyes wash over Rocinante, sweep up the details, and then retire into their sockets. And I found I had nothing to say to him. The "Looks like an early winter," or "Any good fishing hereabouts?" didn't seem to apply. And so we simply brooded at each other.

"Afternoon!"

"Yes, sir," he said.

"Any place nearby where I can buy some eggs?"

"Not real close by 'less you want to go as far as Galva or up to Beach."

"I was set for some scratch-hen eggs."

"Powdered," he said. "My Mrs. gets powdered."

"Lived here long?"

"Yep."

I waited for him to ask something or to say something so we could go on, but he didn't. And as the silence continued, it became more and more impossible to think of something to say. I made one more try. "Does it get very cold here winters?"

"Fairly."

"You talk too much."

He grinned. "That's what my Mrs. says."

"So long," I said, and put the car in gear and moved along. And in my rear-view mirror I couldn't see that he looked after me. He may not be a typical Badlander, but he's one of the few I caught.

A little farther along I stopped at a small house, a section of war-surplus barracks, it looked, but painted white with yellow trim, and with the dying vestiges of a garden, frosted-down geraniums and a few clusters of chrysanthemums, little button things yellow and red-brown. I walked up the path with the certainty that I was being regarded from behind the white window curtains. An old woman answered my knock and gave me the drink of water I asked for and nearly talked my arm off. She was hungry to talk, frantic to talk, about her relatives, her friends, and how she wasn't used to this. For she was not a native and she didn't rightly belong here. Her native clime was a land of milk and honey and had its share of apes and ivory and pea-cocks. Her voice rattled on as though she was terri-fied of the silence that would settle when I was gone. As she talked it came to me that she was afraid of this place and, further, that so was I. I felt I wouldn't like to have the night catch me here.

I went into a state of flight, running to get away from the unearthly landscape. And then the late afternoon changed everything. As the sun angled, the buttes and coulees, the cliffs and sculptured hills and ravines lost their burned and dreadful look and glowed with yellow and rich browns and a hundred variations of red and silver gray, all picked out by streaks of coal black. It was so beau-tiful that I stopped near a thicket of dwarfed and wind-warped cedars and junipers, and once stopped I was caught, trapped in color and dazzled by the clarity of the light. Against the descending sun the battlements were dark and clean-lined, while to the east, where the uninhibited light poured slantwise, the strange landscape shouted with color. And the night, far from being frightful, was lovely beyond thought, for the stars were close, and although there was no moon the starlight made a silver glow in the sky. The air cut the nostrils with dry frost. And for pure pleasure I collected a pile of dry dead cedar branches and built a small fire just to smell the perfume of the burning wood and to hear the excited crackle of the branches. My fire made a dome of yellow light over me, and nearby I heard a screech owl hunting and a barking of coyotes, not howling but the short chuckling bark of the dark of the moon. This is one of the few places I have ever seen where the night was friendlier than the day. And I can easily see how people are driven back to the Bad Lands.

Before I slept I spread a map on my bed, a Charley-tromped map. Beach was not far away, and that would be the end of North Dakota. And coming up would be Montana, where I had never been. That night was so cold that I put on my insulated underwear for pajamas, and when Charley had done his duties and had his biscuits and consumed his usual gallon of water and finally curled up in his place under the bed, I dug out an extra blanket and covered him—all except the tip of his nose—and he sighed and wriggled and gave a great groan of pure ecstatic comfort. And I thought how every safe generality I gathered in my travels was canceled by another. In the night the Bad Lands had become Good Lands. I can't explain it. That's how it was.

THE NEXT PASSAGE IN MY JOURNEY IS A love affair. I am in love with Montana. For other states I have admiration, respect, recognition, even some affection, but with Montana it is love, and it's difficult to analyze love when you're in it. Once, when I raptured in a violet glow given off by the Queen of the World, my father asked me why, and I thought he was crazy not to see. Of course I know now she was a mouse-haired, freckle-nosed, scabby-kneed little girl with a voice like a bat and the loving kindness of a gila monster, but then she lighted up the landscape and me. It seems to me that Montana is a great splash of grandeur. The scale is huge but not overpowering. The land is rich with grass and color, and the mountains are the kind I would create if mountains were ever put on my agenda. Montana seems to me to be what a small boy would think Texas is like from hearing Texans. Here for the first time I heard a definite regional accent unaffected by TV-ese, a slow-paced warm speech. It seemed to me that the frantic bustle of America was not in Montana. Its people did not seem afraid of shadows in a John Birch Society sense. The calm of the mountains and the rolling grasslands had got into the inhabitants. It was hunting season when I drove through the state. The men I talked to seemed to me not moved to a riot of seasonal slaughter but simply to be going out to kill edible meat. Again my attitude may be informed by love, but it seemed to me that the towns were places to live in rather than nervous hives. People had time to pause in their occupations to undertake the passing art of neighborliness.

I found I did not rush through the towns to get them over with. I even found things I had to buy to make myself linger. In Billings I bought a hat, in Livingston a jacket, in Butte a rifle I didn't particularly need, a Remington bolt-action 222, second-hand but in beautiful condition. Then I found a telescope sight I had to have, and waited while it was mounted on the rifle, and in the process got to know everyone in the shop and any customers who entered. With the gun in a vise and the bolt out, we zeroed the new sight on a chimney three blocks away, and later when I got to shooting the little gun I found no reason to change it. I spent a good part of a morning at this, mostly because I wanted to stay. But I see that, as usual, love is inarticulate. Montana has a spell on me. It is grandeur and warmth. If Montana had a seacoast, or if I could live away from the sea, I would instantly move there and petition for admission. Of all the states it is my favorite and my love.

At Custer we made a side trip south to pay our respects to General Custer and Sitting Bull on the battlefield of Little Big Horn. I don't suppose there is an American who doesn't carry Remington's painting of the last defense of the center column of the 7th Cavalry in his head. I removed my hat in memory of brave men, and Charley saluted in his own manner but I thought with great respect.

The whole of eastern Montana and the western Dakotas is memory-marked as Injun country, and the memories are not very old either. Some years ago my neighbor was Charles Erskine Scott Wood, who wrote *Heavenly Discourse*. He was a very old man when I knew him, but as a young lieutenant just out of military academy he had been assigned to General Miles and he served in the Chief Joseph campaign. His memory of it was very clear and very sad. He said it was one of the most gallant retreats in all history. Chief Joseph and the Nez Percés with squaws and children, dogs, and all their possessions, retreated under heavy fire for over a thousand miles, trying to escape to Canada. Wood said they fought every step of the way against odds until finally they were surrounded by the cavalry under General Miles and the large part of them wiped out. It was the saddest duty he had ever performed, Wood said, and he had never lost his respect for the fighting qualities of the Nez Percés. "If they hadn't had their families with them we could never have caught them," he said. "And if we had been evenly matched in men and weapons, we couldn't have beaten them. They were men," he said, "real men."

I MUST CONFESS TO A LAXNESS IN THE MATter of National Parks. I haven't visited many of them. Perhaps this is because they enclose the unique, the spectacular, the astounding—the greatest waterfall, the deepest canyon, the highest cliff, the most stupendous works of man or nature. And I would rather see a good Brady photograph than Mount Rushmore. For it is my opinion that we enclose and celebrate the freaks of our nation and of our civilization. Yellowstone National Park is no more representative of America than is Disneyland.

This being my natural attitude, I don't know what made me turn sharply south and cross a state line to take a look at Yellowstone. Perhaps it was a fear of my neighbors. I could hear them say, "You mean you were that near to Yellowstone and didn't go? You must be crazy." Again it might have been the American tendency in travel. One goes, not so much to see but to tell afterward. Whatever my purpose in going to Yellowstone, I'm glad I went because I discovered something about Charley I might never have known.

A pleasant-looking National Park man checked me in and then he said, "How about that dog? They aren't permitted in except on leash."

"Why?" I asked.

"Because of the bears."

"Sir," I said, "this is an unique dog. He does not

live by tooth or fang. He respects the right of cats to be cats although he doesn't admire them. He turns his steps rather than disturb an earnest caterpillar. His greatest fear is that someone will point out a rabbit and suggest that he chase it. This is a dog of peace and tranquility. I suggest that the greatest danger to your bears will be pique at being ignored by Charley."

The young man laughed. "I wasn't so much worried about the bears," he said. "But our bears have developed an intolerance for dogs. One of them might demonstrate his prejudice with a clip on the chin, and then—no dog."

"I'll lock him in the back, sir. I promise you Charley will cause no ripple in the bear world, and as an old bear-looker, neither will I."

"I just have to warn you," he said. "I have no doubt your dog has the best of intentions. On the other hand, our bears have the worst. Don't leave food about. Not only do they steal but they are critical of anyone who tries to reform them. In a word, don't believe their sweet faces or you might get clobbered. And don't let the dog wander. Bears don't argue."

We went on our way into the wonderland of nature gone nuts, and you will have to believe what happened. The only way I can prove it would be to get a bear.

Less than a mile from the entrance I saw a bear beside the road, and it ambled out as though to flag me down. Instantly a change came over Charley. He shrieked with rage. His lips flared, showing wicked teeth that have some trouble with a dog biscuit. He screeched insults at the bear, which hearing, the bear reared up and seemed to me to overtop Rocinante. Frantically I rolled the windows shut and, swinging quickly to the left, grazed the animal, then scuttled on while Charley raved and ranted beside me, describing in detail what he would do to that bear if he could get at him. I was never so astonished in my life. To the best of my knowledge Charley had never seen a bear, and in his whole history had showed great tolerance for every living thing. Besides all this, Charley is a coward, so deep-seated a coward that he has developed a technique for concealing it. And yet he showed every evidence of wanting to get out and murder a bear that outweighed him a thousand to one. I don't understand it.

A little farther along two bears showed up, and the effect was doubled. Charley became a maniac. He leaped all over me, he cursed and growled, snarled and screamed. I didn't know he had the ability to snarl. Where did he learn it? Bears were in good supply, and the road became a nightmare. For the first time in his life Charley resisted reason, even resisted a cuff on the ear. He became a primitive killer lusting for the blood of his enemy, and up to this moment he had had no enemies. In a bearless stretch, I opened the cab, took Charley by the collar, and locked him in the house. But that did no good. When we passed other bears he leaped on the table and scratched at the windows trying to get out at them. I could hear canned goods crashing as he struggled in his mania. Bears simply brought out the Hyde in my Jekyll-headed dog. What could have caused it? Was it a pre-breed memory of a time when the wolf was in him? I know him well. Once in a while he tries a bluff, but it is a palpable lie. I swear that this was no lie. I am certain that if he were released he would have charged every bear we passed and found victory or death.

It was too nerve-wracking, a shocking spectacle, like seeing an old, calm friend go insane. No amount of natural wonders, of rigid cliffs and belching waters, of smoking springs could even engage my attention while that pandemonium went on. After about the fifth encounter I gave up, turned Rocinante about, and retraced my way. If I had stopped the night and bears had gathered to my cooking, I dare not think what would have happened.

At the gate the park guard checked me out. "You didn't stay long. Where's the dog?"

"Locked up back there. And I owe you an apology. That dog has the heart and soul of a bear-killer and I didn't know it. Heretofore he has been a little tender-hearted toward an underdone steak."

"Yeah!" he said. "That happens sometimes. That's why I warned you. A bear dog would know his chances, but I've seen a Pomeranian go up like a puff of smoke. You know, a well-favored bear can bat a dog like a tennis ball."

I moved fast, back the way I had come, and I was reluctant to camp for fear there might be some un-official non-government bears about. That night I spent in a pretty auto court near Livingston. I had my dinner in a restaurant, and when I had settled in with a drink and a comfortable chair and my bathed bare feet on a carpet with red roses, I inspected Charley. He was dazed. His eyes held a far-away look and he was totally exhausted, emotion-ally no doubt. Mostly he reminded me of a man coming out of a long, hard drunk—worn out, depleted, collapsed. He couldn't eat his dinner, he refused the evening walk, and once we were in he collapsed on the floor and went to sleep. In the night I heard him whining and yapping, and when I turned on the light his feet were making running gestures and his body jerked and his eyes were wide open, but it was only a night bear. I awakened him and gave him some water. This time he went to sleep and didn't stir all night. In the morning he was still tired. I wonder why we think the thoughts and emotions of animals are simple.

I REMEMBER AS A CHILD READING OR HEAR-
ing the words "The Great Divide" and being
stunned by the glorious sound, a proper sound for
the granite backbone of a continent. I saw in my
mind escarpments rising into the clouds, a kind of
natural Great Wall of China. The Rocky Mountains are too big, too long, too important to have
to be imposing. In Montana to which I had returned, the rise is gradual, and were it not for a
painted sign I never would have known when I
crossed it. It wasn't very high as elevations go. I
passed it as I saw the sign, but I stopped and backed
up and got out and straddled it. As I stood over
it facing south it had a strange impact on me that
rain falling on my right foot must fall into the
Pacific Ocean, while that on my left foot would
eventually find its way after uncountable miles to
the Atlantic. The place wasn't impressive enough
to carry a stupendous fact like that.

It is impossible to be in this high spinal country
without giving thought to the first men who crossed
it, the French explorers, the Lewis and Clark men.
We fly it in five hours, drive it in a week, dawdle
it as I was doing in a month or six weeks. But Lewis
and Clark and their party started in St. Louis in
1804 and returned in 1806. And if we get to thinking we are men, we might remember that in the
two and a half years of pushing through wild and
unknown country to the Pacific Ocean and then

back, only one man died and only one deserted. And we get sick if the milk delivery is late and nearly die of heart failure if there is an elevator strike. What must these men have thought as a really new world unrolled—or was the progress so slow that the impact was lost? I can't believe they were unimpressed. Certainly their report to the government is an excited and an exciting document. They were not confused. They knew what they had found.

I drove across the upraised thumb of Idaho and through real mountains that climbed straight up, tufted with pines and deep-dusted with snow. My radio went dead and I thought it was broken, but it was only that the high ridges cut off the radio waves. The snow started to fall, but my luck held, for it was only a light gay snow. The air was softer than it had been on the other side of the Great Divide and I seemed to remember reading that the warm airs from over the Japanese current penetrate deep inland. The underbrush was thick and very green, and everywhere was a rush of waters. The roads were deserted except for an occasional hunting party in red hats and yellow jackets, and sometimes with a deer or an elk draped over the hood of the car. A few mountain cabins were incised into the steep slopes, but not many.

I was having to make many stops for Charley's sake. Charley was having increasing difficulty in evacuating his bladder, which is Nellie talk for the sad symptoms of not being able to pee. This sometimes caused him pain and always caused him embarrassment. Consider this dog of great *élan*, of impeccable manner, of *ton, enfin* of a certain majesty. Not only did he hurt, but his feelings were hurt.

I would stop beside the road and let him wander, and turn my back on him in kindness. It took him a very long time. If it had happened to a human male I would have thought it was prostatitis. Charley is an elderly gentleman of the French persuasion. The only two ailments the French will admit to are that and a bad liver.

And so, while waiting for him and pretending to inspect plants and small water courses, I tried to reconstruct my trip as a single piece and not as a series of incidents. What was I doing wrong? Was it going as I wished? Before I left, I was briefed, instructed, directed, and brain-washed by many of my friends. One among them is a well-known and highly respected political reporter. He had been grass-rooting with the presidential candidates, and when I saw him he was not happy, because he loves his country, and he felt a sickness in it. I might say further that he is a completely honest man.

He said bitterly, "If anywhere in your travels you come on a man with guts, mark the place. I want to go to see him. I haven't seen anything but cowardice and expediency. This used to be a nation of giants. Where have they gone? You can't defend a nation with a board of directors. That takes men. Where are they?"

"Must be somewhere," I said.

"Well, you try to root a few out. We need them. I swear to God the only people in this country with any guts seem to be Negroes. Mind you," he said, "I don't want to keep Negroes out of the hero business, but I'm damned if I want them to corner the market. You dig me up ten white, able-bodied Americans who aren't afraid to have a conviction, an idea, or an opinion in an unpopular field, and I'll have the major part of a standing army."

His obvious worry in this matter impressed me, so I did listen and look along the way. And it is true I didn't hear many convictions. I saw only two real-man fights, with bare fists and enthusiastic inaccuracy, and both of those were over women.

Charley came back apologizing for needing more time. I wished I could help him but he wanted to be alone. And I remembered another thing my friend said.

"There used to be a thing or a commodity we put great store by. It was called the People. Find out where the People have gone. I don't mean the square-eyed toothpaste-and-hair-dye people or the new-car-or-bust people, or the success-and-coronary people. Maybe they never existed, but if there ever were the People, that's the commodity the Declaration was talking about, and Mr. Lincoln. Come to think of it, I've known a few, but not many. Wouldn't it be silly if the Constitution had been talking about a young man whose life centers around a whistle, a wink, and Wildroot?"

I remember retorting, "Maybe the People are always those who used to live the generation before last."

Charley was pretty stiff. I had to help him into the cab of Rocinante. And we proceeded up the mountain. A very light dry snow blew like white dust on the highway, and the evening was coming earlier now, I thought. Just under the ridge of a pass I stopped for gasoline in a little put-together, do-it-yourself group of cabins, square boxes, each with a stoop, a door, and one window, and no vestige of a garden or gravel paths. The small combined store, repair shop, and lunch room behind the gas pumps was as unprepossessing as any I have ever seen. The blue restaurant signs were old and autographed by the flies of many past summers. "Pies like mother would of made if mother could of cooked." "We don't look in your mouth. Don't look in our kitchen." "No checks cashed unless accompanied by fingerprints." The standard old ones. There would be no cellophane on the food here.

No one came to the gas pump, so I went into the lunch room. A sound of a quarrel came from the back room, which was probably the kitchen—a deep voice and a lighter male voice yammering back and forth. I called, "Anybody home?" and the voices stopped. Then a burly man came through the door, still scowling from the fracas.

"Want something?"

"Fill-up of gas. But if you have a cabin, I might stay the night."

"Take your pick. Ain't a soul here."

"Can I have a bath?"

"I'll bring you a bucket of hot water. Winter rates two dollars."

"Good. Can I get something to eat?"

"Baked ham and beans, ice cream."

"Okay. I've got a dog."

"It's a free country. The cabins are all open. Take your pick. Sing out if you need something."

No effort had been spared to make the cabins uncomfortable and ugly. The bed was lumpy, the walls dirty yellow, the curtains like the underskirts of a slattern. And the close room had a mixed aroma of mice and moisture, mold and the smell of old, old dust, but the sheets were clean and a little airing got rid of the memories of old inhabitants. A naked globe hung from the ceiling and the room was heated by kerosene stove.

There was a knock on the door, and I admitted a young man of about twenty, dressed in gray flannel slacks, two-tone shoes, a polka-dotted ascot, and a blazer with the badge of a Spokane high school. His dark, shining hair was a masterpiece of over-combing, the top hair laid back and criss-crossed with long side strands that just cleared the ears. He was a shock to me after the ogre of the lunch counter.

"Here's your hot water," he said, and his was the voice of the other quarreler. The door was open, and I saw his eyes go over Rocinante and linger on the license plate.

"You really from New York?"

"Yep."

"I want to go there sometime."

"Everybody there wants to come out here."

"What for? There's nothing here. You can just rot here."

"If it's rotting you want, you can do it any place."

"I mean there's no chance for advancing yourself."

"What do you want to advance toward?"

"Well, you know, there's no theater and no music, no one to—talk to. Why it's even hard to get late magazines unless you subscribe."

"So you read *The New Yorker?*"

"How did you know? I subscribe."

"And *Time* magazine?"

"Of course."

"You don't have to go anywhere."

"Beg pardon?"

"You've got the world at your fingertips, the world of fashion, of art, and the world of thought right in your own back yard. Going would only confuse you further."

"One likes to see for one's self," he said. I swear he said it.

"That your father?"

"Yes, but I'm more like an orphan. All he likes is fishing and hunting and drinking."

"And what do you like?"

"I want to get ahead in the world. I'm twenty years old. I've got to think of my future. There he is yelling for me. He can't say anything without yelling. You going to eat with us?"

"Sure."

I bathed slowly in the crusted galvanized bucket. For a moment I thought of digging out New York clothes and putting on a puff for the boy, but I dropped that one and settled for clean chino slacks and a knitted shirt.

The burly proprietor's face was red as a ripe raspberry when I went into the lunch counter. He thrust his jaw at me. "As if I ain't carrying enough trouble, you got to be from New York."

"Is that bad?"

"For me it is. I just got that kid quieted down and you put burrs under his blanket."

"I didn't give New York a good name."

"No, but you come from there and now he's all riled up again. Oh, hell, what's the use? He's no damn good around here. Come on, you might as well eat with us out back."

Out back was kitchen, larder, pantry, dining room—and the cot covered with army blankets made it bedroom too. A great gothic wood stove clicked and purred. We were to eat at a square table covered with white, knife-scarred oilcoth. The keyed-up boy dished up bowls of bubbling navy beans and fat-back.

"I wonder if you could rig me a reading light?"

"Hell, I turn off the generator when we go to bed. I can give you a coal-oil lamp. Pull up. Got a canned baked ham in the oven."

The moody boy served the beans listlessly.

The red-faced man spoke up. "I thought he'd just finish high school and that would be the end of it, but not him, not Robbie. He took a night course—now get this—not in high school. He paid for it. Don't know where he got the money."

"Sounds pretty ambitious."

"Ambitious my big fat foot. You don't know what the course was—hairdressing. Not barbering —hairdressing—for women. Now maybe you see why I got worries."

Robbie turned from carving the ham. The slender knife was held rigidly in his right hand. He searched my face for the look of contempt he expected.

I strove to look stern, thoughtful, and noncommittal all at once. I pulled at my beard, which is said to indicate concentration. "Whatever I say, one or the other of you is going to sic the dog on me. You've got me in the middle."

Papa took a deep breath and let it out slowly. "By God, you're right," he said, and then he chuckled and the tension went out of the room.

Robbie brought the plates of ham to the table and he smiled at me, I think in gratitude.

"Now that we got our hackles down, what do you

think of this hair-dressing beautician stuff?" Papa said.

"You're not going to like what I think."

"How do I know if you don't say it?"

"Well, okay, but I'm going to eat fast in case I have to run for it."

I went through my beans and half my ham before I answered him.

"All right," I said. "You've hit on a subject I've given a lot of thought to. I know quite a few women and girls—all ages, all kinds, all shapes—no two alike except in one thing—the hairdresser. It is my considered opinion that the hairdresser is the most influential man in any community."

"You're making a joke."

"I am not. I've made a deep study of this. When women go to the hairdresser, and they all do if they can afford it, something happens to them. They feel safe, they relax. They don't have to keep up any kind of pretense. The hairdresser knows what their skin is like under the make-up, he knows their age, their face-liftings. This being so, women tell a hairdresser things they wouldn't dare confess to a priest, and they are open about matters they'd try to conceal from a doctor."

"You don't say."

"I do say. I tell you I'm a student of this. When women place their secret lives in the hairdresser's hands, he gains an authority few other men ever attain. I have heard hairdressers quoted with complete conviction in art, literature, politics, economics, child care, and morals."

"I think you're kidding but on the level."

"I'm not smiling when I say it. I tell you that a clever, thoughtful, ambitious hairdresser wields a power beyond the comprehension of most men."

"Jesus Christ! You hear that, Robbie? Did you know all that?"

"Some of it. Why, in the course I took there was a whole section on psychology."

"I never would of thought of it," Papa said. "Say, how about a little drink?"

"Thanks, not tonight. My dog's not well. I'm going to push on early and try to find a vet."

"Tell you what—Robbie will rig up a reading light for you. I'll leave the generator on. Will you want some breakfast?"

"I don't think so. I'm going to get an early start."

When I came to my cabin after trying to help Charley in his travail, Robbie was tying a trouble light to the iron frame of my sad bed.

He said quietly, "Mister, I don't know if you believe all that you said, but you sure gave me a hand up."

"You know, I think most of it might be true. If it is, that's a lot of responsibility, isn't it, Robbie?"

"It sure is," he said solemnly.

It was a restless night for me. I had rented a cabin not nearly as comfortable as the one I carried with me, and once installed I had interfered in a matter that was none of my business. And while it is true that people rarely take action on advice of others unless they were going to do it anyway, there was the small chance that in my enthusiasm for my hairdressing thesis I might have raised up a monster.

In the middle of the night Charley awakened me with a soft apologetic whining, and since he is not a whining dog I got up immediately. He was in trouble, his abdomen distended and his nose and ears hot. I took him out and stayed with him, but he could not relieve the pressure.

I wish I knew something of veterinary medicine. There's a feeling of helplessness with a sick animal. It can't explain how it feels, though on the other hand it can't lie, build up its symptoms, or indulge in the pleasures of hypochondria. I don't mean they are incapable of faking. Even Charley, who is as honest as they come, is prone to limp when his feelings are hurt. I wish someone would write a good, comprehensive book of home dog medicine. I would do it myself if I were qualified.

Charley was a really sick dog, and due to get sicker unless I could find some way to relieve the growing pressure. A catheter would do it, but who has one in the mountains in the middle of the night? I had a plastic tube for siphoning gasoline, but the diameter was too great. Then I remembered something about pressure causing muscular tension which increases the pressure, etc., so that the first step is to relax the muscles. My medicine chest was not designed for general practice, but I did have a bottle of sleeping pills—seconal, one and a half grains. But how about dosage? That is where the home medicine book would be helpful. I took a capsule apart and unloaded half of it and fitted it together again. I slipped the capsule back beyond the bow in Charley's tongue where he could not push it out, then held up his head and massaged it down his throat. Then I lifted him on the bed and covered him. At the end of an hour there was no change in him, so I opened a second capsule and gave him another half. I think that, for his weight, one and a half grains is a pretty heavy dose, but Charley must have a high tolerance. He resisted it for three quarters of an hour before his breathing slowed and he went to sleep. I must have dozed off, too. The next thing I knew, he hit the floor. In his drugged condition his legs buckled under him. He got up, stumbled, and got up again. I opened the door and let him out. Well, the method worked all right, but I don't see how one medium-sized dog's body could have held that much fluid. Finally he staggered in and collapsed on a piece of carpet and was asleep immediately. He was so completely out that I worried over the dosage. But his temperature had dropped and his breathing was normal and his heart beat was strong and steady. My sleep was restless, and when dawn came I saw that Charley had not moved. I awakened him and he was quite agreeable when I got his attention. He smiled, yawned, and went back to sleep.

I lifted him into the cab and drove hell for leather for Spokane. I don't remember a thing about the country on the way. On the outskirts I looked up a veterinary in the phone book, asked directions, and rushed Charley into the examination room as an emergency. I shall not mention the doctor's name, but he is one more reason for a good home book on dog medicine. The doctor was, if not elderly, pushing his luck, but who am I to say he had a hangover? He raised Charley's lip with a shaking hand, then turned up an eyelid and let it fall back.

"What's the matter with him?" he asked, with no interest whatever.

"That's why I'm here—to find out."

"Kind of dopey. Old dog. Maybe he had a stroke."

"He had a distended bladder. If he's dopey, it's

because I gave him one and a half grains of seconal."

"What for?"

"To relax him."

"Well, he's relaxed."

"Was the dosage too big?"

"I don't know."

"Well, how much would you give?"

"I wouldn't give it at all."

"Let's start fresh—what's wrong with him?"

"Probably a cold."

"Would that cause bladder symptoms?"

"If the cold was there—yes, sir."

"Well, look—I'm on the move. I'd like a little closer diagnosis."

He snorted. "Look here. He's an old dog. Old dogs get aches and pains. That's just the way it is."

I must have been snappish from the night. "So do old men," I said. "That doesn't keep them from doing something about it." And I think for the first time I got through to him.

"Give you something to flush out his kidneys," he said. "Just a cold."

I took the little pills and paid my bill and got out of there. It wasn't that this veterinary didn't like animals. I think he didn't like himself, and when that is so the subject usually must find an area for dislike outside himself. Else he would have to admit his self-contempt.

On the other hand, I yield to no one in my distaste for the self-styled dog-lover, the kind who heaps up his frustrations and makes a dog carry them around. Such a dog-lover talks baby talk to mature and thoughtful animals, and attributes his own sloppy characteristics to them until the dog becomes in his mind an alter ego. Such people, it seems to me, in what they imagine to be kindness, are capable of inflicting long and lasting tortures on an animal, denying it any of its natural desires and fulfillments until a dog of weak character breaks down and becomes the fat, asthmatic, be-furred bundle of neuroses. When a stranger ad-dresses Charley in baby talk, Charley avoids him. For Charley is not a human; he's a dog, and he likes it that way. He feels that he is a first-rate dog and has no wish to be a second-rate human. When the alcoholic vet touched him with his unsteady, inept hand, I saw the look of veiled contempt in Charley's eyes. He knew about the man, I thought, and perhaps the doctor knew he knew. And maybe that was the man's trouble. It would be very pain-ful to know that your patients had no faith in you.

After Spokane, the danger of early snows had passed, for the air was changed and mulsed by the strong breath of the Pacific. The actual time on the way from Chicago was short, but the overwhelming size and variety of the land, the many incidents and people along the way, had stretched time out of all bearing. For it is not true that an uneventful time in the past is remembered as fast. On the con-trary, it takes the time-stones of events to give a memory past dimension. Eventlessness collapses time.

The Pacific is my home ocean; I knew it first, grew up on its shore, collected marine animals along the coast. I know its moods, its color, its na-ture. It was very far inland that I caught the first smell of the Pacific. When one has been long at sea, the smell of land reaches far out to greet one. And the same is true when one has been long inland. I believe I smelled the sea rocks and the kelp and the excitement of churning sea water, the sharpness of iodine and the under odor of washed and ground calcareous shells. Such a far-off and remembered odor comes subtly so that one does not consciously smell it, but rather an electric excitement is released—a kind of boisterous joy. I found myself plunging over the roads of Washington, as dedicated to the sea as any migrating lemming.

I remembered lush and lovely eastern Washington very well and the noble Columbia River, which left its mark on Lewis and Clark. And, while there were dams and power lines I hadn't seen, it was not greatly changed from what I remembered. It was only as I approached Seattle that the unbelievable change became apparent.

Of course, I had been reading about the population explosion on the West Coast, but for West Coast most people substitute California. People swarming in, cities doubling and trebling in numbers of inhabitants, while the fiscal guardians groan over the increasing weight of improvements and the need to care for a large new spate of indigents. It was here in Washington that I saw it first. I remembered Seattle as a town sitting on hills beside a matchless harborage—a little city of space and trees and gardens, its houses matched to such a background. It is no longer so. The tops of hills are shaved off to make level warrens for the rabbits of the present. The highways eight lanes wide cut like glaciers through the uneasy land. This Seattle had no relation to the one I remembered. The traffic rushed with murderous intensity. On the outskirts of this place I once knew well I could not find my way. Along what had been country lanes rich with berries, high wire fences and mile-long factories stretched, and the yellow smoke of progress hung over all, fighting the sea winds' efforts to drive them off.

This sounds as though I bemoan an older time, which is the preoccupation of the old, or cultivate an opposition to change, which is the currency of the rich and stupid. It is not so. This Seattle was not something changed that I once knew. It was a new thing. Set down there not knowing it was Seattle, I could not have told where I was. Everywhere frantic growth, a carcinomatous growth. Bulldozers rolled up the green forests and heaped the resulting trash for burning. The torn white lumber from concrete forms was piled beside gray walls. I wonder why progress looks so much like destruction.

Next day I walked in the old port of Seattle, where the fish and crabs and shrimps lay beautifully on white beds of shaved ice and where the washed and shining vegetables were arranged in pictures. I drank clam juice and ate the sharp crab cocktails at stands along the waterfront. It was not much changed—a little more run-down and dingy than it was twenty years ago. And here a generality concerning the growth of American cities, seemingly true of all of them I know. When a city begins to grow and spread outward, from the edges, the center which was once its glory is in a sense abandoned to time. Then the buildings grow dark and a kind of decay sets in; poorer people move in as the rents fall, and small fringe businesses take the place of once flowering establishments. The district is still too good to tear down and too outmoded to be desirable. Besides, all the energy has flowed out to the new developments, to the semi-rural supermarkets, the outdoor movies, new houses with wide lawns and stucco schools where children are confirmed in their illiteracy. The old port with narrow streets and cobbled surfaces, smoke-grimed, goes into a period of desolation inhabited at night by the vague ruins of men, the lotus eaters who struggle daily toward unconsciousness by way of raw alcohol. Nearly every city I know has such a dying mother of violence and despair where at night the brightness of the street lamps is sucked away and policemen walk in pairs. And then one day perhaps the city returns and rips out the sore and builds a monument to its past.

The rest during my stay in Seattle had improved Charley's condition. I wondered whether in his advancing age the constant vibration of the truck might not have been the cause of his trouble.

Quite naturally, as we moved down the beautiful coast my method of travel was changed. Each evening I found a pleasant auto court to rest in, beautiful new places that have sprung up in recent years. Now I began to experience a tendency in the West that perhaps I am too old to accept. It is the principle of do it yourself. At breakfast a toaster is on your table. You make your own toast. When I drew into one of these gems of comfort and convenience, registered, and was shown to my comfortable room after paying in advance, of course, that was the end of any contact with the management. There were no waiters, no bell boys. The chambermaids crept in and out invisibly. If I wanted ice, there was a machine near the office. I got my own ice, my own papers. Everything was convenient, centrally located, and lonesome. I lived in the utmost luxury. Other guests came and went silently. If one con-

fronted them with "Good evening," they looked
a little confused and then responded, "Good evening." It seemed to me that they looked at me for
a place to insert a coin.

Somewhere in Oregon, on a rainy Sunday, the
gallant Rocinante bespoke my attention. I have not
spoken of my faithful vehicle except in formal
terms of passing praise. Is it not always so? We
value virtue but do not discuss it. The honest bookkeeper, the faithful wife, the earnest scholar get
little of our attention compared to the embezzler,
the tramp, the cheat. If Rocinante has been neglected in this account, it is because she performed
perfectly. Neglect did not extend to the mechanical,
however. Meticulously I had changed the oil and
attended to the greasing. I hate to see a motor
neglected or mistreated or worked beyond its
capacity.

Rocinante responded to my kindness as she must,
with purring motor and perfect performance. In
only one thing was I thoughtless, or perhaps over-
zealous. I carried too much of everything—too much
food, too many books, tools enough to assemble a
submarine. If I found sweet-tasting water I filled
her tank, and thirty gallons of water weigh three
hundred pounds. A spare container of butane gas
for safety's sake weighs seventy-five pounds. Her
springs were deeply depressed but seemingly safe,
and on hard-pitching roads I slowed and eased her
through, and because of her ready goodness I
treated her like the honest bookkeeper, the faithful
wife: I ignored her. And in Oregon on a rainy
Sunday, moving through an endless muddy puddle,
a right rear tire blew out with a damp explosion. I
have known and owned mean, ugly-natured cars

which would have done this thing out of pure evil and malice, but not Rocinante.

All in the day's work, I thought; that's the way the ball bounces. Well, this ball had bounced in eight inches of muddy water, and the spare tire, under the cab, had been let down into the mud. The changing tools had been put away under the floor under the table, so that my total load had to be unpacked. The new jack, never used and bright with factory paint, was stiff and unruly, and it was not designed for the overhang of Rocinante. I lay on my stomach and edged my way, swam my way under the truck, holding my nostrils clear of the surface of the water. The jack handle was slippery with greasy mud. Mud balls formed in my beard. I lay panting like a wounded duck, quietly cursing as I inched the jack forward under an axle that I had to find by feel, since it was under water. Then, with superhuman gruntings and bubblings, my eyes starting from their sockets, I levered the great weight. I could feel my muscles tearing apart and separating from their anchoring bones. In actual time, not over an hour elapsed before I had the spare tire on. I was unrecognizable under many layers of yellow mud. My hands were cut and bleeding. I rolled the bad tire to a high place and inspected it. The whole side wall had blown out. Then I looked at the left rear tire, and to my horror saw a great rubber bubble on its side and, farther along, another. It was obvious that the other tire might go at any moment, and it was Sunday and it was raining and it was Oregon. If the other tire blew, there we were, on a wet and lonesome road, having no recourse except to burst into tears and wait for death. And perhaps some kind birds might cover us with leaves. I peeled off mud and clothes together and changed to new finery, which got muddy in the process.

No car has ever had such obsequious treatment as did Rocinante as we moved slowly on. Every irregularity in the road hurt me clear through. We crawled along at not more than five miles an hour. And that ancient law went into effect which says that when you need towns they are very far apart. I needed more than a town. I needed two new heavy-duty rear tires. The men who had designed my truck had not anticipated the load I would carry.

After forty years in the painful wet desert with no cloud by day nor pillar of fire by night to guide us, we came to a damp little shut-up town whose name escapes me because I never learned it. Everything was closed—everything but one small service station. The owner was a giant with a scarred face and an evil white eye. If he were a horse I wouldn't buy him. He was a mostly silent man. "You got trouble," he said.

"You're telling me. Don't you sell tires?"

"Not your size. Have to send to Portland for those. Could phone tomorrow and get them maybe the next day."

"Isn't there any place in town that might have them?"

"There's two. Both closed. I don't think they got that size. You going to need bigger tires." He scratched his beard, peered long at the bubbles on the left rear, and poked them with a forefinger like a file. Finally he went into his little office, pushed a litter of brake linings and fan belts and catalogues aside, and from underneath dug out a telephone.

And if ever my faith in the essential saintliness of humans becomes tattered, I shall think of that evil-looking man.

After three calls he found a dealer who had one of the kind and size required, but this man was tied up with a wedding and couldn't tear himself away. Three calls later, he turned up a rumor of another tire, but it was eight miles away. The rain continued to fall. The process was endless because between each call there was a line of cars waiting to be filled with gas and oil, and all this had to be done with a stately slowness.

A brother-in-law was finally aroused. He had a farm up the road a piece. He didn't want to get out in the rain, but my evil saint exerted some kind of pressure on him. That brother-in-law drove to the two places far apart where the tires might be, found them, and brought them to me. In a little less than four hours I was equipped, riding on big heavy-duty tires of a kind that should have been there in the first place. I could have knelt in the mud and kissed the man's hands, but I didn't. I tipped him rather royally and he said, "You didn't ought to do that. Jus' remember one thing," he said. "Them new tires is bigger. They're gonna change your speedometer reading. You'll be goin' faster'n the needle says and you get some itchy cop, why, he might pick you up."

I was so full of humble gratefulness, I could hardly speak. That happened on Sunday in Oregon in the rain, and I hope that evil-looking service-station man may live a thousand years and people the earth with his offspring.

Now, THERE IS NOT ANY QUESTION THAT Charley was rapidly becoming a tree expert of enormous background. He could probably get a job as a consultant with the Davies people. But from the first I had withheld from him any information about the giant redwoods. It seemed to me that a Long Island poodle who had made his devoirs to *Sequoia sempervirens* or *Sequoia gigantia* might be set apart from other dogs—might even be like that Galahad who saw the Grail. The concept is staggering. After this experience he might be translated mystically to another plane of existence, to another dimension, just as the redwoods seem to be out of time and out of our ordinary thinking. The experience might even drive him mad. I had thought of that. On the other hand, it might make of him a consummate bore. A dog with an experience like that could become a pariah in the truest sense of the word.

The redwoods, once seen, leave a mark or create a vision that stays with you always. No one has ever successfully painted or photographed a redwood tree. The feeling they produce is not transferable. From them comes silence and awe. It's not only their unbelievable stature, nor the color which seems to shift and vary under your eyes, no, they are not like any trees we know, they are ambassadors from another time. They have the mystery of ferns that disappeared a million years ago into the coal of the carboniferous era. They carry their own light and shade. The vainest, most slap-happy and irreverent of men, in the presence of redwoods, goes under a spell of wonder and respect. Respect —that's the word. One feels the need to bow to unquestioned sovereigns. I have known these great ones since my earliest childhood, have lived among them, camped and slept against their warm monster bodies, and no amount of association has bred contempt in me. And the feeling is not limited to me.

A number of years ago, a newcomer, a stranger, moved to my country near Monterey. His senses must have been blunted and atrophied with money and the getting of it. He bought a grove of sempervirens in a deep valley near the coast, and then, as was his right by ownership, he cut them down and sold the lumber, and left on the ground the wreckage of his slaughter. Shock and numb outrage filled the town. This was not only murder but sacrilege. We looked on that man with loathing, and he was marked to the day of his death.

Of course, many of the ancient groves have been lumbered off, but many of the stately monuments remain and will remain, for a good and interesting reason. States and governments could not buy and protect these holy trees. This being so, clubs, organizations, even individuals, bought them and dedicated them to the future. I don't know any other similar case. Such is the impact of the sequoias on the human mind. But what would it be on Charley?

Approaching the redwood country, in southern Oregon, I kept him in the back of Rocinante, hooded as it were. I passed several groves and let them go as not quite adequate—and then on a level meadow by a stream we saw the grandfather, standing alone, three hundred feet high and with the girth of a small apartment house. The branches with their flat, bright green leaves did not start below a hundred and fifty feet up. Under that was the straight, slightly tapering column with its red to purple to blue. Its top was noble and lightning-riven by some ancient storm. I coasted off the road and pulled to within fifty feet of the godlike thing, so close that I had to throw back my head and raise my eyes to vertical to see its branches. This was the time I had waited for. I opened the back door and let Charley out and stood silently watching, for this could be dog's dream of heaven in the highest.

Charley sniffed and shook his collar. He sauntered to a weed, collaborated with a sapling, went to the stream and drank, then looked about for new things to do.

"Charley," I called. "Look!" I pointed at the grandfather. He wagged his tail and took another drink. I said, "Of course. He doesn't raise his head high enough to see the branches to prove it's a tree." I strolled to him and raised his muzzle straight up. "Look, Charley. It's the tree of all trees. It's the end of the Quest."

Charley got a sneezing fit, as all dogs do when the nose is elevated too high. I felt the rage and hatred one has toward non-appreciators, toward those who through ignorance destroy a treasured plan. I dragged him to the trunk and rubbed his nose against it. He looked coldly at me and forgave me and sauntered away to a hazlenut bush.

"If I thought he did it out of spite or to make a joke," I said to myself, "I'd kill him out of hand.

I can't live without knowing." I opened my pocket knife and moved to the creekside, where I cut a branch from a small willow tree, a Y-branch well tufted with leaves. I trimmed the branch ends neatly and finally sharpened the butt end, then went to the serene grandfather of Titans and stuck the little willow in the earth so that its greenery rested against the shaggy redwood bark. Then I whistled to Charley and he responded amiably enough. I pointedly did not look at him. He cruised casually about until he saw the willow with a start of surprise. He sniffed its new-cut leaves delicately and then, after turning this way and that to get range and trajectory, he fired.

I STAYED TWO DAYS CLOSE TO THE BODIES OF the giants, and there were no trippers, no chattering troupes with cameras. There's a cathedral hush here. Perhaps the thick soft bark absorbs sound and creates a silence. The trees rise straight up to zenith; there is no horizon. The dawn comes early and remains dawn until the sun is high. Then the green fernlike foliage so far up strains the sunlight to a green gold and distributes it in shafts or rather in stripes of light and shade. After the sun passes zenith it is afternoon and quickly evening with a whispering dusk as long as was the morning.

Thus time and the ordinary divisions of the day are changed. To me dawn and dusk are quiet times, and here in the redwoods nearly the whole of daylight is a quiet time. Birds move in the dim light or flash like sparks through the stripes of sun, but they make little sound. Underfoot is a mattress of needles deposited for over two thousand years. No sound of footsteps can be heard on this thick blanket. To me there's a remote and cloistered feeling here. One holds back speech for fear of disturbing something—what? From my earliest childhood I've felt that something was going on in the groves, something of which I was not a part. And if I had forgotten the feeling, I soon got it back.

At night, the darkness is black—only straight up a patch of gray and an occasional star. And there's a breathing in the black, for these huge things that control the day and inhabit the night are living things and have presence, and perhaps feeling, and, somewhere in deep-down perception, perhaps communication. I have had lifelong association with these things. (Odd that the word "trees" does not apply.) I can accept them and their power and their age because I was early exposed to them. On the other hand, people lacking such experience begin to have a feeling of uneasiness here, of danger, of being shut in, enclosed and overwhelmed. It is not only the size of these redwoods but their strangeness that frightens them. And why not? For these are the last remaining members of a race that flourished over four continents as far back in geologic time as the upper Jurassic period. Fossils of these ancients have been found dating from the Cretaceous era while in the Eocene and Miocene they were spread over England and Europe and America. And then the glaciers moved down and wiped the Titans out beyond recovery. And only these few are left—a stunning memory of what the world was like once long ago. Can it be that we do not love to be reminded that we are very young and callow in a world that was old when we came into it? And could there be a strong resistance to the certainty that a living world will continue its stately way when we no longer inhabit it?

I FIND IT DIFFICULT TO WRITE ABOUT MY native place, northern California. It should be the easiest, because I knew that strip angled against the Pacific better than any place in the world. But I find it not one thing but many—one printed over another until the whole thing blurs. What it is is warped with memory of what it was and that with what happened there to me, the whole bundle wracked until objectiveness is nigh impossible. This four-lane concrete highway slashed with speeding cars I remember as a narrow, twisting mountain road where the wood teams moved, drawn by steady mules. They signaled their coming with the high, sweet jangle of hame bells. This was a little little town, a general store under a tree and a blacksmith shop and a bench in front on which to sit and listen to the clang of hammer on anvil. Now little houses, each one like the next, particularly since they try to be different, spread for a mile in all directions. That was a woody hill with live oaks dark green against the parched grass where the coyotes sang on moonlit nights. The top is shaved off and a television relay station lunges at the sky and feeds a nervous picture to thousands of tiny houses clustered like aphids beside the roads.

And isn't this the typical complaint? I have never resisted change, even when it has been called progress, and yet I felt resentment toward the strangers swamping what I thought of as my country with noise and clutter and the inevitable rings of junk. And of course these new people will resent the newer people. I remember how when I was a child we responded to the natural dislike of the stranger. We who were born here and our parents also felt a strange superiority over newcomers, barbarians, *forestieri*, and they, the foreigners, resented us and even made a rude poem about us:

> The miner came in forty-nine,
> The whores in fifty-one.
> And when they got together,
> They made a Native Son.

And we were an outrage to the Spanish-Mexicans and they in their turn on the Indians. Could that be why the sequoias make folks nervous? Those natives were grown trees when a political execution took place on Golgotha. They were well toward middle age when Caesar destroyed the Roman republic in the process of saving it. To the sequoias everyone is a stranger, a barbarian.

Sometimes the view of change is distorted by a change in oneself. The room which seemed so large is shrunk, the mountain has become a hill. But this is no illusion in this case. I remember Salinas, the town of my birth, when it proudly announced four thousand citizens. Now it is eighty thousand and leaping pell mell on in a mathematical progression —a hundred thousand in three years and perhaps two hundred thousand in ten, with no end in sight. Even those people who joy in numbers and are impressed with bigness are beginning to worry, gradually becoming aware that there must be a saturation point and the progress may be a progression toward strangulation. And no solution has been found. You can't forbid people to be born—at least not yet.

I spoke earlier of the emergence of the trailer home, the mobile unit, and of certain advantages to their owners. I had thought there were many of them in the East and the Middle West, but California spawns them like herrings. The trailer courts are everywhere, lapping up the sides of hills, spilling into river beds. And they bring with them a new problem. These people partake of all the local facilities, the hospitals, the schools, police protection, welfare programs, and so far they do not pay taxes. Local facilities are supported by real-estate taxes, from which the mobile home is immune. It is true that the state imposes a license fee, but that fee does not come to the counties or the towns except for road maintenance and extension. Thus the owners of immovable property find themselves supporting swarms of guests, and they are getting pretty angry about it. But our tax laws and the way we think about them were long developing. The mind shies away from a head tax, a facility tax. The concept of real property is deeply implanted in us as the source and symbol of wealth. And now a vast number of people have found a way to bypass it. This might be applauded, since we generally admire those who can escape taxes, were it not that the burden of this freedom falls with increasing weight on others. It is obvious that within a very short time a whole new method of taxation will have to be devised, else the burden on real estate will be so great that no one will be able to afford it; far from being a source of profit, ownership will be a penalty, and this will be the apex of a pyramid of paradoxes. We have in the past been forced into reluctant change by weather, calamity, and plague. Now the pressure comes from our biologic success as a species. We have overcome all enemies but ourselves.

When I was a child growing up in Salinas we called San Francisco "the City." Of course it was the only city we knew, but I still think of it as the City, and so does everyone else who has ever associated with it. A strange and exclusive word is "city." Besides San Francisco, only small sections of London and Rome stay in the mind as the City. New Yorkers say they are going to town. Paris has no title but Paris. Mexico City is the Capital.

Once I knew the City very well, spent my attic days there, while others were being a lost generation in Paris. I fledged in San Francisco, climbed its hills, slept in its parks, worked on its docks, marched and shouted in its revolts. In a way I felt I owned the City as much as it owned me.

San Francisco put on a show for me. I saw her across the bay, from the great road that bypasses Sausalito and enters the Golden Gate Bridge. The afternoon sun painted her white and gold—rising on her hills like a noble city in a happy dream. A city on hills has it over flat-land places. New York makes its own hills with craning buildings, but this gold and white acropolis rising wave on wave against the blue of the Pacific sky was a stunning thing, a painted thing like a picture of a medieval Italian city which can never have existed. I stopped in a parking place to look at her and the necklace bridge over the entrance from the sea that led to her. Over the green higher hills to the south, the evening fog rolled like herds of sheep coming to cote in the golden city. I've never seen her more lovely. When I was a child and we were going to the City, I couldn't sleep for several nights before, out of bursting excitement. She leaves a mark.

Then I crossed the great arch hung from filaments and I was in the city I knew so well.

It remained the City I remembered, so confident of its greatness that it can afford to be kind. It had been kind to me in the days of my poverty and it did not resent my temporary solvency. I might have stayed indefinitely, but I had to go to Monterey to send off my absentee ballot.

In my young days in Monterey County, a hundred miles south of San Francisco, everyone was a Republican. My family was Republican. I might still be one if I had stayed there. President Harding stirred me toward the Democratic party and President Hoover cemented me there. If I indulge in personal political history, it is because I think my experience may not be unique.

I arrived in Monterey and the fight began. My sisters are still Republicans. Civil war is supposed to be the bitterest of wars, and surely family politics are the most vehement and venomous. I can discuss politics coldly and analytically with strangers. That was not possible with my sisters. We ended each session panting and spent with rage. On no point was there any compromise. No quarter was asked or given.

Each evening we promised, "Let's just be friendly and loving. No politics tonight." And ten minutes later we would be screaming at each other. "John Kennedy was a so-and-so—"

"Well, if that's your attitude, how can you reconcile Dick Nixon?"

"Now let's be calm. We're reasonable people. Let's explore this."

"I have explored it. How about the scotch whisky?"

"Oh, if you take that line, how about the grocery in Santa Ana? How about Checkers, my beauty?"

"Father would turn in his grave if he heard you."

"No, don't bring him in, because he would be a Democrat today."

"Listen to you. Bobby Kennedy is out buying sacks full of votes."

"You mean no Republican ever bought a vote? Don't make me laugh."

It was bitter and it was endless. We dug up obsolete convention weapons and insults to hurl back and forth.

"You talk like a Communist."

"Well, you sound suspiciously like Genghis Khan."

It was awful. A stranger hearing us would have called the police to prevent bloodshed. And I don't think we were the only ones. I believe this was going on all over the country in private. It must have been only publicly that the nation was tongue-tied.

The main purpose of this homecoming seemed to be fighting over politics, but in between I visited old places. There was a touching reunion in Johnny Garcia's bar in Monterey, with tears and embraces, speeches and endearments in the *poco* Spanish of my youth. There were Jolón Indians I remembered as shirttail *chamacos*. The years rolled away. We danced formally, hands locked behind us. And we sang the southern county anthem, "There wass a

jung guy from Jolón—got seek from leeving halone.
He wan to Keeng Ceety to gat sometheeng pretty—
Puta chingada cabrón." I hadn't heard it in years.
It was old home week. The years crawled back in
their holes. It was the Monterey where they used
to put a wild bull and a grizzly bear in the ring
together, a place of sweet and sentimental violence,
and a wise innocence as yet unknown and therefore
undirtied by undiapered minds.

We sat at the bar, and Johnny Garcia regarded
us with his tear-blown Gallego eyes. His shirt was
open and a gold medal on a chain hung at his
throat. He leaned close over the bar and said to the
nearest man, "Look at it! Juanito here gave it to
me years ago, brought it from Mexico—la Morena,
La Virgincita de Guadeloupe, and look!" He
turned the gold oval. "My name and his."

I said, "Scratched with a pin."

"I have never taken it off," said Johnny.

A big dark *paisano* I didn't know stood on the
rail and leaned over the bar. *"Favor?"* he asked,
and without looking Johnny extended the medal.
The man kissed it, said *"Gracias,"* and went
quickly out through the swinging doors.

Johnny's chest swelled with emotion and his eyes
were wet. "Juanito," he said. "Come home! Come
back to your friends. We love you. We need you.
This is your seat, *compadre,* do not leave it vacant."

I must admit I felt the old surge of love and
oratory and I haven't a drop of Galician blood.
"Cuñado mio," I said sadly, "I live in New York
now."

"I don't like New York," Johnny said.

"You've never been there."

"I know. That's why I don't like it. You have to come back. You belong here."

I drank deeply, and darned if I didn't find myself making a speech. The old words unused for so long came rattling back to me. "Let your heart have ears, my uncle, my friend. We are not baby skunks, you and I. Time has settled some of our problems."

"Silence," he said. "I will not hear it. It is not true. You still love wine, you still love girls. What has changed? I know you. *No me cagas, niño.*"

"*Te cago nunca.* There was a great man named Thomas Wolfe and he wrote a book called *You Can't Go Home Again.* And that is true."

"Liar," said Johnny. "This is your cradle, your home." Suddenly he hit the bar with the oaken indoor ball bat he used in arguments to keep the peace. "In the fullness of time—maybe a hundred years—this should be your grave." The bat fell from his hand and he wept at the prospect of my future demise. I puddled up at the prospect myself.

I gazed at my empty glass. "These Gallegos have no manners."

"Oh, for God's sake," Johnny said. "Oh, forgive me!" and he filled us up.

The line-up at the bar was silent now, dark faces with a courteous lack of expression.

"To your home-coming, *compadre,*" Johnny said. "John the Baptist, get the hell out of those potato chips."

"*Conejo de mi Alma,*" I said. "Rabbit of my soul, hear me out."

The big dark one came in from the street, leaned over the bar and kissed Johnny's medal, and went out again.

I said irritably, "There was a time when a man could be listened to. Must I buy a ticket? Must I make a reservation to tell a story?"

Johnny turned to the silent bar. "Silence!" he said fiercely, and took up his indoor ball bat.

"I will now tell you true things, brother-in-law. Step into the street—strangers, foreigners, thousands of them. Look to the hills, a pigeon loft. Today I walked the length of Alvarado Street and back by the Calle Principál and I saw nothing but strangers. This afternoon I got lost in Peter's Gate. I went to the Field of Love back of Joe Duckworth's house by the Ball Park. It's a used-car lot. My nerves are jangled by traffic lights. Even the police are strangers, foreigners. I went to the Carmel Valley where once we could shoot a thirty-thirty in any direction. Now you couldn't shoot a marble knuckles down without wounding a foreigner. And Johnny, I don't mind people, you know that. But these are rich people. They plant geraniums in big pots. Swimming pools where frogs and crayfish used to wait for us. No, my goatly friend. If this were my home, would I get lost in it? If this were my home could I walk the streets and hear no blessing?"

Johnny was slumped casually over the bar. "But here, Juanito, it's the same. We don't let them in."

I looked down the line of faces. "Yes, here it is better. But can I live on a bar stool? Let us not fool ourselves. What we knew is dead, and maybe the greatest part of what we were is dead. What's out there is new and perhaps good, but it's nothing we know."

Johnny held his temples between his cupped hands and his eyes were bloodshot.

"Where are the great ones? Tell me, where's Willie Trip?"

"Dead," Johnny said hollowly.

"Where is Pilon, Johnny, Pom Pom, Miz Gragg, Stevie Field?"

"Dead, dead, dead," he echoed.

"Ed Ricketts, Whitey's Number One and Two, where's Sonny Boy, Ankle Varney, Jesús María Corcoran, Joe Portagee, Shorty Lee, Flora Wood, and that girl who kept spiders in her hat?"

"Dead—all dead," Johnny moaned.

"It's like we was in a bucket of ghosts," said Johnny.

"No. They're not true ghosts. We're the ghosts."

The big dark one came in and Johnny held out his medal for kissing without being asked.

Johnny turned and walked with widespread legs back to the bar mirror. He studied his face for a moment, picked up a bottle, took out the cork, smelled it, tasted it. Then he looked at his fingernails. There was a stir of restlessness along the bar, shoulders hunched, legs were uncrossed.

There's going to be trouble, I said to myself.

Johnny came back and delicately set the bottle on the bar between us. His eyes were wide and dreamy.

Johnny shook his head. "I guess you don't like us any more. I guess maybe you're too good for us." His fingertips played slow chords on an invisible keyboard on the bar.

For just a moment I was tempted. I heard the wail of trumpets and the clash of arms. But hell, I'm too old for it. I made the door in two steps. I turned. "Why does he kiss your medal?"

"He's placing bets."

"Okay. See you tomorrow, Johnny."

The double door swung to behind me. I was on Alvarado Street, slashed with neon light—and around me it was nothing but strangers.

In my flurry of nostalgic spite, I have done the Monterey Peninsula a disservice. It is a beautiful place, clean, well run, and progressive. The beaches are clean where once they festered with fish guts and flies. The canneries which once put up a sickening stench are gone, their places filled with restaurants, antique shops, and the like. They fish for tourists now, not pilchards, and that species they are not likely to wipe out. And Carmel, begun by starveling writers and unwanted painters, is now a community of the well-to-do and the retired. If Carmel's founders should return, they could not afford to live there, but it wouldn't go that far. They would be instantly picked up as suspicious characters and deported over the city line.

The place of my origin had changed, and having gone away I had not changed with it. In my memory it stood as it once did and its outward appearance confused and angered me.

What I am about to tell must be the experience of very many in this nation where so many wander and come back. I called on old and valued friends. I thought their hair had receded a little more than mine. The greetings were enthusiastic. The memories flooded up. Old crimes and old triumphs were brought out and dusted. And suddenly my attention wandered, and looking at my ancient friend, I saw that his wandered also. And it was true what

I had said to Johnny Garcia—I was the ghost. My town had grown and changed and my friend along with it. Now returning, as changed to my friend as my town was to me, I distorted his picture, muddied his memory. When I went away I had died, and so became fixed and unchangeable. My return caused only confusion and uneasiness. Although they could not say it, my old friends wanted me gone so that I could take my proper place in the pattern of remembrance—and I wanted to go for the same reason. Tom Wolfe was right. You can't go home again because home has ceased to exist except in the mothballs of memory.

My departure was flight. But I did do one formal and sentimental thing before I turned my back. I drove up to Fremont's Peak, the highest point for many miles around. I climbed the last spiky rocks to the top. Here among these blackened granite outcrops General Frémont made his stand against a Mexican army, and defeated it. When I was a boy we occasionally found cannon balls and rusted bayonets in the area. This solitary stone peak overlooks the whole of my childhood and youth, the great Salinas Valley stretching south for nearly a hundred miles, the town of Salinas where I was born now spreading like crab grass toward the foothills. Mount Toro, on the brother range to the west, was a rounded benign mountain, and to the north Monterey Bay shone like a blue platter. I felt and smelled and heard the wind blow up from the long valley. It smelled of the brown hills of wild oats.

I remembered how once, in that part of youth that is deeply concerned with death, I wanted to be buried on this peak where without eyes I could see everything I knew and loved, for in those days there was no world beyond the mountains. And I remembered how intensely I felt about my interment. It is strange and perhaps fortunate that when one's time grows nearer one's interest in it flags as death becomes a fact rather than a pageantry. Here on these high rocks my memory myth repaired itself. Charley, having explored the area, sat at my feet, his fringed ears blowing like laundry on a line. His nose, moist with curiosity, sniffed the windborne pattern of a hundred miles.

"You wouldn't know, my Charley, that right down there, in that little valley, I fished for trout with your namesake, my Uncle Charley. And over there—see where I'm pointing—my mother shot a wildcat. Straight down there, forty miles away, our family ranch was—old starvation ranch. Can you see that darker place there? Well, that's a tiny canyon with a clear and lovely stream bordered with wild azaleas and fringed with big oaks. And on one of those oaks my father burned his name with a hot iron together with the name of the girl he loved. In the long years the bark grew over the burn and covered it. And just a little while ago, a man cut that oak for firewood and his splitting wedge uncovered my father's name and the man sent it to me. In the spring, Charley, when the valley is carpeted with blue lupines like a flowery sea, there's the smell of heaven up here, the smell of heaven."

I printed it once more on my eyes, south, west, and north, and then we hurried away from the permanent and changeless past where my mother is always shooting a wildcat and my father is always burning his name with his love.

IT WOULD BE PLEASANT TO BE ABLE TO SAY of my travels with Charley, "I went out to find the truth about my country and I found it." And then it would be such a simple matter to set down my findings and lean back comfortably with a fine sense of having discovered truths and taught them to my readers. I wish it were that easy. But what I carried in my head and deeper in my perceptions was a barrel of worms. I discovered long ago in collecting and classifying marine animals that what I found was closely intermeshed with how I felt at the moment. External reality has a way of being not so external after all.

This monster of a land, this mightiest of nations, this spawn of the future, turns out to be the macrocosm of microcosm me. If an Englishman or a Frenchman or an Italian should travel my route, see what I saw, hear what I heard, their stored pictures would be not only different from mine but equally different from one another. If other Americans reading this account should feel it true, that agreement would only mean that we are alike in our Americanness.

From start to finish I found no strangers. If I had, I might be able to report them more objectively. But these are my people and this my country. If I found matters to criticize and to deplore, they were tendencies equally present in myself. If I were to prepare one immaculately inspected generality it would be this: For all of our enormous geographic range, for all of our sectionalism, for all of our interwoven breeds drawn from every part of the ethnic world, we are a nation, a new breed. Americans are much more American than they are Northerners, Southerners, Westerners, or Easterners. And descendants of English, Irish, Italian, Jewish, German, Polish are essentially American. This is not patriotic whoop-de-do; it is carefully observed fact. California Chinese, Boston Irish, Wisconsin German, yes, and Alabama Negroes, have more in common than they have apart. And this is the more remarkable because it has happened so quickly. It is a fact that Americans from all sections and of all racial extractions are more alike than the Welsh are like the English, the Lancashireman like the Cockney, or for that matter the Lowland Scot like the Highlander. It is astonishing that this has happened in less than two hundred years and most of it in the last fifty. The American identity is an exact and provable thing.

Starting on my return journey, I realized by now that I could not see everything. My impressionable gelatin plate was getting muddled. I determined to inspect two more sections and then call it a day—Texas and a sampling of the Deep South. From my reading, it seemed to me that Texas is emerging as a separate force and that the South is in the pain of labor with the nature of its future child still unknown. And I have thought that such is the bitterness of the labor that the child has been forgotten.

This journey had been like a full dinner of many courses, set before a starving man. At first he tries to eat all of everything, but as the meal progresses he finds he must forgo some things to keep his appetite and his taste buds functioning.

I bucketed Rocinante out of California by the shortest possible route—one I knew well from the old days of the 1930s. From Salinas to Los Banos, through Fresno and Bakersfield, then over the pass and into the Mojave Desert, a burned and burning desert even this late in the year, its hills like piles of black cinders in the distance, and the rutted floor sucked dry by the hungry sun. It's easy enough now, on the high-speed road in a dependable and comfortable car, with stopping places for shade and every service station vaunting its refrigeration. But I can remember when we came to it with prayer, listening for trouble in our laboring old motors, drawing a plume of steam from our boiling radiators. Then the broken-down wreck by the side of the road was in real trouble unless someone stopped to offer help. And I have never crossed it without sharing something with those early families foot-dragging through this terrestrial hell, leaving the white skeletons of horses and cattle which still mark the way.

The Mojave is a big desert and a frightening one. It's as though nature tested a man for endurance and constancy to prove whether he was good enough to get to California. The shimmering dry heat made visions of water on the flat plain. And even when you drive at high speed, the hills that mark the boundaries recede before you. Charley, always a dog for water, panted asthmatically, jarring his whole body with the effort, and a good eight inches of his tongue hung out flat as a leaf and dripping. I pulled off the road into a small gulley to give him water from my thirty-gallon tank. But before I let him drink I poured water all over him and on my hair and shoulders and shirt. The air is so dry that evaporation makes you feel suddenly cold.

I opened a can of beer from my refrigerator and sat well inside the shade of Rocinante, looking out at the sun-pounded plain, dotted here and there with clumps of sagebrush.

About fifty yards away two coyotes stood watching me, their tawny coats blending with sand and sun. I knew that with any quick or suspicious movement of mine they could drift into invisibility. With the most casual slowness I reached down my new rifle from its sling over my bed—the .222 with its bitter little high-speed, long-range stings. Very slowly I brought the rifle up. Perhaps in the shade of my house I was half hidden by the blinding light outside. The little rifle has a beautiful telescope sight with a wide field. The coyotes had not moved.

I got both of them in the field of my telescope, and the glass brought them very close. Their tongues lolled out so that they seemed to smile mockingly. They were favored animals, not starved, but well furred, the golden hair tempered with black guard hairs. Their little lemon-yellow eyes were plainly visible in the glass. I moved the cross hairs to the breast of the right-hand animal, and pushed the safety. My elbows on the table steadied the gun. The cross hairs lay unmoving on the brisket. And then the coyote sat down like a dog and its right rear paw came up to scratch the right shoulder.

My finger was reluctant to touch the trigger. I must be getting very old and my ancient conditioning worn thin. Coyotes are vermin. They steal chickens. They thin the ranks of quail and all other game birds. They must be killed. They are the enemy. My first shot would drop the sitting beast, and the other would whirl to fade away. I might very well pull him down with a running shot because I am a good rifleman.

And I did not fire. My training said, "Shoot!" and my age replied, "There isn't a chicken within thirty miles, and if there are any they aren't my chickens. And this waterless place is not quail country. No, these boys are keeping their figures with kangaroo rats and jackrabbits, and that's vermin eat vermin. Why should I interfere?"

"Kill them," my training said. "Everyone kills them. It's a public service." My finger moved to the trigger. The cross was steady on the breast just below the panting tongue. I could imagine the splash and jar of angry steel, the leap and struggle until the torn heart failed, and then, not too long later, the shadow of a buzzard, and another. By that time I would be long gone—out of the desert and across the Colorado River. And beside the sagebrush there would be a naked, eyeless skull, a few picked bones, a spot of black dried blood and a few rags of golden fur.

I guess I'm too old and too lazy to be a good citizen. The second coyote stood sidewise to my rifle. I moved the cross hairs to his shoulder and held steady. There was no question of missing with that rifle at that range. I owned both animals. Their lives were mine. I put the safety on and laid the rifle on the table. Without the telescope they were not so intimately close. The hot blast of light tousled the air to shimmering.

Then I remembered something I heard long ago

that I hope is true. It was unwritten law in China, so my informant told me, that when one man saved another's life he became responsible for that life to the end of its existence. For, having interfered with a course of events, the savior could not escape his responsibility. And that has always made good sense to me.

Now I had a token responsibility for two live and healthy coyotes. In the delicate world of relationships, we are tied together for all time. I opened two cans of dog food and left them as a votive.

I have driven through the Southwest many times, and even more often have flown over it—a great and mysterious wasteland, a sun-punished place. It is a mystery, something concealed and waiting. It seems deserted, free of parasitic man, but this is not entirely so. Follow the double line of wheel tracks through sand and rock and you will find a habitation somewhere huddled in a protected place, with a few trees pointing their roots at under-earth water, a patch of starveling corn and squash, and strips of jerky hanging on a string. There is a breed of desert men, not hiding exactly but gone to sanctuary from the sins of confusion.

At night in this waterless air the stars come down just out of reach of your fingers. In such a place lived the hermits of the early church piercing to infinity with unlittered minds. The great concepts of oneness and of majestic order seem always to be born in the desert. The quiet counting of the stars, and observation of their movements, came first from desert places. I have known desert men who chose their places with quiet and slow passion, rejecting the nervousness of a watered world. These men have not changed with the exploding times except to die and be replaced by others like them.

And always there are mysteries in the desert, stories told and retold of secret places in the desert mountains where surviving clans from an older era wait to re-emerge. Usually these groups guard treasures hidden from the waves of conquest, the golden artifacts of an archaic Montezuma, or a mine so rich that its discovery would change the world. If a stranger discovers their existence, he is killed or so absorbed that he is never seen again. These stories have an inevitable pattern untroubled by the question, If none return, how is it known what is there? Oh, it's there all right, but if you find it you will never be found.

And there is another monolithic tale which never changes. Two prospectors in partnership discover a mine of preternatural richness—of gold or diamonds or rubies. They load themselves with samples, as much as they can carry, and they mark the place in their minds by landmarks all around. Then, on the way out to the other world, one dies of thirst and exhaustion, but the other crawls on, discarding most of the treasure he has grown too weak to carry. He comes at last to a settlement, or perhaps is found by other prospecting men. They examine his samples with great excitement. Sometimes in the story the survivor dies after leaving directions with his rescuers, or again he is nursed back to strength. Then a well-equipped party sets out to find the treasure, and it can never be found again. That is the invariable end of the story—it is never found again. I have heard this story many times, and it never changes. There is nourishment in the desert for myth, but myth must somewhere have its roots in reality.

And there are true secrets in the desert. In the war of sun and dryness against living things, life has its secrets of survival. Life, no matter on what level, must be moist or it will disappear. I find most interesting the conspiracy of life in the desert to circumvent the death rays of the all-conquering sun. The beaten earth appears defeated and dead, but it only appears so. A vast and inventive organization of living matter survives by seeming to have lost. The gray and dusty sage wears oily armor to protect its inward small moistness. Some plants engorge themselves with water in the rare rainfall and store it for future use. Animal life wears a hard, dry skin or an outer skeleton to defy the desiccation. And every living thing has developed techniques for finding or creating shade. Small reptiles and rodents burrow or slide below the surface or cling to the shaded side of an outcropping. Movement is slow to preserve energy, and it is a rare animal which can or will defy the sun for long. A rattlesnake will die in an hour of full sun. Some insects of bolder inventiveness have devised personal refrigeration systems. Those animals which must drink moisture get it at second hand—a rabbit from a leaf, a coyote from the blood of a rabbit.

One may look in vain for living creatures in the daytime, but when the sun goes and the night gives consent, a world of creatures awakens and takes up its intricate pattern. Then the hunted come out and the hunters, and hunters of the hunters. The night awakes to buzzing and to cries and barks.

When, very late in the history of our planet, the incredible accident of life occurred, a balance of chemical factors, combined with temperature, in quantities and in kinds so delicate as to be unlikely, all came together in the retort of time and a new thing emerged, soft and helpless and unprotected in the savage world of unlife. Then processes of change and variation took place in the organisms, so that one kind became different from all others. But one ingredient, perhaps the most important of all, is planted in every life form—the factor of survival. No living thing is without it, nor could life exist without this magic formula. Of course, each form developed its own machinery for survival, and some failed and disappeared while others peopled the earth. The first life might easily have been snuffed out and the accident may never have happened again—but, once it existed, its first quality, its duty, preoccupation, direction, and end, shared by every living thing, is to go on living. And so it does and so it will until some other accident cancels it. And the desert, the dry and sun-lashed desert, is a good school in which to observe the cleverness and the infinite variety of techniques of survival under pitiless opposition. Life could not change the sun or water the desert, so it changed itself.

The desert, being an unwanted place, might well be the last stand of life against unlife. For in the rich and moist and wanted areas of the world, life pyramids against itself and in its confusion has finally allied itself with the enemy non-life. And what the scorching, searing, freezing, poisoning weapons of non-life have failed to do may be accomplished to the end of its destruction and extinction by the tactics of survival gone sour. If the most versatile of living forms, the human, now fights for survival as it always has, it can eliminate not only itself but all other life. And if that should transpire, unwanted places like the desert might be the harsh mother of repopulation. For the inhabitants of the desert are well trained and well armed against desolation. Even our own misguided species might re-emerge from the desert. The lone man and his sun-toughened wife who cling to the shade in an unfruitful and uncoveted place might, with their brothers in arms—the coyote, the jackrabbit, the horned toad, the rattlesnake, together with a host of armored insects—these trained and tested fragments of life might well be the last hope of life against non-life. The desert has mothered magic things before this.

MUCH EARLIER I SPOKE OF THE CHANGES AT state lines, changes in Highway English, in prose forms on the signs, changes in permitted speeds. The states' rights guaranteed under the Constitution seem to be passionately and gleefully exercised. California searches vehicles for vegetables and fruits which might carry pernicious insects and diseases, and regulations of these are enforced with almost religious intensity.

Some years ago I knew a gay and inventive family from Idaho. Planning to visit relatives in California, they took a truckload of potatoes to sell along the way to help pay expenses. They had disposed of over half their cargo when they were stopped at the California line and their potatoes refused entrance. They were not financially able to abandon their potatoes, so they cheerfully set up camp right on the state line, where they ate potatoes, sold potatoes, bartered potatoes. At the end of two weeks the truck was empty. Then they went through the inspector's station in good standing and continued on their way.

The separateness of the states, which has been bitterly called Balkanization, creates many problems. Rarely do two states have the same gasoline tax, and these taxes largely support the building and maintenance of highways. The enormous interstate trucks make use of the roads and by their very weight and speed increase the maintenance costs.

Thus the states have weighing stations for trucks where the loads are assessed and taxed. And if there is a differential in gasoline tax, the tanks are measured and the tax applied. The signs say, "All trucks stop." Being a truck, I stopped, only to be waved on over the scales. They were not looking for such as I. But sometimes I stopped and talked to the inspectors when they were not too busy. And this brings me to the subject of state police. Like most Americans I am no lover of cops, and the consistent investigation of city forces for bribery, brutality, and a long and picturesque list of malfeasances is not designed to reassure me. However, my hostility does not extend to the state troopers now maintained in most parts of the country. By the simple expedient of recruiting intelligent and educated men, paying them adequately, and setting them beyond political coercion, many states have succeeded in creating elite corps of men, secure in their dignity and proud of their service. Eventually our cities may find it necessary to reorganize their police on the pattern of the state police. But this will never happen while political organizations retain the slightest power to reward or to punish.

Across the Colorado River from Needles, the dark and jagged ramparts of Arizona stood up against the sky, and behind them the huge tilted plain rising toward the backbone of the continent again. I know this way so well from many crossings —Kingman, Ash Fork, Flagstaff with its mountain peak behind it, then Winslow, Holbrook, Sanders, down hill and up again, and then Arizona passed. The towns were a little larger and more brightly lighted than I remembered them, the motels bigger and more luxurious.

I crossed into New Mexico, rushed past Gallup in the night, and camped on the Continental Divide—and much more spectacular it is here than in the north. The night was very cold and dry, and the stars were cut glass. I drove into a little canyon out of the wind and parked by a mound of broken bottles—whisky and gin bottles, thousands of them. I don't know why they were there.

And I sat in the seat and faced what I had concealed from myself. I was driving myself, pounding out the miles because I was no longer hearing or seeing. I had passed my limit of taking in or, like a man who goes on stuffing in food after he is filled, I felt helpless to assimilate what was fed in through my eyes. Each hill looked like the one just passed. I have felt this way in the Prado in Madrid after looking at a hundred paintings—the stuffed and helpless inability to see more.

This would be a time to find a sheltered place beside a stream to rest and refurbish. Charley, in the dark seat beside me, mentioned a difficulty with a little moaning sigh. I had even forgotten him. I let him out and he staggered to the hill of broken bottles, sniffed at them, and took another way.

The night air was very cold, shivery cold, so that I lighted the cabin and turned up the gas to warm the air. The cabin was not neat. My bed was unmade and breakfast dishes lay desolate in the sink. I sat on the bed and stared into gray dreariness. Why had I thought I could learn anything about the land? For the last hundreds of miles I had avoided people. Even at necessary stops for gasoline I had answered in monosyllables and retained no picture. My eye and brain had welshed on me. I was fooling myself that this was important or even instructive. There was a ready remedy, of course. I reached out the whisky bottle without getting up, poured half a tumbler, smelled it, and poured it back in the bottle. No remedy was there.

Charley had not returned. I opened the door and whistled him and got no response. That shook me out of it. I grabbed my searchlight and turned its spearing beam up the canyon. The light flashed on two eyes about fifty yards away. I ran up the trail and found him standing staring into space, just as I had been.

"What's the matter, Charley, aren't you well?"

His tail slowly waved his replies. "Oh, yes. Quite well, I guess."

"Why didn't you come when I whistled?"

"I didn't hear you whistle."

"What are you staring at?"

"I don't know. Nothing I guess."

"Well, don't you want your dinner?"

"I'm really not hungry. But I'll go through the motions."

Back in the cabin he flopped down on the floor and put his chin down on his paws.

"Come on up on the bed, Charley. Let's be miserable together." He complied but without enthusiasm and I riffled my fingers in his topknot and behind his ears the way he likes it. "How's that?"

He shifted his head. "A little more to the left. There. That's the place."

"We'd be lousy explorers. A few days out and we get the mullygrubs. The first white man through here—I think he was named Narváez and I'm under the impression his little jaunt took six years. Move over. I'll look it up. Nope, it was eight years —1528 to 1536. And Narváez himself didn't make it this far. Four of his men did, though. I wonder if they ever got the mullygrubs. We're soft, Charley. Maybe it's time for a little gallantry. When's your birthday?"

"I don't know. Maybe it's like horses, the first of January."

"Think it might be today?"

"Who knows?"

"I could make you a cake. Have to be hotcake mix because that's what I have. Plenty of syrup and a candle on top."

Charley watched the operation with some interest. His silly tail made delicate conversation. "Anybody saw you make a birthday cake for a dog that he don't even know when's his birthday would think you were nuts."

"If you can't manage any better grammar than that with your tail, maybe it's a good thing you can't talk."

It turned out pretty well—four layers of hotcakes with maple syrup between and a stub of a miner's candle on top. I drank Charley's health in straight whisky as he ate and licked up the syrup. And then we both felt better. But there was Narváez' party —eight years. There were men in those days.

Charley licked the syrup from his whiskers. "What makes you so moony?"

"It's because I've stopped seeing. When that happens you think you'll never see again."

He stood up and stretched himself, first fore and then aft. "Let's take a stroll up the hill," he suggested. "Maybe you've started again."

We inspected the pile of broken whisky bottles and then continued up the trail. The dry, frozen air came out of us in plumes of steam. Some fairly large animal went leaping up the broken stone hill, or maybe a small animal and a big little avalanche.

"What does your nose say that was?"

"Nothing I recognize. Kind of a musky smell. Nothing I'm going to chase, either."

So dark was the night that it was prickled with fiery dots. My light brought an answering flash up the steep rocky bank. I climbed up, slipping and floundering, lost the echoed light and found it again, a good little new-split stone with a piece of mica in it—not a fortune but a good thing to have. I put it in my pocket and we went to bed.

PART FOUR

WHEN I STARTED THIS NARRATIVE, I KNEW that sooner or later I would have to have a go at Texas, and I dreaded it. I could have bypassed Texas about as easily as a space traveler can avoid the Milky Way. It sticks its big old Panhandle up north and it slops and slouches along the Rio Grande. Once you are in Texas it seems to take forever to get out, and some people never make it.

Let me say in the beginning that even if I wanted to avoid Texas I could not, for I am wived in Texas and mother-in-lawed and uncled and aunted and cousined within an inch of my life. Staying away from Texas geographically is no help whatever, for Texas moves through our house in New York, our fishing cottage at Sag Harbor, and when we had a flat in Paris, Texas was there too. It permeates the world to a ridiculous degree. Once, in Florence, on seeing a lovely little Italian princess, I said to her father, "But she doesn't look Italian. It may seem strange, but she looks like an American Indian." To which her father replied, "Why shouldn't she? Her grandfather married a Cherokee in Texas."

Writers facing the problem of Texas find themselves floundering in generalities, and I am no exception. Texas is a state of mind. Texas is an obsession. Above all, Texas is a nation in every sense of the word. And there's an opening covey of generalities. A Texan outside of Texas is a foreigner. My wife refers to herself as the Texan that got away, but that is only partly true. She has virtually no accent until she talks to a Texan, when she instantly reverts. You would not have to scratch deep to find her origin. She says such words as yes, air, hair, guess, with two syllables—yayus, ayer, hayer, gayus. And sometimes in a weary moment the word ink becomes ank. Our daughter, after a stretch in Austin, was visiting New York friends. She said, "Do you have a pin?"

"Certainly, dear," said her host. "Do you want a straight pin or a safety pin?"

"Aont a fountain pin," she said.

I've studied the Texas problem from many angles and for many years. And of course one of my truths is inevitably canceled by another. Outside their state I think Texans are a little frightened and very tender in their feelings, and these qualities cause boasting, arrogance, and noisy complacency—the outlets of shy children. At home Texans are none of these things. The ones I know are gracious, friendly, generous, and quiet. In New York we hear them so often bring up their treasured uniqueness. Texas is the only state that came into the Union by treaty. It retains the right to secede at will. We have heard them threaten to secede so often that I formed an enthusiastic organization—The American Friends for Texas Secession. This stops the subject cold. They want to be able to secede but they don't want anyone to want them to.

Like most passionate nations Texas has its own private history based on, but not limited by, facts. The tradition of the tough and versatile frontiersman is true but not exclusive. It is for the few to know that in the great old days of Virginia there were three punishments for high crimes—death, exile to Texas, and imprisonment, in that order. And some of the deportees must have descendants.

Again—the glorious defense to the death of the Alamo against the hordes of Santa Anna is a fact. The brave bands of Texans did indeed wrest their liberty from Mexico, and freedom, liberty, are holy words. One must go to contemporary observers in Europe for a non-Texan opinion as to the nature of the tyranny that raised need for revolt. Outside observers say the pressure was twofold. The Texans, they say, didn't want to pay taxes and, second, Mexico had abolished slavery in 1829, and Texas, being part of Mexico, was required to free its slaves. Of course there were other causes of revolt, but these two are spectacular to a European, and rarely mentioned here.

I have said that Texas is a state of mind, but I think it is more than that. It is a mystique closely approximating a religion. And this is true to the extent that people either passionately love Texas or passionately hate it and, as in other religions, few people dare to inspect it for fear of losing their bearings in mystery and paradox. Any observations of mine can be quickly cancelled by opinion or counter-observation. But I think there will be little quarrel with my feeling that Texas is one thing. For all its enormous range of space, climate, and physical appearance, and for all the internal squabbles, contentions, and strivings, Texas has a tight cohesiveness perhaps stronger than any other section of America. Rich, poor, Panhandle, Gulf, city, country, Texas is the obsession, the proper study and the passionate possession of all Texans. Some years ago, Edna Ferber wrote a book about a very tiny group of very rich Texans. Her description was accurate, so far as my knowledge extends, but the emphasis was one of disparagement. And instantly the book was attacked by Texans of all groups, classes, and possessions. To attack one Texan is to draw fire from all Texans. The Texas joke, on the other hand, is a revered institution, beloved and in many cases originating in Texas.

The tradition of the frontier cattleman is as tenderly nurtured in Texas as is the hint of Norman blood in England. And while it is true that many families are descended from contract colonists not unlike the present-day braceros, all hold to the dream of the longhorn steer and the unfenced horizon. When a man makes his fortune in oil or government contracts, in chemicals or wholesale groceries, his first act is to buy a ranch, the largest he can afford, and to run some cattle. A candidate for public office who does not own a ranch is said to have little chance of election. The tradition of the land is deep fixed in the Texas psyche. Businessmen wear heeled boots that never feel a stirrup, and men of great wealth who have houses in Paris and regularly shoot grouse in Scotland refer to themselves as little old country boys. It would be easy to make sport of their attitude if one did not know that in this way they try to keep their association with the strength and simplicity of the land. Instinctively they feel that this is the source not only of wealth but of energy. And the energy of Texans is boundless and explosive. The successful man with his traditional ranch, at least in my experience, is no absentee owner. He works at it, oversees his herd and adds to it. The energy, in a climate so hot as to be staggering, is also staggering. And the tradition of hard work is maintained whatever the fortune or lack of it.

The power of an attitude is amazing. Among other tendencies to be noted, Texas is a military nation. The armed forces of the United States are loaded with Texans and often dominated by Texans. Even the dearly loved spectacular sports are run almost like military operations. Nowhere are there larger bands or more marching organizations, with corps of costumed girls whirling glittering batons. Sectional football games have the glory and the despair of war, and when a Texas team takes the field against a foreign state, it is an army with banners.

If I keep coming back to the energy of Texas, it is because I am so aware of it. It seems to me like that thrust of dynamism which caused and permitted whole peoples to migrate and to conquer in earlier ages. The land mass of Texas is rich in recoverable spoil. If this had not been so, I think I believe the relentless energy of Texans would have moved out and conquered new lands. This conviction is somewhat borne out in the restless movement of Texas capital. But now, so far, the conquest has been by purchase rather than by warfare. The oil deserts of the Near East, the opening lands of South America have felt the thrust. Then there are new islands of capital conquest: factories in the Middle West, food-processing plants, tool and die works, lumber and pulp. Even publishing houses have been added to the legitimate twentieth-century Texas spoil. There is no moral in these observations, nor any warning. Energy must have an outlet and will seek one.

In all ages, rich, energetic, and successful nations,

when they have carved their place in the world, have felt hunger for art, for culture, even for learning and beauty. The Texas cities shoot upward and outward. The colleges are heavy with gifts and endowments. Theaters and symphony orchestras sprout overnight. In any huge and boisterous surge of energy and enthusiasm there must be errors and miscalculations, even breach of judgment and taste. And there is always the non-productive brotherhood of critics to disparage and to satirize, to view with horror and contempt. My own interest is attracted to the fact that these things are done at all. There will doubtless be thousands of ribald failures, but in the world's history artists have always been drawn where they are welcome and well treated.

By its nature and its size Texas invites generalities, and the generalities usually end up as paradox —the "little ol' country boy" at a symphony, the booted and blue-jeaned ranchman in Neiman-Marcus, buying Chinese jades.

Politically Texas continues its paradox. Traditionally and nostalgically it is Old South Democrat, but this does not prevent its voting conservative Republican in national elections while electing liberals to city and county posts. My opening statement still holds—everything in Texas is likely to be canceled by something else.

Most areas in the world may be placed in latitude and longitude, described chemically in their earth, sky and water, rooted and fuzzed over with identified flora and peopled with known fauna, and there's an end to it. Then there are others where fable, myth, preconception, love, longing, or prejudice step in and so distort a cool, clear appraisal that a kind of high-colored magical confusion takes permanent hold. Greece is such an area, and those parts of England where King Arthur walked. One quality of such places as I am trying to define is that a very large part of them is personal and subjective. And surely Texas is such a place.

I have moved over a great part of Texas and I know that within its borders I have seen just about as many kinds of country, contour, climate, and conformation as there are in the world saving only the Arctic, and a good north wind can even bring the icy breath down. The stern horizon-fenced plains of the Panhandle are foreign to the little wooded hills and sweet streams in the Davis Mountains. The rich citrus orchards of the Rio Grande valley do not relate to the sagebrush grazing of South Texas. The hot and humid air of the Gulf Coast has no likeness in the cool crystal in the northwest of the Panhandle. And Austin on its hills among the bordered lakes might be across the world from Dallas.

What I am trying to say is that there is no physical or geographical unity in Texas. Its unity lies in the mind. And this is not only in Texans. The word Texas becomes a symbol to everyone in the world. There's no question that this Texas-of-the-mind fable is often synthetic, sometimes untruthful, and frequently romantic, but that in no way diminishes its strength as a symbol.

The foregoing investigation into the nature of the idea of Texas is put down as a prelude to my journeying across Texas with Charley in Rocinante. It soon became apparent that this stretch had to be different from the rest of the trip. In the first place I knew the countryside, and in the second I had friends and relatives by marriage, and such a situation makes objectivity practically impossible, for I know no place where hospitality is practiced so fervently as in Texas.

But before that most pleasant and sometimes exhausting human trait took hold, I had three days of namelessness in a beautiful motor hotel in the middle of Amarillo. A passing car on a gravel road had thrown up pebbles and broken out the large front window of Rocinante and it had to be replaced. But, more important, Charley had been taken with his old ailment again, and this time he was in bad trouble and great pain. I remembered the poor incompetent veterinary in the Northwest, who did not know and did not care. And I remembered how Charley had looked at him with pained wonder and contempt.

In Amarillo the doctor I summoned turned out to be a young man. He drove up in a medium-priced convertible. He leaned over Charley. "What's his problem?" he asked. I explained Charley's difficulty. Then the young vet's hands went down and moved over hips and distended abdomen—trained and knowing hands. Charley sighed a great sigh and his tail wagged slowly up from the floor and down again. Charley put himself in this man's care, completely confident. I've seen this instant rapport before, and it is good to see.

The strong fingers probed and investigated and then the vet straightened up. "It can happen to any little old boy," he said.

"Is it what I think it is?"

"Yep. Prostatitis."

"Can you treat it?"

"Sure. I'll have to relax him first, and then I can give him medication for it. Can you leave him for maybe four days?"

"Whether I can or not, I will."

He lifted Charley in his arms and carried him out and laid him in the front seat of the convertible, and the tufted tail twittered against the leather. He was content and confident, and so was I. And that is how I happened to stay around Amarillo for a while. To complete the episode, I picked up Charley four days later, completely well. The doctor gave me pills to give at intervals while traveling so that the ailment never came back. There's absolutely nothing to take the place of a good man.

I do not intend to dwell long on Texas. Since the death of Hollywood the Lone Star State has taken its place at the top for being interviewed, inspected, and discussed. But no account of Texas would be complete without a Texas orgy, showing men of great wealth squandering their millions on tasteless and impassioned exhibitionism. My wife had come from New York to join me, and we were invited to a Texas ranch for Thanksgiving. It is owned by a friend who sometimes comes to New York, where we give him an orgy. I shall not name him, following the tradition of letting the reader guess. I presume that he is rich, although I have never asked him about it. As invited, we arrived at the ranch on the afternoon before the Thanksgiving orgy. It is a beautiful ranch, rich in water and trees and grazing land. Everywhere bulldozers had pushed up earth dams to hold back the water, making a series of life-giving lakes down the center of the ranch. On well-grassed flats the blooded Herefords grazed, only looking up as we drove by in a cloud of dust. I don't know how big the ranch is. I didn't ask my host.

The house, a one-story brick structure, stood in a grove of cottonwoods on a little eminence over a pool made by a dammed-up spring. The dark surface of the water was disturbed by trout that had been planted there. The house was comfortable, had three bedrooms, each room with a bath—both tub and shower. The living room, paneled in stained pine, served also as a dining room, with a fireplace at one end and a glass-fronted gun case against the side. Through the open kitchen door the staff could be seen—a large dark lady and a giggleful girl. Our host met us and helped carry our bags in.

The orgy began at once. We had a bath and on emerging were given scotch and soda, which we drank thirstily. After that we inspected the barn across the way, the kennels in which there were three pointers, one of them not feeling so well. Then to the corral, where the daughter of the house was working on the training of a quarter horse, an animal of parts named Specklebottom. After that we inspected two new dams with water building slowly behind them, and at several drinking stations communed with a small herd of recently purchased cattle. This violence exhausted us and we went back to the house for a short nap.

We awakened from this to find neighboring friends arriving; they brought a large pot of chili con carne, made from a family recipe, the best I have ever tasted. Now other rich people began to arrive, concealing their status in blue jeans and riding boots. Drinks were passed and a gay conversation ensued having to do with hunting, riding, and cattle-breeding, with many bursts of laughter. I reclined on a window seat and in the gathering dusk watched the wild turkeys come in to roost in the cottonwood trees. They fly up clumsily and distribute themselves and then suddenly they blend with the tree and disappear. At least thirty of them came in to roost.

As the darkness came the window became a mirror in which I could watch my host and his guests without their knowledge. They sat about the little paneled room, some in rocking chairs and three of the ladies on a couch. And the subtlety of their ostentation drew my attention. One of the ladies was making a sweater while another worked a puzzle, tapping her teeth with the eraser of a yellow pencil. The men talked casually of grass and water, of So-and-So who had bought a new champion bull in England and flown it home. They were dressed in jeans of that light blue, lighter and a little frayed at the seams, that can be achieved only by a hundred washings.

But the studied detail did not stop there. Boots were scuffed on the inside and salted with horse sweat, and the heels run over. The open collars of the men's shirts showed dark red lines of sunburn on their throats, and one guest had gone to the trouble and expense of breaking his forefinger, which was splinted and covered with laced leather cut from a glove. My host went to the extreme of serving his guests from a bar which consisted of a tub of ice, quart bottles of soda, two bottles of whisky and a case of pop.

The smell of money was everywhere. The daughter of the house, for example, sat on the floor cleaning a .22 rifle, telling a sophisticated and ribald story of how Specklebottom, her stallion, had leaped a five-bar corral gate and visited a mare in the next county. She thought she had property rights in the foal, Specklebottom's blood line being what it was. The scene verified what we have all heard about fabulous Texas millionaires.

I was reminded of a time in Pacific Grove when I was painting the inside of a cottage my father had built there before I was born. My hired helper worked beside me, and neither of us being expert we were well splattered. Suddenly we found ourselves out of paint. I said, "Neal, run up to Holman's and get a half-gallon of paint and a quart of thinner."

"I'll have to clean up and change my clothes," he said.

"Nuts! Go as you are."

"I can't do it."

"Why not? I would."

Then he said a wise and memorable thing. "You got to be awful rich to dress as bad as you do," he said.

And this isn't funny. It's true. And it was true at the orgy. How unthinkably rich these Texans must be to live as simply as they were.

I took a walk with my wife, around the trout pool and over against the hill. The air was chill and the wind blowing from the north had winter in it. We listened for frogs, but they had shacked up for the winter. But we heard a coyote howl upwind and we heard a cow bawling for her late weaned bairn. The pointers came to the wire mesh of the kennel, wriggling like happy snakes and sneezing with enthusiasm, and even the sickly one came out of his house and fleered at us. Then we stood in the high entrance of the great barn and smelled at the sweetness of alfalfa and the bready odor of rolled barley. At the corral the stock horses snorted at us and rubbed their heads against the bars, and Specklebottom took a kick at a gelded friend just to keep in practice. Owls were flying this night, shrieking to start their prey, and a nighthawk made soft rhythmic whoops in the distance. I wished that Able Baker Charley Dog could have been with us. He would have admired this night. But he was resting under sedatives in Amarillo curing his prostatitis. The sharp north wind clashed the naked branches of the cottonwoods. It seemed to me that winter, which had been on my tail during the whole trip, had finally caught up with me. Somewhere in our, or at least my, recent zoologic past, hibernation must have been a fact of being. Else why does cold night air make me so sleepy? It does and it did, and we went in to the house where the ghosts had already retired and we went to bed.

I awakened early. I had seen two trout rods leaning against the screen outside our room. I went down the grassed hill, slipping in the frost to the edge of the dark pool. A fly was ready fastened on the line, a black gnat, a little frayed but still hairy enough. And as it touched the surface of the pool the water boiled and churned. I brought in a ten-inch rainbow trout and skidded him up on the grass and knocked him on the head. I cast four times and had four trout. I cleaned them and threw the innards to their friends.

In the kitchen the cook gave me coffee and I sat in an alcove while she dipped my fish in corn meal and fried them crisp in bacon fat and served them to me under a coverlet of bacon that crumbled in my mouth. It was a long time since I had eaten trout like that, five minutes from water to pan. You take him in your fingers delicately by head and tail and nibble him from off his backbone, and finally you eat the tail, crisp as a potato chip. Coffee has a special taste of a frosty morning, and the third cup is as good as the first. I would have lingered in the kitchen discussing nothing with the staff, but she cleared me out because she had to stuff two turkeys for the Thanksgiving orgy.

In the mid-morning sunshine we went quail-hunting, I with my old and shiny 12-bore with the dented barrel, which I carried in Rocinante. That gun was no great shakes when I bought it second-hand fifteen years ago, and it has never got any better. But I suppose it is as good as I am. If I can hit them the gun will pull them down. But before we started I looked with a certain longing through the glass door at a Luigi Franchi 12-gauge double with a Purdy lock so beautiful that I was filled with covetousness. The carving on the steel had the pearly gleam of a Damascus blade, while the stock flowed into lock and lock into barrels as though they had grown that way from a magic planted seed. I'm sure that if my host had seen my envy he would have loaned me the beauty, but I didn't ask. Suppose I tripped and fell, or dropped it, or knocked its lovely tubes against a rock? No, it would be like carrying the crown jewels through a mine field. My old beat-up gun is no bargain, but at least anything that can happen to it has, and there's no worrying.

For a week our host had noted where the coveys were gathering. We spread out and moved through brush and thicket, down into water, out, and up, while the spring-steel pointers worked ahead of us and a fat old bitch pointer named Duchess with flame in her eyes outworked them all, and us too. We found quail tracks in the dust, quail tracks in the sand and mud of stream beds, bits of quail-feather fluff in the dry tips of the sage. We walked for miles, slowly, guns up and ready to throw shot at a drumming flight. And we never saw a quail. The dogs never saw or smelled a quail. We told stories and some lies about previous quail hunts, but it did no good. The quail had gone, really gone. I am only a reasonable quail shot but the men with me were excellent, the dogs were professional, keen, hard, and hard-working. No quail. But there's one nice thing about hunting. Even with no birds, you'd rather go than not.

My host thought my heart was breaking. He said, "Look. You take that little 222 of yours this afternoon and shoot yourself a wild turkey."

"How many are there?" I asked.

"Well, two years ago I planted thirty. I think there are about eighty now."

"I counted thirty in the band that flew up near the house last night."

"There's two other bands," he said.

I really didn't want a turkey. What would I do with it in Rocinante? I said, "Wait a year. When they top a hundred birds, I'll come down and hunt with you."

We came back to the house and showered and shaved, and because it was Thanksgiving we put on white shirts and jackets and ties. The orgy came off on schedule at two o'clock. I'll skip through the details quickly in order not to shock the readers, and also I see no reason to hold these people up to scorn. After two good drinks of whisky, the two brown and glazed turkeys were brought in, carved by our host and served by us. We said grace and afterward drank a toast all around and ate ourselves into a proper insensibility. Then, like decadent Romans at Petronius's board, we took a walk and retired for the necessary and inevitable nap. And that was my Thanksgiving orgy in Texas.

Of course I don't think they do it every day. They couldn't. And somewhat the same thing happens when they visit us in New York. Of course they want to see shows and go to night clubs. And at the end of a few days of this they say, "We just don't see how you can live like this." To which we reply, "We don't. And when you go home, we won't."

And now I feel better for having exposed to the light of scrutiny the decadent practices of the rich Texans I know. But I don't for one moment think they eat chili con carne or roast turkey every day.

WHEN I LAID THE GROUND PLAN OF MY journey, there were definite questions to which I wanted matching answers. It didn't seem to me that they were impossible questions. I suppose they could all be lumped into the single question: "What are Americans like today?"

In Europe it is a popular sport to describe what the Americans are like. Everyone seems to know. And we are equally happy in this game. How many times have I not heard one of my fellow countrymen, after a three-week tour of Europe, describe with certainty the nature of the French, the British, the Italians, the Germans, and above all the Russians? Traveling about, I early learned the difference between an American and the Americans. They are so far apart that they might be opposites. Often when a European has described the Americans with hostility and scorn he has turned to me and said, "Of course, I don't mean you. I am speaking of those others." It boils down to this: the Americans, the British are that faceless clot you don't know, but a Frenchman or an Italian is your acquaintance and your friend. He has none of the qualities your ignorance causes you to hate.

I had always considered this a kind of semantic deadfall, but moving about in my own country I am not at all sure that is so. Americans as I saw them and talked to them were indeed individuals, each one different from the others, but gradually I began to feel that the Americans exist, that they really do have generalized characteristics regardless of their states, their social and financial status, their education, their religious, and their political convictions. But if there is indeed an American image built of truth rather than reflecting either hostility or wishful thinking, what is this image? What does it look like? What does it do? If the same song, the same joke, the same style sweeps through all parts of the country at once, it must be that all Americans are alike in something. The fact that the same joke, the same style, has no effect in France or England or Italy makes this contention valid. But the more I inspected this American image, the less sure I became of what it is. It appeared to me increasingly paradoxical, and it has been my experience that when paradox crops up too often for comfort, it means that certain factors are missing in the equation.

Now I had moved through a galaxy of states, each with its own character, and through clouds and myriads of people, and ahead of me lay an area, the South, that I dreaded to see and yet knew I must see and hear. I am not drawn to pain and violence. I never gaze at accidents unless I can help, or attend street fights for kicks. I faced the South with dread. Here, I knew, were pain and confusion and all the manic results of bewilderment and fear. And the South being a limb of the nation, its pain spreads out to all America.

I knew, as everyone knows, the true but incomplete statement of the problem—that an original sin of the fathers was being visited on the children of succeeding generations. I have many Southern friends, both Negro and white, many of them of superb minds and characters, and often, when not the problem but the mere suggestion of the Negro-white subject has come up, I have seen and felt them go into a room of experience into which I cannot enter.

Perhaps I, more than most people from the so-called North, am kept out of real and emotional understanding of the agony not because I, a white, have no experience with Negroes but because of the nature of my experience.

In Salinas in California, where I was born and grew and went to school gathering the impressions that formed me, there was only one Negro family. The name was Cooper and the father and mother were there when I was born, but they had three sons, one a little older than I, one my age, and one a year younger, so that in grade school and high school there was always a Cooper in the grade ahead, one in my class, and one in the class below. In a word, I was bracketed with Coopers. The father, universally called Mr. Cooper, ran a little trucking business—ran it well and made a good living. His wife was a warm and friendly woman who was good for a piece of gingerbread any time we wanted to put the hustle on her.

If there was any color prejudice in Salinas I never heard or felt a breath of it. The Coopers were respected, and their self-respect was in no way forced. Ulysses, the oldest, was one of the best pole-vaulters our town ever developed, a tall, quiet boy. I remember the lean grace of his movements in a track suit and I remember envying his smooth and perfect timing. He died in his third year in high school and I was one of his pallbearers, and

I think I was guilty of the sin of pride at being chosen. The second son, Ignatius, my classmate, was not my favorite, I discover now, because he was far and away the best student. In arithmetic and later in mathematics he topped our grades, and in Latin he not only was a better student but he didn't cheat. And who can like a classmate like that? The youngest Cooper—the baby—was all smiles. It's odd that I do not remember his first name. He was a musician from the start, and when I last saw him he was deep in composition which seemed, to my partially instructed ear, bold and original and good. But beyond this giftedness, the Cooper boys were my friends.

Now, these were the only Negroes I knew or had contact with in the days of my flypaper childhood, and you can see how little I was prepared for the great world. When I heard, for example, that Negroes were an inferior race, I thought the authority was misinformed. When I heard that Negroes were dirty I remembered Mrs. Cooper's shining kitchen. Lazy? The drone and clop of Mr. Cooper's horse-drawn dray in the street outside used to awaken us in the dawn. Dishonest? Mr. Cooper was one of the very few Salinians who never let a debt cross the fifteenth of the month.

I realize now that there was something else about the Coopers that set them apart from other Negroes I have seen and met since. Because they were not hurt or insulted, they were not defensive or combative. Because their dignity was intact, they had no need to be overbearing, and because the Cooper boys had never heard that they were inferior, their minds could grow to their true limits.

That was my Negro experience until I was well

grown, perhaps too far grown to reform the inflexible habits of childhood. Oh, I have seen plenty since and have felt the shattering waves of violence and despair and confusion. I have seen Negro children who really cannot learn, particularly those who in their gelatin plate of babyness have been told they were inferior. And, remembering the Coopers and how we felt about them, I think my main feeling is sorrow at the curtain of fear and anger drawn down between us. And I've just thought of an amusing possibility. If in Salinas anyone from a wiser and more sophisticated world had asked, "How would you like your sister to marry a Cooper?" I think we would have laughed. For it might have occurred to us that a Cooper might not have wanted to marry our sister, good friends though we all were.

Thus it remains that I am basically unfitted to take sides in the racial conflict. I must admit that cruelty and force exerted against weakness turn me sick with rage, but this would be equally true in the treatment of any weak by any strong.

Beyond my failings as a racist, I knew I was not wanted in the South. When people are engaged in something they are not proud of, they do not welcome witnesses. In fact, they come to believe the witness causes the trouble.

In all this discussion of the South I have been speaking only about the violence set loose by the desegregation movements—the children going to school, the young Negroes demanding the questionable privilege of lunch counters, buses, and toilets. But I am particularly interested in the school business, because it seems to me that the blight can disappear only when there are millions of Coopers.

Recently a dear Southern friend instructed me passionately in the theory of "equal but separate." "It just happens," he said, "that in my town there are three new Negro schools not equal but superior to the white schools. Now wouldn't you think they would be satisfied with that? And in the bus station the washrooms are exactly the same. What's your answer to that?"

I said, "Maybe it's a matter of ignorance. You could solve it and really put them in their places if you switched schools and toilets. The moment they realized that your schools weren't as good as theirs, they would realize their error."

And do you know what he said? He said, "You trouble-making son of a bitch." But he said it smiling.

WHILE I WAS STILL IN TEXAS, LATE IN 1960, the incident most reported and pictured in the newspapers was the matriculation of a couple of tiny Negro children in a New Orleans school. Behind these small dark mites were the law's majesty and the law's power to enforce—both the scales and the sword were allied with the infants—while against them were three hundred years of fear and anger and terror of change in a changing world. I had seen photographs in the papers every day and motion pictures on the television screen. What made the newsmen love the story was a group of stout middle-aged women who, by some curious definition of the word "mother," gathered every day to scream invectives at children. Further, a small group of them had become so expert that they were known as the Cheerleaders, and a crowd gathered every day to enjoy and to applaud their performance.

This strange drama seemed so improbable that I felt I had to see it. It had the same draw as a five-legged calf or a two-headed foetus at a sideshow, a distortion of normal life we have always found so interesting that we will pay to see it, perhaps to prove to ourselves that we have the proper number of legs or heads. In the New Orleans show, I felt all the amusement of the improbable abnormal, but also a kind of horror that it could be so.

At this time the winter which had been following my track ever since I left home suddenly struck with a black norther. It brought ice and freezing sleet and sheeted the highways with dark ice. I gathered Charley from the good doctor. He looked half his age and felt wonderful, and to prove it he ran and jumped and rolled and laughed and gave little yips of pure joy. It felt very good to have him with me again, sitting up right in the seat beside me, peering ahead at the unrolling road, or curling up to sleep with his head in my lap and his silly ears available for fondling. That dog can sleep through any amount of judicious caresses.

Now we stopped dawdling and laid our wheels to the road and went. We could not go fast because of the ice, but we drove relentlessly, hardly glancing at the passing of Texas beside us. And Texas was achingly endless—Sweetwater and Balinger and Austin. We bypassed Houston. We stopped for gasoline and coffee and slabs of pie. Charley had his meals and his walks in gas stations. Night did not stop us, and when my eyes ached and burned from peering too long and my shoulders were side hills of pain, I pulled into a turnout and crawled like a mole into my bed, only to see the highway writhe along behind my closed lids. No more than two hours could I sleep, and then out into the bitter cold night and on and on. Water beside the road was frozen solid, and people moved about with shawls and sweaters wrapped around their ears.

Other times I have come to Beaumont dripping with sweat and lusting for ice and air-conditioning. Now Beaumont with all its glare of neon signs was what they called froze up. I went through Beaumont at night, or rather in the dark well after midnight. The blue-fingered man who filled my gas tank looked in at Charley and said, "Hey, it's a dog! I thought you had a nigger in there." And he laughed delightedly. It was the first of many repetitions. At least twenty times I heard it—"Thought you had a nigger in there." It was an unusual joke —always fresh—and never Negro or even Nigra, always Nigger or rather Niggah. That word seemed terribly important, a kind of safety word to cling to lest some structure collapse.

And then I was in Louisiana, with Lake Charles away to the side in the dark, but my lights glittered on ice and glinted on diamond frost, and those people who forever trudge the roads at night were mounded over with cloth against the cold. I dogged it on through La Fayette and Morgan City and came in the early dawn to Houma, which is pronounced Homer and is in my memory one of the pleasantest places in the world. There lives my old friend Doctor St. Martin, a gentle, learned man, a Cajun who has lifted babies and cured colic among the shell-heap Cajuns for miles around. I guess he knows more about Cajuns than anyone living, but I remembered with longing other gifts of Doctor St. Martin. He makes the best and most subtle martini in the world by a process approximating magic. The only part of his formula I know is that he uses distilled water for his ice and distills it himself to be sure. I have eaten black duck at his table—two St. Martin martinis and a brace of black duck with a burgundy delivered from the bottle as a baby might be delivered, and this in a darkened house where the shades have been closed at dawn and the cool night air preserved. At that table with its silver soft and dull, shining as pewter, I remember the raised glass of the grape's holy blood, the stem caressed by the doctor's strong artist fingers, and even now I can hear the sweet little health and welcome in the singing language of Acadia which once was French and now is itself. This picture filled my frosty windshield, and if there had been traffic would have made me a dangerous driver. But it was pale yellow frozen dawn in Houma and I knew that if I stopped to pay my respects, my will and my determination would drift away on the particular lotus St. Martin purveys and we would be speaking of timeless matters when the evening came, and another evening. And so I only bowed in the direction of my friend and scudded on toward New Orleans, for I wanted to catch a show of the Cheerleaders.

Even I know better than to drive a car near trouble, particularly Rocinante, with New York license plates. Only yesterday a reporter had been beaten and his camera smashed, for even convinced voters are reluctant to have their moment of history recorded and preserved.

So, well on the edge of town I drove into a parking lot. The attendant came to my window. "Man, oh man, I thought you had a nigger in there. Man, oh man, it's a dog. I see that big old black face and I think it's a big old nigger."

"His face is blue-gray when he's clean," I said coldly.

"Well I see some blue-gray niggers and they wasn't clean. New York, eh?"

It seemed to me a chill like the morning air came into his voice. "Just driving through," I said.

"I want to park for a couple of hours. Think you can get me a taxi?"

"Tell you what I bet. I bet you're going to see the Cheerleaders."

"That's right."

"Well, I hope you're not one of those trouble-makers or reporters."

"I just want to see it."

"Man, oh man, you going to see something. Ain't those Cheerleaders something? Man, oh man, you never heard nothing like it when they get going."

I locked Charley in Rocinante's house after giving the attendant a tour of the premises, a drink of whisky, and a dollar. "Be kind of careful about opening the door when I'm away," I said. "Charley takes his job pretty seriously. You might lose a hand." This was an outrageous lie, of course, but the man said, "Yes, sir. You don't catch me fooling around with no strange dog."

The taxi driver, a sallow, yellowish man, shriveled like a chickpea with the cold, said, "I wouldn't take you more than a couple of blocks near. I don't go to have my cab wrecked."

"Is it that bad?"

"It ain't is it. It's can it get. And it can get that bad."

"When do they get going?"

He looked at his watch. "Except it's cold, they been coming in since dawn. It's quarter to. You get along and you won't miss nothing except it's cold."

I had camouflaged myself in an old blue jacket and my British navy cap on the supposition that in a seaport no one ever looks at a sailor any more than a waiter is inspected in a restaurant. In his natural haunts a sailor has no face and certainly no plans beyond getting drunk and maybe in jail for fighting. At least that's the general feeling about sailors. I've tested it. The most that happens is a kindly voice of authority saying, "Why don't you go back to your ship, sailor? You wouldn't want to sit in the tank and miss your tide, now would you, sailor?" And the speaker wouldn't recognize you five minutes later. And the Lion and Unicorn on my cap made me even more anonymous. But I must warn anyone testing my theory, never try it away from a shipping port.

"Where you from?" the driver asked with a complete lack of interest.

"Liverpool."

"Limey, huh? Well, you'll be all right. It's the goddamn New York Jews cause all the trouble."

I found myself with a British inflection and by no means one of Liverpool. "Jews—what? How do they cause trouble?"

"Why, hell, mister. We know how to take care of this. Everybody's happy and getting along fine. Why, I *like* niggers. And them goddamn New York Jews come in and stir the niggers up. They just stay in New York there wouldn't be no trouble. Ought to take them out."

"You mean lynch them?"

"I don't mean nothing else, mister."

He let me out and I started to walk away. "Don't try to get too close, mister," he called after me. "Just you enjoy it but don't mix in."

"Thanks," I said, and killed the "awfully" that came to my tongue.

As I walked toward the school I was in a stream of people all white and all going in my direction.

They walked intently like people going to a fire after it has been burning for some time. They beat their hands against their hips or hugged them under coats, and many men had scarves under their hats and covering their ears.

Across the street from the school the police had set up wooden barriers to keep the crowd back, and they paraded back and forth, ignoring the jokes called to them. The front of the school was deserted but along the curb United States marshals were spaced, not in uniform but wearing armbands to identify them. Their guns bulged decently under their coats but their eyes darted about nervously, inspecting faces. It seemed to me that they inspected me to see if I was a regular, and then abandoned me as unimportant.

It was apparent where the Cheerleaders were, because people shoved forward to try to get near them. They had a favored place at the barricade directly across from the school entrance, and in that area a concentration of police stamped their feet and slapped their hands together in unaccustomed gloves.

Suddenly I was pushed violently and a cry went up: "Here she comes. Let her through. . . . Come on, move back. Let her through. Where you been? You're late for school. Where you been, Nellie?"

The name was not Nellie. I forget what it was. But she shoved through the dense crowd quite near enough to me so that I could see her coat of imitation fleece and her gold earrings. She was not tall, but her body was ample and full-busted. I judge she was about fifty. She was heavily powdered, which made the line of her double chin look very dark.

She wore a ferocious smile and pushed her way through the milling people, holding a fistful of clippings high in her hand to keep them from being crushed. Since it was her left hand I looked particularly for a wedding ring, and saw that there was none. I slipped in behind her to get carried along by her wave, but the crush was dense and I was given a warning too. "Watch it, sailor. Everybody wants to hear."

Nellie was received with shouts of greeting. I don't know how many Cheerleaders there were. There was no fixed line between the Cheerleaders and the crowd behind them. What I could see was that a group was passing newspaper clippings back and forth and reading them aloud with little squeals of delight.

Now the crowd grew restless, as an audience does when the clock goes past curtain time. Men all around me looked at their watches. I looked at mine. It was three minutes to nine.

The show opened on time. Sound of sirens. Motorcycle cops. Then two big black cars filled with big men in blond felt hats pulled up in front of the school. The crowd seemed to hold its breath. Four big marshals got out of each car and from somewhere in the automobiles they extracted the littlest Negro girl you ever saw, dressed in shining starchy white, with new white shoes on feet so little they were almost round. Her face and little legs were very black against the white.

The big marshals stood her on the curb and a jangle of jeering shrieks went up from behind the barricades. The little girl did not look at the howling crowd but from the side the whites of her eyes showed like those of a frightened fawn. The men turned her around like a doll, and then the strange procession moved up the broad walk toward the school, and the child was even more a mite because the men were so big. Then the girl made a curious hop, and I think I know what it was. I think in her whole life she had not gone ten steps without skipping, but now in the middle of her first skip the weight bore her down and her little round feet took measured, reluctant steps between the tall guards. Slowly they climbed the steps and entered the school.

The papers had printed that the jibes and jeers were cruel and sometimes obscene, and so they were, but this was not the big show. The crowd was waiting for the white man who dared to bring his white child to school. And here he came along the guarded walk, a tall man dressed in light gray, leading his frightened child by the hand. His body was tensed as a strong leaf spring drawn to the breaking strain; his face was grave and gray, and his eyes were on the ground immediately ahead of him. The muscles of his cheeks stood out from clenched jaws, a man afraid who by his will held his fears in check as a great rider directs a panicked horse.

A shrill, grating voice rang out. The yelling was not in chorus. Each took a turn and at the end of each the crowd broke into howls and roars and whistles of applause. This is what they had come to see and hear.

No newspaper had printed the words these women shouted. It was indicated that they were indelicate, some even said obscene. On television the sound track was made to blur or had crowd noises cut in to cover. But now I heard the words, bestial and filthy and degenerate. In a long and unprotected life I have seen and heard the vomitings of demoniac humans before. Why then did these screams fill me with a shocked and sickened sorrow?

The words written down are dirty, carefully and selectedly filthy. But there was something far worse here than dirt, a kind of frightening witches' Sabbath. Here was no spontaneous cry of anger, of insane rage.

Perhaps that is what made me sick with weary nausea. Here was no principle good or bad, no direction. These blowzy women with their little hats and their clippings hungered for attention. They wanted to be admired. They simpered in happy, almost innocent triumph when they were applauded. Theirs was the demented cruelty of egocentric children, and somehow this made their insensate beastliness much more heartbreaking. These were not mothers, not even women. They were crazy actors playing to a crazy audience.

The crowd behind the barrier roared and cheered and pounded one another with joy. The nervous strolling police watched for any break over the barrier. Their lips were tight but a few of them smiled and quickly unsmiled. Across the street the U.S. marshals stood unmoving. The gray-clothed man's legs had speeded for a second, but he reined them down with his will and walked up the school pavement.

The crowd quieted and the next cheer lady had her turn. Her voice was the bellow of a bull, a deep and powerful shout with flat edges like a circus barker's voice. There is no need to set down her words. The pattern was the same; only the rhythm and tonal quality were different. Anyone who has been near the theater would know that these speeches were not spontaneous. They were tried and memorized and carefully rehearsed. This was theater. I watched the intent faces of the listening crowd and they were the faces of an audience. When there was applause, it was for a performer.

My body churned with weary nausea, but I could not let an illness blind me after I had come so far to look and to hear. And suddenly I knew something was wrong and distorted and out of drawing. I knew New Orleans, I have over the years had many friends there, thoughtful, gentle people, with a tradition of kindness and courtesy. I remembered Lyle Saxon, a huge man of soft laughter. How many days I have spent with Roark Bradford, who took Louisiana sounds and sights and created God and the Green Pastures to which He leadeth us. I looked in the crowd for such faces of such people and they were not there. I've seen this kind bellow for blood at a prize fight, have orgasms when a man is gored in the bull ring, stare with vicarious lust at a highway accident, stand patiently in line for the privilege of watching any pain or any agony. But where were the others—the ones who would be proud they were of a species with the gray man —the ones whose arms would ache to gather up the small, scared black mite?

I don't know where they were. Perhaps they felt as helpless as I did, but they left New Orleans misrepresented to the world. The crowd, no doubt, rushed home to see themselves on television, and what they saw went out all over the world, unchallenged by the other things I know are there.

THE SHOW WAS OVER AND THE RIVER OF US began to move away. Second show would be when school-closing bell rang and the little black face had to look out at her accusers again. I was in New Orleans of the great restaurants. I know them all and most of them know me. And I could no more have gone to Gallatoir's for an omelet and champagne than I could have danced on a grave. Even setting this down on paper has raised the weary, hopeless nausea in me again. It is not written to amuse. It does not amuse me.

I bought a poor-boy sandwich and got out of town. Not too far along I found a pleasant resting place where I could sit and munch and contemplate and stare out over the stately brown, slow-moving Father of Waters as my spirit required. Charley did not wander about but sat close and pressed his shoulder against my knee, and he does that only when I am ill, so I suppose I was ill with a kind of sorrow.

I lost track of time, but a while after the sun had passed top a man came walking and we exchanged good afternoons. He was a neatly dressed man well along in years, with a Greco face and fine wind-lifted white hair and a clipped white mustache. I asked him to join me, and when he accepted I went into my house and set coffee to cooking and, remembering how Roark Bradford liked it, I doubled the dosage, two heaping tablespoons of coffee to each cup and two heaping for the pot. I cracked an egg and cupped out the yolk and dropped white and shells into the pot, for I know nothing that polishes coffee and makes it shine like that. The air was still very cold and a cold night was coming, so that the brew, rising from cold water to a rolling boil, gave the good smell that competes successfully with other good smells.

My guest was satisfied, and he warmed his hands against the plastic cup. "By your license, you're a stranger here," he said. "How do you come to know about coffee?"

"I learned on Bourbon Street from giants in the earth," I said. "But they would have asked the bean of a darker roast and they would have liked a little chicory for bite."

"You do know," he said. "You're not a stranger after all. And can you make diablo?"

"For parties, yes. You come from here?"

"More generations than I can prove beyond doubt, except classified under *ci gît* in St. Louis."

"I see. You're of that breed. I'm glad you stopped by. I used to know St. Louis, even collected epitaphs."

"Did you, sir? You'll remember the queer one, then."

"If it's the same one, I tried to memorize it. You mean that one that starts, 'Alas that one whose darnthly joy . . . ?' "

"That's it. Robert John Cresswell, died 1845 aged twenty-six."

"I wish I could remember it."

"Have you a paper? You can write it down."

And when I had a pad on my knee he said, "Alas that one whose darnthly joy had often to trust in heaven should canty thus sudden to from all its hopes benivens and though thy love for off remore that dealt the dog pest thou left to prove thy sufferings while below."

"It's wonderful," I said. "Lewis Carroll could have written it. I almost know what it means."

"Everyone does. Are you traveling for pleasure?"

"I was until today. I saw the Cheerleaders."

"Oh, yes, I see," he said, and a weight and a darkness fell on him.

"What's going to happen?"

"I don't know. I just don't know. I don't dare think about it. Why do I have to think about it? I'm too old. Let the others take care of it."

"Can you see an end?"

"Oh, certainly an end. It's the means—it's the means. But you're from the North. This isn't your problem."

"I guess it's everybody's problem. It isn't local. Would you have another cup of coffee and talk to me about it? I don't have a position. I mean I want to hear."

"There's nothing to learn," he said. "It seems to change its face with who you are and where you've been and how you feel—not think, but feel. You didn't like what you saw?"

"Would you?"

"Maybe less than you because I know all of its aching past and some of its stinking future. That's an ugly word, sir, but there's no other."

"The Negroes want to be people. Are you against that?"

"Bless you, no, sir. But to get to be people they must fight those who aren't satisfied to be people."

"You mean the Negroes won't be satisfied with any gain?"

"Are you? Is anyone you know?"

"Would you be content to let them be people?"

"Content enough, but I wouldn't understand it. I've got too many *ci gîts* here. How can I tell you? Well, suppose your dog here, he looks a very intelligent dog—"

"He is."

"Well, suppose he could talk and stand on his hind legs. Maybe he could do very well in every way. Perhaps you could invite him to dinner, but could you think of him as people?"

"Do you mean, how would I like my sister to marry him?"

He laughed. "I'm only telling you how hard it is to change a feeling about things. And will you believe that it will be just as hard for Negroes to change their feeling about us as it is for us to change about them? This isn't new. It's been going on a long time."

"Anyway, the subject skims the joy off a pan of conversation."

"That it does, sir. I think I'm what you might call an enlightened Southerner mistaking an insult for a compliment. As such a new-born hybrid, I know what will happen over the ages. It's starting now in Africa and in Asia."

"You mean absorption—the Negroes will disappear?"

"If they outnumber us, we will disappear, or more likely both will disappear into something new."

"And meanwhile?"

"It's the meanwhile frightens me, sir. The ancients placed love and war in the hands of closely related gods. That was no accident. That, sir, was a profound knowledge of man."

"You reason well."

"The ones you saw today do not reason at all. They're the ones who may alert the god."

"Then you do think it can't happen in peace?"

"I don't know," he cried. "I guess that's the worst. I just don't know. Sometimes I long to assume my rightful title Ci Gît."

"I wish you would ride along with me. Are you on the move?"

"No. I have a little place just off there below that grove. I spend a lot of time there, mostly reading—old things—mostly looking at—old things. It's my intentional method of avoiding the issue because I'm afraid of it."

"I guess we all do some of that."

He smiled. "I have an old Negro couple as old as I am to take care of me. And sometimes in the evening we forget. They forget to envy me and I forget they might, and we are just three pleasant . . . things living together and smelling the flowers."

"Things," I repeated. "That's interesting—not man and beast, not black and white, but pleasant things. My wife told me of an old old man who said, 'I remember a time when Negroes had no souls. It was much better and easier then. Now it's confusing.'"

"I don't remember, but it must be so. It is my guess that we can cut and divide our inherited guilt like a birthday cake," he said, and save for the mustache he looked like the Greco San Pablo who holds the closed book in his hands. "Surely my ancestors had slaves, but it is possible that yours caught them and sold them to us."

"I have a puritan strain that might well have done so."

"If by force you make a creature live and work like a beast, you must think of him as a beast, else empathy would drive you mad. Once you have classified him in your mind, your feelings are safe." He stared at the river, and the breeze stirred his hair like white smoke. "And if your heart has human vestiges of courage and anger, which in a man are virtues, then you have fear of a dangerous beast, and since your heart has intelligence and inventiveness and the ability to conceal them, you live with terror. Then you must crush his manlike tendencies and make of him the docile beast you want. And if you can teach your child from the beginning about the beast, he will not share your bewilderment."

"I've been told the good old-time Negro sang and danced and was content."

"He also ran away. The fugitive laws suggest how often."

"You're not what the North thinks of as a Southerner."

"Perhaps not. But I'm not alone." He stood up and dusted his trousers with his fingers. "No—not alone. I'll go along to my pleasant things now."

"I have not asked your name, sir, nor offered mine."

"Ci Gît," he said. "Monsieur Ci Gît—a big family, a common name."

When he went away I felt a sweetness like music, if music could pleasure the skin with a little chill.

To me, it had been a day larger than a day, not

to be measured against other days with any chance of matching. With little sleep the night before I knew I should stop. I was very tired, but sometimes fatigue can be a stimulant and a compulsion. It forced me to fill my gas tank and compelled me to stop and offer a ride to an old Negro who trudged with heavy heels in the grass-grown verge beside the concrete road. He was reluctant to accept and did so only as though helpless to resist. He wore the battered clothes of a field hand and an ancient broadcloth coat highly polished by age and wear. His face was coffee-colored and cross-hatched with a million tiny wrinkles, and his lower lids showed red rims like a bloodhound's eyes. He clasped his hands in his lap, knotted and lumpy as cherry twigs, and all of him seemed to shrink in the seat as though he sucked in his outline to make it smaller.

He never looked at me. I could not see that he looked at anything. But first he asked, "Dog bite, captain, sir?"

"No. He's friendly."

After a long silent while I asked, "How are things going with you?"

"Fine, just fine, captain, sir."

"How do you feel about what's going on?"

He didn't answer.

"I mean about the schools and the sit-ins."

"I don't know nothing about that, captain, sir."

"Work on a farm?"

"Crop a cotton lot, sir."

"Make a living at it?"

"I get along fine, captain, sir."

We went in silence for a stretch upriver. The trees and the tropic grass were burned and sad from the ferocious northern freeze. After a time I said, more to myself than to him, "After all, why should you trust me? A question is a trap and an answer is your foot in it." I remembered a scene—something that happened in New York—and was moved to tell him about it, but I quickly abandoned the impulse because out of the corner of my eye I could see that he had drawn away and squeezed himself against the far side of the cab. But the memory was strong.

I lived then in a small brick house in Manhattan, and, being for the moment solvent, employed a Negro. Across the street and on the corner there was a bar and restaurant. One winter dusk when the sidewalks were iced I stood in my window looking out and saw a tipsy woman come out of the bar, slip on the ice, and fall flat. She tried to struggle up but slipped and fell again and lay there screaming maudlinly. At that moment the Negro who worked for me came around the corner, saw the woman, and instantly crossed the street, keeping as far from her as possible.

When he came in I said, "I saw you duck. Why didn't you give that woman a hand?"

"Well, sir, she's drunk and I'm Negro. If I touched her she could easy scream rape, and then it's a crowd, and who believes me?"

"It took quick thinking to duck that fast."

"Oh, no sir!" he said. "I've been practicing to be a Negro a long time."

And now in Rocinante I was foolishly trying to destroy a lifetime of practice.

"I won't ask you any more questions," I said.

But he squirmed with restlessness. "Would you let me down here, please, captain? I live nearby."

I let him down and saw in the mirror how he took up his trudging beside the road. He didn't live nearby at all, but walking was safer than riding with me.

Weariness flagged me down and I stopped in a pleasant motel. The beds were good but I could not sleep. The gray man walked across my eyes, and the faces of the Cheerladies, but mostly I saw the old man squeezed as far away from me as he could get, as though I carried the infection, and perhaps I did. I came out to learn. What was I learning? I had not felt one moment free from the tension, a weight of savage fear. No doubt I felt it more being newcome, but it was there; I hadn't brought it. Everyone, white and black, lived in it and breathed it—all ages, all trades, all classes. To them it was a fact of existence. And it was building pressure like a boil. Could there be no relief until it burst?

I had seen so little of the whole. I didn't see a great deal of World War II—one landing out of a hundred, a few separated times of combat, a few thousand dead out of millions—but I saw enough and felt enough to believe war was no stranger. So here—a little episode, a few people, but the breath of fear was everywhere. I wanted to get away—a cowardly attitude, perhaps, but more cowardly to deny. But the people around me lived here. They accepted it as a permanent way of life, had never known it otherwise nor expected it to stop. The Cockney children in London were restless when the bombing stopped and disturbed a pattern to which they had grown accustomed.

I tossed about until Charley grew angry with me and told me "Ftt" several times. But Charley doesn't have our problems. He doesn't belong to a species clever enough to split the atom but not clever enough to live in peace with itself. He doesn't even know about race, nor is he concerned with his sisters' marriage. It's quite the opposite. Once Charley fell in love with a dachshund, a romance racially unsuitable, physically ridiculous, and mechanically impossible. But all these problems Charley ignored. He loved deeply and tried dogfully. It would be difficult to explain to a dog the good and moral purpose of a thousand humans gathered to curse one tiny human. I've seen a look in dogs' eyes, a quickly vanishing look of amazed contempt, and I am convinced that basically dogs think humans are nuts.

I didn't choose my first customer the next day. He picked me. He sat on a stool next to me eating a hamburger whose twin I held in my hand. He was somewhere between thirty and thirty-five, long and stringy, and nice-looking. His long lank hair was nearly ash-blond, worn long and treasured since he whopped it with a pocket comb unconsciously and often. He wore a light gray suit that was travel-wrinkled and stained; he carried the jacket over his shoulder. His white shirt was open at the collar, permitted so by pulling down the knot of his pale paisley tie. His speech was the deepest south I had heard so far. He asked where I was going and, when I told him I aimed toward Jackson and Montgomery, begged a ride with me. When he saw Charley he thought at first I had a nigger in there. It had got to be a pattern.

We settled ourselves comfortably. He combed back his hair and complimented me on Rocinante. "Of course," he said, "I could tell right off you're from the North."

"You've got a good ear," I said, I thought facetiously.

"Oh, I get around," he admitted.

I think I was responsible for what happened. If I could have kept my mouth shut I might have learned something of value. There's the restless night to blame and the length of the journey and the nervousness. Then, too, Christmas was coming and I found myself thinking of getting home more often than was helpful.

We established that I was traveling for pleasure and that he was on the lookout for a job.

"You come up the river," he said. "Did you see the doings in New Orleans?"

"Yes, I did."

"Wasn't they something, especially that Nellie? She really ripped the roof off."

"Yes, she did."

"Does your heart good to see somebody do their duty."

I think it was there that I went haywire. I should have grunted and let him read what he wanted in it. But a nasty little worm of anger began to stir in me. "They doing it out of duty?"

"Sure, God bless them. Somebody got to keep the goddamn niggers out of our schools." The sublimity of self-sacrifice activating the Cheerleaders overwhelmed him. "Comes a time when a man's got to sit down and think, and that's the time you got to make up your mind to sell your life for something you believe in."

"Did you decide to do it?"

"I sure did, and a lot more like me."

"What do you believe in?"

"I'm not just about to allow my kids to go to

school with no niggers. Yes, sir. I'll sell my life first but I aim to kill me a whole goddamn flock of niggers before I go."

"How many children do you have?"

He swung around toward me. "I don't have any but I aim to have some and I promise you they won't go to school with no niggers."

"Do you propose to sell your life before or after you have children?"

I had to watch the road so I only got a glimpse of his expression, and it wasn't pleasant. "You sound to me like a nigger-lover. I might of known it. Trouble-makers—come down here and tell us how to live. Well, you won't get away with it, mister. We got an eye on you Commie nigger-lovers."

"I just had a brave picture of you selling your life."

"By God, I was right. You are a nigger-lover."

"No, I'm not. And I'm not a white-lover either, if it includes those noble Cheerladies."

His face was very near to me. "You want to hear what I think of you?"

"No. I heard Nellie use the words yesterday." I put on the brake and pulled Rocinante off the road.

He looked puzzled. "What are you stopping for?"

"Get out," I said.

"Oh, you want to go round."

"No. I want to get rid of you. Get out."

"You going to make me?"

I reached into the space between the seat and the door where there is nothing.

"Okay, okay," he said, and got out and slammed the door so hard that Charley wailed with annoyance.

I started instantly, but I heard him scream, and in the mirror saw his hating face and his open spit-ringed mouth. He shrilled "Nigger-lover, nigger-lover, nigger-lover," as long as I could see him and I don't know how long after. It's true I goaded him, but I couldn't help it. I guess when they're drafting peacemakers they'd better pass me by.

I picked up one more passenger between Jackson and Montgomery, a young Negro student with a sharp face and the look and feel of impatient fierceness. He carried three fountain pens in his breast pocket, and his inner pocket bulged with papers. I knew he was a student because I asked him. He was alert. License plate and speech relaxed him as much as he is ever likely to relax.

We discussed the sit-ins. He had taken part in them, and in the bus boycott. I told him what I had seen in New Orleans. He had been there. He had expected what I was shocked at.

Finally we spoke of Martin Luther King and his teaching of passive but unrelenting resistance.

"It's too slow," he said. "It will take too long."

"There's improvement, there's constant improvement. Gandhi proved it's the only weapon that can win against violence."

"I know all that. I've studied it. The gains are drops of water and time is passing. I want it faster, I want action—action now."

"That might defeat the whole thing."

"I might be an old man before I'm a man at all. I might be dead before."

"That's true. And Gandhi's dead. Are there many like you who want action?"

"Yes. I mean, some—I mean, I don't know how many."

We talked of many things then. He was a passionate and articulate young man with anxiety and fierceness just below the surface. But when I dropped him in Montgomery he leaned through the window of the cab and he laughed. "I'm ashamed," he said. "It's just selfishness. But I want to see it—me—not dead. Here! Me! I want to see it—soon." And then he swung around and wiped his eyes with his hand and he walked quickly away.

With all the polls and opinion posts, with newspapers more opinion than news so that we no longer know one from the other, I want to be very clear about one thing. I have not intended to present, nor do I think I have presented, any kind of cross-section so that a reader can say, "He thinks he has presented a true picture of the South." I don't. I've only told what a few people said to me and what I saw. I don't know whether they were typical or whether any conclusion can be drawn. But I do know it is a troubled place and a people caught in a jam. And I know that the solution when it arrives will not be easy or simple. I feel with Monsieur Ci Gît that the end is not in question. It's the means—the dreadful uncertainty of the means.

IN THE BEGINNING OF THIS RECORD I TRIED to explore the nature of journeys, how they are things in themselves, each one an individual and no two alike. I speculated with a kind of wonder on the strength of the individuality of journeys and stopped on the postulate that people don't take trips—trips take people. That discussion, however, did not go into the life span of journeys. This seems to be variable and unpredictable. Who has not known a journey to be over and dead before the traveler returns? The reverse is also true: many a trip continues long after movement in time and space have ceased. I remember a man in Salinas who in his middle years traveled to Honolulu and back, and that journey continued for the rest of his life. We could watch him in his rocking chair on his front porch, his eyes squinted, half-closed, endlessly traveling to Honolulu.

My own journey started long before I left, and was over before I returned. I know exactly where and when it was over. Near Abingdon, in the dogleg of Virginia, at four o'clock of a windy afternoon, without warning or good-by or kiss my foot, my journey went away and left me stranded far from home. I tried to call it back, to catch it up—a foolish and hopeless matter, because it was definitely and permanently over and finished. The road became an endless stone ribbon, the hills obstructions, the trees green blurs, the people simply moving figures with heads but no faces. All the food along the way tasted like soup, even the soup. My bed was unmade. I slipped into it for naps at long uneven intervals. My stove was unlighted and a loaf of bread gathered mold in my cupboard. The miles rolled under me unacknowledged. I know it was cold, but I didn't feel it; I know the countryside must have been beautiful, but I didn't see it. I bulldozed blindly through West Virginia, plunged into Pennsylvania and grooved Rocinante to the great wide turnpike. There was no night, no day, no distance. I must have stopped to fill my gas tank, to walk and feed Charley, to eat, to telephone, but I don't remember any of it.

It is very strange. Up to Abingdon, Virginia, I can reel back the trip like film. I have almost total recall, every face is there, every hill and tree and color, and sound of speech and small scenes ready to replay themselves in my memory. After Abingdon—nothing. The way was a gray, timeless, eventless tunnel, but at the end of it was the one shining reality—my own wife, my own house in my own street, my own bed. It was all there, and I lumbered my way toward it. Rocinante could be fleet, but I had not driven her fast. Now she leaped under my heavy relentless foot, and the wind shrieked around the corners of the house. If you think I am indulging in fantasy about the trip, how can you explain that Charley knew it was over too? He at least is no dreamer, no coiner of moods. He went to sleep with his head in my lap, never looked out the window, never said "Ftt," never urged me to a turn-out. He carried out his functions like a sleepwalker, ignored whole rows of garbage cans. If that doesn't prove the truth of my statement, nothing can.

New Jersey was another turnpike. My body was in a nerveless, tireless vacuum. The increasing river of traffic for New York carried me along, and suddenly there was the welcoming maw of Holland Tunnel and at the other end home.

A policeman waved me out of the snake of traffic and flagged me to a stop. "You can't go through the tunnel with that butane," he said.

"But officer, it's turned off."

"Doesn't matter. It's the law. Can't take gas into the tunnel."

And suddenly I fell apart, collapsed into a jelly of weariness. "But I want to get home," I wailed. "How am I going to get home?"

He was very kind to me, and patient too. Maybe he had a home somewhere. "You can go up and take George Washington Bridge, or you can take a ferry."

It was rush hour, but the gentle-hearted policeman must have seen a potential maniac in me. He held back the savage traffic and got me through and directed me with great care. I think he was strongly tempted to drive me home.

Magically I was on the Hoboken ferry and then ashore, far downtown with the daily panic rush of commuters leaping and running and dodging in front, obeying no signals. Every evening is Pamplona in lower New York. I made a turn and then another, entered a one-way street the wrong way and had to back out, got boxed in the middle of a crossing by a swirling rapids of turning people.

Suddenly I pulled to the curb in a no-parking area, cut my motor, and leaned back in the seat and laughed, and I couldn't stop. My hands and arms and shoulders were shaking with road jitters.

An old-fashioned cop with a fine red face and a frosty blue eye leaned in toward me. "What's the matter with you, Mac, drunk?" he asked.

I said, "Officer, I've driven this thing all over the country—mountains, plains, deserts. And now I'm back in my own town, where I live—and I'm lost."

He grinned happily. "Think nothing of it, Mac," he said. "I got lost in Brooklyn only Saturday. Now where is it you were wanting to go?"

And that's how the traveler came home again.

ABOUT THE AUTHOR

JOHN STEINBECK was born in Salinas, California in 1902. His first three books were financial failures, and he worked at various kinds of jobs to survive, including fruit picking. His first success was *Tortilla Flat* (1935), which was followed by *In Dubious Battle* and a number of shorter works, leading up to his great masterpiece, *The Grapes of Wrath*, Pulitzer Prize-winner of 1940.

In 1962 Steinbeck became the sixth American to win the Nobel Prize for Literature. He is the author of such books as *The Red Pony, The Short Reign of Pippin IV, Sweet Thursday, The Winter of Our Discontent,* and, most recently, *Travels with Charley.*

STEINBECK'S PEOPLE

**Your Key
to the
Year's Most
Exciting Reading
Experience**

JAMES A. MICHENER

Whether he is chronicling the history and life of a new nation, describing a powerful political event, or writing about love in exotic settings, James Michener always captures the drama and excitement that makes reading an adventure!

THE BRIDGE AT ANDAU	50¢
THE BRIDGES AT TOKO-RI	45¢
SAYONARA	75¢
RETURN TO PARADISE	75¢
THE FIRES OF SPRING	95¢
HAWAII	95¢
CARAVANS	95¢

Get these fine Michener books wherever Bantam paperbacks are sold, or write:

God Tells
the Man
Who Cares

A.W. Tozer

God Tells the Man Who Cares

CHRISTIAN PUBLICATIONS, INC.
Harrisburg, Pennsylvania

Christian Publications, Inc.
25 S. 10th Street, P.O. Box 3404
Harrisburg, PA 17105

The mark of $\mathcal{OP}$ *vibrant faith*

Contents

Introduction

GOD SPEAKS only to those who take time to listen. It is the man who cares who communes with the Most High and learns the secrets of the Lord. Such a man also sees the sorrow and feels the woe of the world. He shares the burdens of his brothers.

Because A. W. Tozer lived in the presence of God he saw clearly and he spoke as a prophet to the church. He sought for God's honor with the zeal of Elijah and mourned with Jeremiah at the apostasy of God's people. But he was not a prophet of despair.

The chapters in this book are messages of concern. They expose the weaknesses of the church and denounce compromise. They warn and exhort. But they are messages of hope as well, for God is always there, ever faithful to restore and to fulfill His Word to those who hear and obey.

Anita M. Bailey

Managing Editor
The Alliance Witness

Acknowledgments

With the exception of one chapter, the material in this book originally appeared in *The Alliance Witness*, which Dr. Tozer edited from 1950 to 1963. "We Are Becoming What We Love" was written for *Eternity* Magazine and it is included here with their permission.

God Tells the Man Who Cares

THE BIBLE was written in tears and to tears it will yield its best treasures. God has nothing to say to the frivolous man.

It was to Moses, a trembling man, that God spoke on the mount, and that same man later saved the nation when he threw himself before God with the offer to have himself blotted out of God's book for Israel's sake. Daniel's long season of fasting and prayer brought Gabriel from heaven to tell him the secret of the centuries. When the beloved John wept much because no one could be found worthy to open the seven-sealed book, one of the elders comforted him with the joyous news that the Lion of the tribe of Judah had prevailed.

The psalmists often wrote in tears, the prophets could hardly conceal their heavyheartedness, and the apostle Paul in his otherwise joyous epistle to the Philippians broke into tears when he thought of the many who were enemies of the cross of Christ and whose end was destruction. Those Christian leaders who shook the world were one and all men of sorrows whose witness to mankind welled out of heavy hearts. There is no power in tears per se, but tears and power ever lie close together in the Church of the First-born.

It is not a reassuring thought that the writings

of the grief-stricken prophets are often pored over by persons whose interests are curious merely and who never shed one tear for the woes of the world. They have a prying inquisitiveness about the schedule of future events, forgetting apparently that the whole purpose of Bible prophecy is to prepare us morally and spiritually for the time to come.

The doctrine of Christ's return has fallen into neglect, on the North American continent at least, and as far as I can detect, today exercises no power whatever over the rank and file of Bible-believing Christians. For this there may be a number of contributing factors; but the chief one is, I believe, the misfortune suffered by prophetic truth between the two world wars when men without tears undertook to instruct us in the writings of the tear-stained prophets. Big crowds and big offerings resulted until events proved the teachers wrong on too many points; then the reaction set in and prophecy lost favor with the masses. This was a neat trick of the devil and it worked too well. We should and must learn that we cannot handle holy things carelessly without suffering serious consequences.

Another field where tearless men have done us untold harm is in prayer for the sick. There have always been reverent, serious men who felt it their sacred duty to pray for the sick that they might be healed in the will of God. It was said of Spurgeon that his prayers raised up more sick persons than the ministrations of any doctor in London. When tearless promoters took up the doctrine it was turned into a lucrative racket. Smooth, persuasive men used superior salesmanship methods to make impressive fortunes out of their campaigns. Their big ranches and heavy financial investments prove how successful they have been in separating the sick and suffering from their money. And this in the name of the Man of Sorrows who had not where to lay His head!

Whatever is done without heart is done in the dark no matter how scriptural it may appear to be. By the law of just compensation the heart of the religious trifler will be destroyed by the exceeding brightness of the truth he touches. Tearless eyes are finally blinded by the light at which they gaze.

We of the nonliturgical churches tend to look with some disdain upon those churches that follow a carefully prescribed form of service, and certainly there must be a good deal in such services that has little or no meaning for the average participant—this not because it is carefully prescribed but because the average participant is what he is. But I have observed that our familiar impromptu service, planned by the leader twenty minutes before, often tends to follow a ragged and tired order almost as standardized as the Mass. The liturgical service is at least beautiful; ours is often ugly. Theirs has been carefully worked out through the centuries to capture as much of beauty as possible and to preserve a spirit of reverence among the worshipers. Ours is often an off-the-cuff makeshift with nothing to recommend it. Its so-called liberty is often not liberty at all but sheer slovenliness.

The theory is that if the meeting is unplanned

the Holy Spirit will work freely, and that would be true if all the worshipers were reverent and Spirit-filled. But mostly there is neither order nor Spirit, just a routine prayer that is, except for minor variations, the same week after week, and a few songs that were never much to start with and have long ago lost all significance by meaningless repetition.

In the majority of our meetings there is scarcely a trace of reverent thought, no recognition of the unity of the body, little sense of the divine Presence, no moment of stillness, no solemnity, no wonder, no holy fear. But so often there is a dull or a breezy song leader full of awkward jokes, as well as a chairman announcing each "number" with the old radio continuity patter in an effort to make everything hang together.

The whole Christian family stands desperately in need of a restoration of penitence, humility and tears. May God send them soon.

The Voice of God Speaking

I THINK it may be accepted as axiomatic that God is constantly trying to speak to men. He desires to communicate Himself, to impart holy ideas to those of His creatures capable of receiving them.

This divine impulse toward self-expression may account for the creation, particularly for God's having made intelligent and moral beings who could hear and understand truth. Among these beings man stands at the top, having been created in the image of God and so possessing purer and finer organs for the apprehension of whatever can be known of God. The Second Person of the Godhead is called the Word of God, that is, the mind of God in expression.

Concerning God's speaking to men there are two views, opposed to each other, it is true, but alike in that both are erroneous. One is that God spoke the Holy Scriptures into being and then elapsed into silence, a silence that will not be broken till God calls all men before Him to judgment. God will then speak again as in olden days, but in the meantime we have the Bible as a deposit of embalmed truth which scribe and theologian must decipher as they can.

This view is held by the majority of evangelicals, allowing for some variation in detail, and is extremely injurious to the Christian's soul. It is injurious because it contains two false notions, one that God is no longer speaking and the other that we are shut up to our intellects for the understanding and apprehension of truth. According to this view, God is far away and wholly noncommunicative; and we, whether we like to admit it or not, are forced into a kind of evangelical rationalism, since according to this notion the human mind becomes the final arbiter of truth as well as the organ for its reception into the soul.

Now, the blessed fact is that God is not silent and has never been silent, but is speaking in His universe. The written Word is effective because, and only because, the Living Word is speaking in heaven and the Living Voice is sounding in the earth. "And it is the Spirit that beareth witness, because the Spirit is truth. For there are three that bear record in heaven, the Father, the Word, and the Holy Ghost: and these three are one."

That the creative voice of God is constantly sounding throughout the creation is a truth forgotten by modern Christianity. Yet it was by His word that He called the world into being and it is by His word that all things are held together. It is the still voice of God in the heart of every human being that renders everyone culpable before the bar of God's judgment and convicts of sin even those who have never been exposed to the written Word.

The idea that the only mortal sin is the rejection of Christ and that men are not held accountable for sin in those parts of the world where the gospel has not been preached is a monstrous error. There is a light that lighteth every man that cometh into the world. It is sin against light that destroys men, not the rejection of Christ, though that rejection leaves the sinner desolate in his sin and shuts him out forever from the forgiving love of God.

It is written that Christ upholds all things by the word of His power; and the word that upholds all things is the power-filled voice of God sounding vibrantly throughout the creation. The Bible is not, as some appear to think, God's last will and testament; it is, rather, the written expression of the mind of the Living God, inactive until the same breath that first inspired it breathes on it again.

The other and opposite error from the God-has-once-spoken error is that held by various kinds of liberals. It is that since God is vocal in His universe, there is no such thing as an inspired canon of Scripture containing a full body of revealed truth that can serve as the one final source of doctrine and practice. According to these gentlemen, the two ideas contradict each other. If God is still speaking, then we must keep our minds open to further revelation given, it may be, through poets, philosophers, scientists and novelists, as well as religionists of various kinds. Wherever new truth is discovered or new and advanced ideas are brought forth, there God is speaking again as He once spoke by the prophet and seer in olden days.

Certainly we must grant these men the right to believe what they will, as well as the right to teach what they believe. But one thing is settled: Whoever, for whatever reason, denies the finality of the Biblical revelation and insists upon a continuing revelation having the same authority as the Sacred Scriptures has shut himself out from the name of Christian. He is simply not a Christian in the scriptural and historic meaning of the word.

Between the ideas of a fixed Biblical canon and a constantly speaking God there is no contradiction. In the Scriptures God has caused to be written a full and sufficient body of truth. Holy men were moved by the Holy Spirit to record the words God knew would be best suited to teach doctrine, and to reprove, correct and instruct in righteousness. The point I make here is that if the living voice of God were not speaking in the world and in the hearts of men the written Word could have no real meaning for us. Because God is speaking in His world we are able to hear Him speak in His Word.

We Must Be Still to Know

"Be still, and know that I am God."—Psalm 46:10.

OUR FATHERS had much to say about stillness, and by stillness they meant the absence of motion or the absence of noise or both.

They felt that they must be still for at least a part of the day, or that day would be wasted. God can be known in the tumult of the world if His providence has for the time placed us there, but He is known best in the silence. So they held, and so the Sacred Scriptures declare. Inward assurance comes out of the stillness. We must be still to know.

There has hardly been another time in the history of the world when stillness was needed more than it is today, and there has surely not been another time when there was so little of it or when it was so hard to find.

16

Christ is every man's contemporary. His presence and His power are offered to us in this time of mad activity and mechanical noises as certainly as to fishermen on the quiet lake of Galilee or to shepherds on the plains of Judea. The only condition is that we get still enough to hear His voice and that we believe and heed what we hear.

Some things can be learned in the din of modern life. Amid the noises we may become engineers or scientists or architects. In the humdrum we may learn how to fly a jet plane or to manage a department store. We may win an athletic contest, conduct an orchestra, earn a degree or get ourselves elected to public office. We do these things by accepting civilization at its face value and getting adjusted to it. Thus we become children of the twentieth century and our psychology takes its complexion from the times. We move as gracefully as we are able through the complicated steps of the dance of circumstance, the noise actually aiding our motion; or, not knowing where we are headed, we march with the multitude to booming music that keeps us in step and adds a bit of pleasure to the effort.

These things men can do and are doing. But when we begin to doubt the validity of a philosophy built on physical science and to question the soundness of a civilization that produced the H-bomb, and especially when we begin to grope after God if perchance we may find Him, something strange and wonderful happens. As we draw nearer to the ancient Source of our being we find that we are no longer learned or ignorant, modern or old-fashioned, crude or cultured, white or colored; in that awesome Presence we are just *men*. Artificial distinctions fade away. Thousands of years of education disappear in a moment and we stand again where Adam and Eve stood after the Fall, where Cain stood, and Abel, outside the Garden, frightened and undone and fugitive from the terror of the broken law.

There before the judgment seat which suddenly becomes as real to the trembling sinner as if it were the very last judgment itself, no modern religious techniques avail; none of the carefully thought out methods work. The civilized man surrounded by his lately invented and noisy gadgets passes back in his heart through the centuries of "Progress" and becomes again a terrified, whimpering human thing desperately in need of a Saviour.

Because this is true, any evangelism which by appeal to common interests and chatter about current events seeks to establish a common ground where the sinner can feel at home is as false as the altars of Baal ever were. Every effort to smooth out the road for men and to take away the guilt and the embarrassment is worse than wasted; it is evil and dangerous to the souls of men.

One of the most popular current errors, and the one out of which springs most of the noisy, blustering religious activity being carried on in evangelical circles these days, is the notion that as times change the church must change with them. Christians must adapt their methods by the demands of the people. If they want ten-minute sermons, give them ten-minute sermons. If they want truth in capsule form, give it to them. If they want pictures, give them plenty of pictures. If they like stories, tell them stories. If they prefer to absorb their religious instruction through the drama, go along with them—give them what they want. "The message is the same, only the method changes," say the advocates of compromise.

"Whom the gods would destroy they first make mad," the old Greeks said, and they were wiser than they knew. That mentality which mistakes Sodom for Jerusalem and Hollywood for the Holy City is too gravely astray to be explained otherwise than as a judicial madness visited upon professed Christians for affronts committed against the Spirit of God. "Hear ye indeed, but understand not; and see ye indeed, but perceive not. Make the heart of this people fat, and make their ears heavy, and shut their eyes; lest they see with their eyes, and hear with their ears, and understand with their heart, and convert, and be healed" (Isa. 6:9, 10).

But, some earnest persons reason, since there is no stillness in this mechanized world we must learn to get along without it. We cannot hope to bring back the still waters and the quiet pastures where David once led his sheep. This rat race of civilization is too noisy for us to hear the still, small Voice, so we must learn to hear God speak in the earthquake and the storm. And if modern evangelism is geared to the tumult and the agitation of the times, why should anyone complain? Does it not represent an honest effort to be all things to all men that by any means some should be saved?

The answer is that the soul of man does not change fundamentally, no matter how external conditions may change. The aborigine in his hut, the college professor in his study, the truck driver in the bedlam of city traffic have all the same basic need: to be rid of their sins, to obtain eternal life and to be brought into communion with God. Civilized noises and activities are surface phenomena, a temporary rash on the epidermis of the human race. To attribute sound values to them and then to try to bring religion into harmony with them is to commit a moral blunder so huge as to stagger the imagination, and one for which we shall surely be paying long after this frenetic extravaganza we call civilization has ended in tragedy and everlasting grief.

What certain religious teachers fail to understand is that true Christian experience takes place in the human spirit, far in and beneath the changing surface of things. It is only the surface that responds to noise and agitation. The deep-in part of the man lies in primeval silence waiting that quickening word that shall give it second birth. Because this far-in spirit of the man is separated from God the whole life is out of order; so the flesh and the imagination take over and direct the thinking, the willing and the doing of the individual man and the race of which he is a part. These create the dance macabre, the dance of death we know as society and in which as natural men we find ourselves.

Popular Christianity parrots the language of New Testament theology, but it accepts the world's opinion of itself and sedulously apes its ways (except for a few evil practices which even the world itself admits are wrong). Then Christ is offered as something added, a Friend Up There, a Guarantor against the time when the tumult and the shouting dies and we are called in from the playground and forced to go to sleep.

Be it remembered that the great essential facts have not changed. Men are still what they were and the Son of Man is forever who and what He was. He calls to the eternal in us. Deep calls unto deep and the call, if it is heard at all, is heard by that in us which is neither savage nor civilized, old nor young, Western nor Oriental, but simply human and once made in the image of God.

It is significant that the psalm in which the words "Be still" occur is filled with noise and commotion. The earth shakes, the waters roar and are troubled, the mountains threaten to tumble into the midst of the sea, the nations rage, the kingdoms are moved and the sound of war is heard throughout the land. Then a voice is heard out of the silence saying, "Be still, and know that I am God."

So today we must listen till our inner ears hear the words of God. When the Voice is heard it will not be as the excited shouting of the nervous world; rather it will be the reassuring call of One of whom it was said, "He shall not strive, nor cry; neither shall any man hear his voice in the streets."

It cannot be heard in the street, but it may be heard plainly enough in the heart. And that is all that matters at last.

The Kingdoms of the World and the Glory of Them

SATAN once tried to bring about the downfall of Christ by offering Him all the kingdoms of the world and the glory of them.

Here is sufficient proof that the devil is wise, but not wise enough.

He knew fallen human nature and just how to handle it. He knew the power of pomp and circumstance to charm the sinful heart and bring it into captivity. In presenting to the Man Jesus the glory of the world he was shrewdly taking advantage of a known weakness in the human race. The trick should have worked, and it would have worked but for one thing: This was no fallen man Satan was attempting to seduce; it was a sinless Man full of the Holy Ghost and wisdom, whose penetrating glance pierced the world's attractive exterior and saw what was inside. What He saw revolted Him. He would have no part of it.

Our Lord saw in the world's glory not what other men saw and, conversely, He saw what other men could not see. He saw not beauty but death, a garish death that must be purchased at the price of the soul. Beneath its gaudy allurements He saw corruption and decay. He knew its glory was but bait to catch foolish victims. He knew its bright promises were all lies.

All this Jesus knew; and Satan for all his wisdom did not know that He knew it. The devil is an assiduous student of the Bible, but still he did not know or he would not have attempted the impossible, and that to his own confusion and permanent loss of face.

The delusive quality of all human glory is taught throughout the Bible, and with bold emphasis in the New Testament. It has been taught also with great clarity by the saints and faithful brethren since the days of the apostles. We sing it in our hymns and repeat it in our prayers, and no Christian but would admit the truth of it.

With the Bible open before us and a long tradition of truth behind us there would seem to be no reason for our present tragic failure to recognize the world's deceptive appeal and to stay clear of it. For there must not be any denial of the facts: the church has been captured by the kingdoms of the world and the glory of them. In spite of the prophetic voices that are raised here and there among us, present-day believers are drawn to the world with irresistible force.

That world which our Saviour once refused to buy at the price of disobedience to God is now wooing His professed followers with every sly, deceptive artifice. The glory which our Lord once rejected with cold scorn is now being admired and sought after by multitudes who make a loud profession of accepting the gospel. The old trick which our Lord saw through so easily is charming His present-day followers into smiling acquiescence.

The devil did not know Christ, but apparently he knows Christians.

A century ago Satan launched a drive to destroy evangelical religion by a direct attack upon the Scriptures. He misjudged the strength of Christian orthodoxy and was thrown back with heavy losses. Today "Modernism" is a word without much meaning, and many liberals now admit that they have lost the beating heart out of their religion. But the evangelical creed is as vigorous as ever, and even in learned circles it is now considered intellectually respectable to believe Christian truth.

No, Satan's effort to destroy Christianity on the doctrinal front has not been a success; there are probably more Bible believers now than at any time in world history. Still the true religion of the cross is in great and serious peril on another front and, strangely enough, many of the very warriors who fought so valiantly when the veracity of the Bible was attacked have failed to recognize the enemy when he has approached from a new direction.

The real peril today arises from within the fold of orthodox believers. It consists of an acceptance of the world's values, a belief that the kingdoms of the world and the glory of them are valid prizes to be pursued by believing men and women. Blind leaders of blind souls are admitting that there is something to be said in favor of the world-glory after all; they insist that Christians should not cut themselves off from the pleasures of the world, except, of course, from those that are too degraded for respectable society. Everything else goes, and the very values that Christ scorned are now being used to attract people to the gospel.

Christ now stands in need of a patron, a celebrity who will sponsor Him before the world. He looks weakly about for some well-known figure upon whose inside popularity He can ride forth as He once rode into Jerusalem on the back of an ass's colt. His ability to draw men unto Him is frankly doubted, so He is provided with a gimmick to do the trick for Him. The cheap and tawdry glory which He once rejected is placed around His head as a crown. The crown they give Him is studded with paste imitations, all borrowed from the world: middleclass prosperity, success, fame, publicity, money, crowds, social acceptance, pomp, display, earthly honor. The lust of the flesh, the lust of the eyes and the pride of life have all been Christianized (not by the liberal, mind you, but by the evangelicals) and are now offered along with Christ to everyone who will "believe."

And on top of this we still pray for revival, with no awareness of our dark betrayal and no intention to repent. All such prayers are vain. We need only humble ourselves to obey the truth and the true revival has already started. An emotional revival superimposed upon an evangelical religion hopelessly sold out to the glory of the world would but increase the confusion and confirm the deception.

O Lord, save Thy people from such a snare.

The Vital Place of the Church

THE HIGHEST expression of the will of God in this age is the church which He purchased with His own blood. To be scripturally valid any religious activity must be part of the church. Let it be clearly stated that there can be no service acceptable to God in this age that does not center in and spring out of the church. Bible schools, tract societies, Christian business men's committees, seminaries, and the many independent groups working at one or another phase of religion need to check themselves reverently and courageously, for they have no true spiritual significance outside of or apart from the church.

According to the Scriptures the church is the habitation of God through the Spirit, and as such is the most important organism beneath the sun. She is not one more good institution along with the home, the state, and the school; she is the most vital of all institutions—the only one that can claim a heavenly origin.

The cynic may inquire which church we mean, and may remind us that the Christian church is so divided that it is impossible to tell which is the true one, even if such a one exists. But we are not too much troubled by the suppressed smile of the doubter. Being inside the church we are probably as well aware of her faults as any person on the outside could possibly be. And we believe in her nevertheless wherever she manifests herself in a world of darkness and unbelief.

The church is found wherever the Holy Spirit has drawn together a few persons who trust Christ for their salvation, worship God in spirit and have no dealings with the world and the flesh. The members may by necessity be scattered over the surface of the earth and separated by distance and circumstances, but in every true member of the church is the homing instinct and the longing of the sheep for the fold and the shepherd. Give a few real Christians half a chance and they will get together and organize and plan regular meetings for prayer and worship. In these meetings they will hear the Scriptures expounded, break bread together in one form or another according to their light, and try as far as possible to spread the saving gospel to the lost world.

Such groups are cells in the Body of Christ, and each one is a true church, a real part of the greater church. It is in and through these cells that the Spirit does His work on earth. Whoever scorns the local church scorns the Body of Christ.

The church is still to be reckoned with. "The gates of hell shall not prevail against her."

Organization: Necessary and Dangerous

BASICALLY, organization is the placing of several parts of a whole in such relation to each other that a desired end may be achieved. This may be by consent or compulsion, depending upon the circumstances.

A certain amount of organization is necessary everywhere throughout the created universe and in all human society. Without it there could be no science, no government, no family unit, no art, no music, no literature, no creative activity of any kind.

Life requires organization. There is no such thing as life apart from the medium through which it expresses itself. It cannot exist as a thing in itself independent of an organized body. It is found only where there is some body, some form in which it may reside. And where there is body and form there is organization. A man, for instance, is the sum of his organized and coordinated parts and in these and through these the mystery of life is afforded expression. When, for any cause, the parts become disorganized life departs and the man dies.

Society requires organization. If men are to

live together in the world they must be organized in some manner. This has been recognized in all times and places and is seen on all levels of human society from the jungle tribe to the world empire. Ideally the object of government is to achieve order with a minimum of restraint while permitting a maximum of freedom to the individual.

That some restraint of individual liberty is good and necessary is admitted by all intelligent persons; that too much restraint is bad is also admitted by everyone. Disagreement arises when we try to define "some" and "too much." Just how much is too much? and how little is some? If this could be settled peace would descend upon Congress and Parliament, the Democrat and the liberal would lie down with the Republican and the conservative, and a little child should lead them.

The difference between the slave state and the free is one of degree only. Even the totalitarian countries enjoy some freedom, and the citizens of the free nations must endure a certain amount of restraint. It is the balance between the two that decides whether a given country is slave or free. No informed citizen believes he is absolutely free. He knows his liberty must be curtailed somewhat for the benefit of all. The best he can hope for is that the curtailment will be kept at a minimum. This minimum of curtailment he calls "freedom," and so precious is it that he is willing to risk his life for it. The Western world fought two major wars within twenty-five years to preserve this balance of liberty and escape the tighter restrictions that Nazism and Facism would have imposed upon it.

Being Christ-centered and church-oriented in his thinking, this writer of course relates everything to the Christian religion. I am and have been for years much distressed about the tendency to over-organize the Christian community, and I have for that reason had it charged against me that I do not believe in organization. The truth is quite otherwise.

The man who would oppose all organization in the church must needs be ignorant of the facts of life. Art is organized beauty; music is organized sound; philosophy is organized thought; science is organized knowledge; government is merely society organized. And what is the true church of Christ but organized mystery?

The throbbing heart of the church is life—in the happy phrase of Henry Scougal, "the life of God in the soul of man." This life, together with the actual presence of Christ within her, constitutes the church a divine thing, a mystery, a miracle. Yet without substance, form and order this divine life would have no dwelling place, and no way to express itself to the community.

For this reason there is much in the New Testament about organization. Paul's pastoral epistles and his letters to the Corinthian Christians reveal that the great apostle was an organizer. He reminded Titus that he had left him in Crete to set in order the things that were wanting and to ordain elders in every city. Surely this can only mean that Titus was commissioned by the apostle to impose some kind of order upon the various companies of believers living in the island, and order can only be achieved through organization.

Christians have tended to err in one of several directions because they have not understood the purpose of organization or the dangers that attend it if it is allowed to get out of hand. Some will have no organization at all, and of course the results are confusion and disorder, and these can never help mankind or bring glory to our Lord. Others substitute organization for life, and while having a name to live they are dead. Still others become so enamored of rules and regulations that they multiply them beyond all reason, and soon the spontaneity is smothered within the church and the life squeezed out of it.

It is with the latter error that I am mainly concerned. Many church groups have perished from too much organization, even as others from too little. Wise church leaders will watch out for both extremes. A man may die as a result of having too low blood pressure as certainly as from having too high, and it matters little which takes him off. He is equally dead either way. The important thing in church organization is to discover the scriptural balance between two extremes and avoid both.

It is painful to see a happy group of Christians, born in simplicity and held together by the bonds of heavenly love, slowly lose their simple character, begin to try to regulate every sweet impulse of the Spirit and slowly die from within. Yet that is the direction almost all Christian denominations have taken throughout history, and in spite of the warnings set out by the Holy Spirit and the Scriptures of truth it is the direction almost all church groups are taking today.

While there is some danger that our present-day evangelical groups may suffer from want of proper organization, the real peril surely lies on the other side. Churches run toward complexity as ducks take to water. What is back of this?

First, I think it arises from a natural but carnal desire on the part of a gifted minority to bring the less gifted majority to heel and get them where they will not stand in the way of their soaring ambitions. The oftquoted (and usually misquoted) saying is true in religion as well as in politics: "Power tends to corrupt and absolute power tends to corrupt absolutely." The itch to have the preeminence is one disease for which no natural cure has ever been found.

Another cause back of our top-heavy and ugly overorganization is fear. Churches and societies founded by saintly men with courage, faith and sanctified imagination appear unable to propagate themselves on the same spiritual level beyond one or two generations. The spiritual fathers were not able to sire others with courage and faith equal to their own. The fathers had God and little else, but their descendants lose their vision and look to methods and constitutions for the power their hearts tell them they lack. Then rules and precedents harden into a protective shell where they can take refuge from trouble. It is always easier and safer to pull in our necks than to fight things out on the field of battle.

In all our fallen life there is a strong gravitational pull toward complexity and away from things simple and real. There seems to be a kind of sad inevitability back of our morbid urge toward spiritual suicide. Only by prophetic insight, watchful prayer and hard work can we reverse the trend and recover the departed glory.

In the old cemetery near historic Plymouth Rock where sleep the Pilgrim Fathers, there is a stone into which has been carved these solemn words (I quote from memory): "That which our fathers at such a great price secured, let us not lightly cast away."

We mid-century evangelicals might be wise to apply these words to our own religious situation. We are still Protestants. We must protest the light casting away of our religious freedom. The simple liberty of early Christianity is being lost to us. One by one we are surrendering those rights purchased for us by the blood of the everlasting covenant—the right to be ourselves, the right to obey the Holy Spirit, the right to think our own private thoughts, the right to do what we will with our lives, the right to determine under God what we shall do with our money.

And remember, our dangers for the moment come not from without, but from within.

The Christian's Witness to the World

THE MISSION of the church is to declare, to proclaim, to witness. She has been left on earth to be a witness to certain great eternal truths which she received from God and which the world could not possibly know unless she told it.

"Go ye therefore, and teach all nations," said Jesus to the infant church. The church was to teach and the world was to listen, and all who received the witness of the church were to be baptized and taught further in the mysteries of the kingdom of God.

That was the order established by the new-risen Christ. Those first Christians had seen and heard such wonders as had first terrified them, then filled them with a high spiritual excitement which they could not contain. With joy they turned their backs on the open tomb from which their Lord had walked forth, and literally raced away to spread the news.

A few days later the Holy Spirit came upon them to confirm the truth and to add a new afflatus of moral power to their testimony.

That is how it all began. The Early Church had the message; the world had only the need for that message. The disciples had seen and touched and handled that Eternal Life which was with the Father and was manifested unto 'men; and driven by an irresistible compulsion they went forth to Jew and Greek, bondman and freeman, high and low, to tell, to witness, to declare, to testify. Succeeding generations of Christians, not having seen Christ with their mortal eyes but having met Him in living encounter and having known and experienced Him by the inward operation of the Holy Spirit, told forth the message with the same zeal as had the original band. They had something to tell the world. They were witnesses eagerly testifying. They were devotees and zealots, convinced that they had the truth the world needed desperately and which it could not afford to ignore.

It has been so wherever the church has had eyesight and hearing. When she has been conscious of One walking among the golden candlesticks with a voice like the sound of many waters she has stood to echo that voice and the world has had to listen. Sometimes that world turned its back upon its benefactors and persecuted them unto death; sometimes it listened as Herod listened to John the Baptist, deeply touched by what it heard but unwilling to obey. Sometimes it listened sympathetically and numbers of people repented and went on to follow Christ. *But always the world was on the receiving end. The church spoke and the world heard.* Thus it was as Christ said it must be.

But hear, O ye heavens, and be astonished, O earth, for a mighty derangement has occurred in the relative position of the church and the world, a transposition so radical and so grotesque as would not have been believed if it had been foretold but a few years ago.

The church has lost her testimony. She has no longer anything to say to the world. Her once robust shout of assurance has faded away to an apologetic whisper. She who one time went out to declare now goes out to inquire. Her dogmatic declaration has become a respectful suggestion, a word of religious advice, given with the understanding that it is after all only an opinion and not meant to sound bigoted.

Not only has the church nothing to say to the world but the tables have actually been turned and the ministers of Christ are now going to the world for light. They sit at Adam's feet for instruction and clear their message with the wise and the prudent before they dare deliver it. But the certainty that comes from seeing and the assurance that springs from hearing—where are they?

But let us be more specific. About whom am I speaking here? The liberal who denies the authenticity of the Scriptures? I wish it were so. No, I write off the liberal as long dead and expect nothing from him. It is of the evangelical church that I speak, and of the so-called gospel churches. I speak of the theology of popular evangelism which quotes the Bible copiously but without one trace of authority, accepts the world at its own estimate, chides sinners like a weak-chinned father of a family who has long ago lost control of his household and doesn't expect to be obeyed, offers Christ as a religious tranquilizer who is without sovereignty and without any semblance of Lordship, adopts the world's methods, courts the favor of rich men, politicians and playboys—with the understanding, of course, that the said playboy will stoop to say a nice word about Jesus now and then.

I refer to a religious journalism ostensibly orthodox but which can scarcely be told in appearance, tone, spirit, language, method or aim from the secular magazine it so sedulously apes. I refer to the Christianity which says to Christ, "We will eat our own bread, and wear our own apparel: only let us be called by thy name, to take away our reproach" (Isa. 4:1). I refer to the masses of Christians who have "accepted" Jesus, but who turn their churches into playhouses, are entirely ignorant of worship, misunderstand the cross and are totally blind to the serious implications of discipleship.

Again I refer to the new crop of borderline liberals who use the language of orthodoxy but are nevertheless fellow travelers with old-line liberals and who seek to escape the reproach of the cross by what they like to believe is a dazzling display of intellectualism.

The church is in her Babylonian captivity, and as Israel could not sing the songs of Zion in a strange land, so Christians in bondage have no authoritative message to declare. They must wait for the news broadcast for a text and read *Time* magazine for a subject. Like the harried editor of a daily newspaper who languishes for a good story when no convenient murder or accident has happened for the last few hours, so the prophet in Babylon waits for a war, a new development in the Middle East or a space exploit to rescue him from enforced silence and give him a new lease on his pulpit.

But what is the church called to declare? What are the hard, bold, everlasting words she has been sent to give to the world? The first is that God is all in all. He is the great Reality which gives meaning to all other realities. "Ye are my witnesses, saith the Lord, and my servant whom I have chosen: that ye may know and believe me, and understand that I am he: before me there was no God formed, neither shall there be after me . . . . Yea, before the day was I am he; and there is none that can deliver out of my hand" (Isa. 43:10, 13).

The next great fact is that we are made *by* God and *for* Him. The answer to the question, "Where did I come from?" is never better answered than by the mother who says "God made you." The pooled knowledge of the world cannot improve upon this simple answer. Scientific research has probed deep into the secrets of how matter operates, but the *origin* of matter lies in deep silence and refuses to give an answer to any questions. God made the heaven and the earth and man upon the earth and He made man for Himself, and there is no other answer to the inquiry, "Why did God make me?"

The Christian is not sent to argue or persuade, nor is he sent to prove or demonstrate; he is sent to declare "Thus saith the Lord." When he has done this he makes God responsible for the outcome. No one knows enough and no one *can* know enough to go beyond this. God made us for Himself: that is the first and last thing that can be said about human existence and whatever more we add is but commentary.

Seeing who God is and who we are, a right relationship between God and us is of vital importance. That God should be glorified in us is so critically important that it stands in lonely grandeur, a moral imperative more compelling than any other which the human heart can acknowledge. To bring ourselves into a place where God will be eternally pleased with us should be the first responsible act of every man.

Knowing our sin and moral ignorance, the impossibility of effecting such a happy relationship becomes instantly evident. Since we cannot go to God, what then shall we do? The answer is found in the Christian witness: it is that God came to us in the Incarnation. "Who is Jesus?" asks the world, and the church answers, "Jesus is God come to us." He is come to seek us, to woo us, to win us to God again. And to do this He needed to die for us redemptively. He must in some manner undo our sins, destroy our record of sins committed and break the power of sins entrenched within us. All this, says the Christian witness, He did upon the cross perfectly, effectually and for good.

"Where is Jesus now?" asks the world, and the Christian answers, "At the right hand of God." He died but He is not dead. He rose again as He said He would, and scores of sober, trustworthy eyewitnesses saw Him after His return from among the dead. Better than all, His Spirit now reveals to the Christian heart not a dead Christ but a living one. This we are sent to declare with all the bold dogmatism of those who know, who have been there and experienced it beyond the possibility of a doubt.

The gospel is the official proclamation that Christ died for us and is risen again, with the added announcement that everyone who will believe, and as a result of that belief will cast in his lot with Christ in full and final committal, shall be saved eternally. He must come with the understanding that he will not be popular and that he will be called to stand where Jesus stood before the world: to be admired by many, loved by a few and rejected at last by the majority of men. He must be willing to pay this price; or let him go his way; Christ has nothing more to say to him now.

The Christian's message to the world must also be one of sin, righteousness and judgment. He must not accept in any measure the world's moral code, but stand boldly to oppose it and warn of the consequences of following it. And this he must do loudly and persistently, meanwhile taking great care that he himself walk so circumspectly that no flaw may be found in his life to give the lie to his testimony.

There is one thing more: the Christian witness includes also the faithful warning that God is a just and holy Being who will not trifle with men nor allow them to trifle with Him. He is long-suffering and waits patiently to be gracious, but after a while the friendly invitation of the gospel is withdrawn. The effort to persuade the incorrigible sinner is discontinued, death fixes the status of the man who loved his sins and he is sent to the place of the rejected where there is for him no further hope. That is hell, and it may be well we know so little about it. What we do know is sufficiently terrifying.

To His own children God has much more to say, so much that it requires a lifetime of eager listening to hear it all; but His message to the world is simple and brief. It is the work of the church to keep on repeating it to each generation of men till it is either accepted or rejected by those who hear.

The Christian must not allow himself to be entrapped by current vogues in religion, and above all he must never go to the world for his message. He is a man of heaven sent to give witness on earth. As he shall give account to the Lord that bought him, let him see to his commission.

The Church Must Not Conform

A STIMULATING little book written by a thoughtful observer of the religious scene attempts to explain Christian sects and denominations as reflections of the social conditions out of which they sprang.

The idea is, if I understand the author's arguments correctly, that differences in doctrine and in forms of church government among various Christian bodies have resulted from different economic, political, racial and cultural patterns throughout Christendom.

According to this theory, a democratic state would tend to produce a democratic church, whereas under a political dictatorship the authoritarian form of government would naturally prevail within the Christian community. In a highly cultured society ritualism would mark the worship of the church along with much rich symbolism and forms of external beauty.

Whether this conforms to historic fact I am not ready to say, though my limited knowledge of history would lead me to believe that this explanation is probably an accommodation of fact to theory and, while partly true, does not tell the whole story. One thing is certain, however; it is that wherever the Christian religion differs from itself there will surely be found elements that are unscriptural and altogether without Biblical authority, and it is always those elements that divide the church against itself.

In whatever language they appear the Scriptures continue century after century to say the same thing to everyone. The Spirit that inspired the Christian revelation never differs from Himself, but remains from age to age the same. God works according to an eternal purpose which He purposed in Christ Jesus before the world began; and our Lord assures us that till heaven and earth pass, one jot or one tittle shall in no wise pass from the Law till all be fulfilled. God's truth is the same wherever it is found and if the church conforms to the truth it will be the same church in doctrine and in practice throughout the entire world.

There are in the Christian religion three major elements: spiritual life, moral practice and community organization, and these all spring out of and follow New Testament doctrine; or more correctly, the first must and the others should. Life is and must necessarily be first. Life comes mysteriously to the soul that believes the truth. "He that heareth my word, and believeth on him that sent me, hath everlasting life, and shall not come into condemnation; but is passed from death unto life" (John 5:24). And again, "He that believeth on me, as the scripture hath said, out of his belly shall flow rivers of living water. (But this spake he of the Spirit, which they that believe on him should receive . . .)."

The message of the cross offers eternal life and the blessedness of the Holy Spirit indwelling the soul. These distinguish Christianity from every other religion; and it is significant that these distinguishing marks are of such a nature as to be wholly above and beyond the reach of man. They are altogether mysterious and divine and are unaffected by race, politics, economics or education. The life of God in the soul of a man is wholly independent of the social status of that man. In the Early Church the Spirit leaped across all artificial lines that separate men from each other and made of all believers a spiritual brotherhood. Jew and Gentile, rich and poor, Greek and barbarian were all baptized into one body, of which Christ was and is the Head.

Along with the gift of eternal life, the entrance of the Holy Spirit into the believer's heart and the induction of the newborn soul into the Body of Christ comes instant obligation to obey the teachings of the New Testament. These teachings are so plain and so detailed that it is difficult to understand how they could appear different to persons living under different political systems or on different cultural levels. That they have so appeared cannot be denied; but always the reasons lie in the imperfect state of the believers composing the different groups. They permitted the unauthorized introduction of extrascriptural matter into their beliefs and suffered spiritual weakness and debility as a consequence.

Undoubtedly Christian groups have been influenced in their moral practices by the society in which they lived, but we should see it for what it is and not try to explain it away. "Whosoever therefore shall break one of these least commandments, and shall teach men so, he shall be called the least in the kingdom of heaven.''

That we Christians modify the moral teachings of Christ at our convenience to avoid the stigma of being thought different is a proof of our backsliding, and the shame of it will not be removed until we have repented and brought our lives completely under the discipline of Christ.

The third element in the Christian religion, that of church polity or the political organization of the religious community in worship and service, is subject to the pressures and influences of society to a greater degree than are the other two. A modern example of this is the Salvation Army, which is to all intents and purposes a Christian denomination imitating the military in its organization and nomenclature. Other examples may be found in the historic denominations which have often followed rather closely the organization of the state. That some may deny this and quote Scripture to justify their organizational pattern does not invalidate my statement.

Christianity does vary from itself from place to place and from time to time as it permits itself to be influenced by political, economic, racial or cultural factors. Without doubt neither I who write this nor you who read it can be said to have escaped completely the molding power of society. As Christians we are somewhat different from what we would have been had we lived in a different period of history.

I think we do well to admit this, but we should not accept it as normal; and certainly we should not accept it as inevitable that we continue to be shaped by the world. Paul said, "Be not conformed to this world: but be ye transformed by the renewing of your mind" (Rom. 12:2). That we have to some extent conformed to the world is a proof of our weakness. We must begin at once to correct matters. By consecration, detachment, obedience and unceasing prayer we must escape the clutches of the world.

Pure Christianity, instead of being shaped by its environment, actually stands in sharp opposition to it, and where the power of God has been present over a sustained period the church has sometimes reversed the direction of things and exercised a purifying effect upon society.

Divisions Are Not Always Bad

WHEN TO UNITE and when to divide, that is the question, and a right answer requires the wisdom of a Solomon.

Some settle the problem by rule of thumb: All union is good and all division bad. It's that easy. But obviously this effortless way of dealing with the matter ignores the lessons of history and overlooks some of the deep spiritual laws by which men live.

If good men were all for union and bad men for division, or vice versa, that would simplify things for us. Or if it could be shown that God always unites and the devil always divides it would be easy to find our way around in this confused and confusing world. But that is not how things are.

To divide what should be divided and unite what should be united is the part of wisdom. Union of dissimilar elements is never good even where it is possible, nor is the arbitrary division of elements that are alike; and this is as certainly true of things moral and religious as of things political or scientific.

The first divider was God who at the creation divided the light from the darkness. This division set the direction for all God's dealings in nature and in grace. Light and darkness are incompatible; to try to have both in the same place at once is to try the impossible and end by having neither the one nor the other, but dimness rather, and obscurity.

In the world of men there are at present scarcely any sharp outlines. The race is fallen. Sin has brought confusion. The wheat grows with the tares, the sheep and the goats coexist, the farms of the just and the unjust lie side by side in the landscape, the mission is next door to the saloon.

But things will not always be so. The hour is coming when the sheep will be divided from the goats and the tares separated from the wheat. God will again divide the light from the darkness and all things will run to their kind. Tares will go into the fire with tares and wheat into the garner with wheat. The dimness will lift like a fog and all outlines will appear. Hell will be seen to be hell all the way through, and heaven revealed as the one home of all who bear the nature of the one God.

For that time we with patience wait. In the meanwhile for each of us, and for the church wherever she appears in human society, the constantly recurring question must be: What shall we unite with and from what shall we separate? The question of coexistence does not enter here, but the question of union and fellowship does. The wheat grows in the same field with the tares, but shall the two cross-pollinate? The sheep graze near the goats, but shall they seek to interbreed? The unjust and the just enjoy the same rain and sunshine, but shall they forget their deep moral differences and intermarry?

To these questions the popular answer is *yes*. Union for union's sake, and men shall brothers be for a' that. Unity is so devoutly to be desired that no price is too high to pay for it and nothing is important enough to keep us apart. Truth is slain to provide a feast to celebrate the marriage of heaven and hell, and all to support a concept of unity which has no basis in the Word of God.

The Spirit-illuminated church will have none of this. In a fallen world like ours unity is no treasure to be purchased at the price of compromise. Loyalty to God, faithfulness to truth and the preservation of a good conscience are jewels more precious than gold of Ophir or diamonds from the mine. For these jewels men have suffered the loss of property, imprisonment and even death; for them, even in recent times, behind the various curtains, followers of Christ have paid the last full measure of devotion and quietly died, unknown to and unsung by the great world, but known to

God and dear to His Father heart. In the day that shall declare the secrets of all souls these shall come forth to receive the deeds done in the body. Surely such as these are wiser philosophers than the religious camp followers of meaningless unity who have not the courage to stand against current vogues and who bleat for brotherhood only because it happens to be for the time popular.

"Divide and conquer" is the cynical slogan of Machiavellian political leaders, but Satan knows also how to *unite* and conquer. To bring a nation to its knees the aspiring dictator must unite it. By repeated appeals to national pride or to the need to avenge some past or present wrong the demagogue succeeds in uniting the populace behind him. It is easy after that to take control of the military and to beat the legislature into submission. Then follows almost perfect unity indeed, but it is the unity of the stockyards and the concentration camp. We have seen this happen several times in this century, and the world will see it at least once more when the nations of the earth are united under Antichrist.

When confused sheep start over a cliff the individual sheep can save himself only by separating from the flock. Perfect unity at such a time can only mean total destruction for all. The wise sheep to save his own hide disaffiliates.

Power lies in the union of things similar and the division of things dissimilar. Maybe what we need in religious circles today is not more union but some wise and courageous division. Everyone desires peace but it could be that revival will follow the sword.

Artificial Divisions Are Harmful

IN THE PRECEDING CHAPTER I remarked on the usefulness of division in certain situations. But I want to explain further.

I feel that we evangelicals are making two serious mistakes. One is insisting upon union where it should not be, and the other is creating divisions artificially where there is no justification for them.

One blessed fact to be kept ever in mind is the organic unity of all true believers in Christ. However ill taught God's children may be on this subject and however widely separated by artificial barriers, they are nonetheless all members of Christ and as surely one as a man's hands and feet and eyes and ears are one by being members of his body. Unity in Christ is not something to be achieved; it is something to be recognized. I think Paul made this sufficiently clear in First Corinthians 12 and Ephesians 4.

The unity of believers was taken for granted by the church at Jerusalem. "And all that believed were together, and had all things common." This very well describes the first naive attitude of those early Christians. Paul, in his epistles, gave the theological explanation of this unity, but the fact preceded the explanation by some years.

In writing to the Ephesians the apostle did not exhort them to seek to achieve unity; he told them rather to try to keep the unity of the Spirit in the bonds of peace *because* there is one body, one Spirit, one hope, one Lord, one faith, one baptism and one God the Father of all. God's sons should act like brethren because they *are* brethren, not in order to become brethren.

Now for the very reason that the church is one body anything that tends to introduce division is an evil, however harmless, or even useful, it may appear to be. Yet the average evangelical church is divided into fragments which live and work separate from, and sometimes in opposition to, each other. In some churches there is simply no time or place for the worship and service of all members unitedly. These churches are organized to make such unity impossible.

Any belief or practice that causes the members of a local church to separate into groups on any pretext whatever is an evil. At first it may seem necessary to form such groups and it may be easy enough to show how many practical advantages follow these divisions; but soon the spirit of separateness unconsciously enters the minds of the persons involved and grows and hardens until it is impossible for them to think of themselves as belonging to the whole church. They may each and all hold the *doctrine* of unity, but the damage has been done; they *think* and *feel* themselves to be separated nevertheless.

One place where the evil manifests itself is in the practice of dividing the church into age groups.

ARTIFICIAL DIVISIONS ARE HARMFUL

As far as I can discover neither the Hebrew worshipers of Old Testament times nor the church of the New Testament ever divided into age groups to worship the Lord. The practice appears to have come in with the modern vogue of glorifying youth and downgrading age as something a bit disgraceful. And this, incidentally, followed the children's rebellion of the last half century, which rebellion was foreseen by the apostle Paul nineteen hundred years ago.

This age-youth division has gone so far in some churches that the old and the young glare at each other from different parts of the church and can have no spiritual fellowship whatsoever. If all are true Christians the basic unity has not been destroyed, but the *spirit* of unity has, with the result that the Lord is grieved and the church weakened. Yet much current religious education aids and abets division.

Another harmful thing is the dividing of Christians into groups crystallizing around their secular professions. So-called Christian guilds built around occupations, trades and professions cannot but be deeply injurious when they exist within a church. Where organizations are formed outside the local church to afford a center of fellowship within one or another secular field, such as student groups in universities or groups for the promotion of Christian fellowship and testimony in the military services, these have a useful function within our quasi-Christian society. They tend to unify, not divide, Christians, and do not come in for censure here.

Deeper and more far-reaching in its effects is the old practice of dividing the Christians in any communion into two classes, called respectively laymen and the clergy. This has grown out of a partial truth and is for that reason extremely hard to correct.

It is true that God has ordained that some in the church should be apostles, some prophets, some evangelists, some pastors and some teachers, and He has, furthermore, invested these with certain limited authority in the congregation of the saints; but the notion that they constitute a superior or privileged class is wholly wrong. They do not, but the exercise of their proper offices within the church easily leads to the idea that they do and this makes for division.

I have identified here only three artificial divisions; the alert reader will have no difficulty in carrying on his own examination of the injuries wrought by arbitrary divisions within the church.

The Responsibility of Leadership

THE HISTORY of Israel and Judah points up a truth taught clearly enough by *all* history, viz., that the masses are or soon will be what their leaders are. The kings set the moral pace for the people.

The public is never capable of acting en masse. Without a leader it is headless and a headless body is powerless. Always someone must lead. Even the mob engaged in pillage and murder is not the disorganized thing it appears to be. Somewhere behind the violence is a leader whose ideas it is simply putting into effect.

Israel sometimes rebelled against her leaders, it is true, but the rebellions were not spontaneous. The people merely switched to a new leader and followed him. The point is, they always had to have a leader.

Whatever sort of man the king turned out to be the people were soon following his leadership. They followed David in the worship of Jehovah, Solomon in the building of the Temple, Jeroboam in the making of a calf and Hezekiah in the restoration of the temple worship.

It is not complimentary to the masses that they are so easily led, but we are not interested in praising or blaming; we are concerned for truth, and the truth is that for better or for worse religious people follow leaders. A good man may change the moral complexion of a whole nation; or a corrupt and worldly clergy may lead a nation into bondage. The transposed proverb, "Like priest, like people," sums up in four words a truth taught plainly in the Scriptures and demonstrated again and again in religious history.

Today Christianity in the Western world is what its leaders were in the recent past and is becoming what its present leaders are. The local church soon becomes like its pastor, and this is true even of those groups who do not believe in pastors. The true pastor of such a group is not hard to identify; he is usually the one who can present the strongest argument against any church having a pastor. The strong-minded leader of the local group who succeeds in influencing the flock through Bible teaching or frequent impromptu talks in the public gatherings is the pastor, no matter how earnestly he may deny it.

The poor condition of the churches today may be traced straight to their leaders. When, as sometimes happens, the members of a local church rise up and turn their pastor out for preaching the truth, they are still following a leader. Behind their act is sure to be found a carnal (and often well-to-do) deacon or elder who usurps the right to determine who the pastor shall be and what he shall say twice each Sunday. In such cases the pastor is unable to lead the flock. He merely *works* for the leader; a pitiful situation indeed.

A number of factors contribute to bad spiritual leadership. Here are a few:

1. *Fear.* The wish to be liked and admired is strong even among the clergy, so rather than risk public disapproval the pastor is tempted simply to sit on his hands and smile ingratiatingly at the people. "The fear of man bringeth a snare," says the Holy Spirit, and nowhere more than in the ministry.

2. *The economic squeeze.* The Protestant ministry is notoriously underpaid and the pastor's family is often large. Put these two facts together and you have a situation ready-made to bring trouble and temptation to the man of God. The ability of the congregation to turn off the flow of money to the church when the man in the pulpit gets on their toes is well known. The average pastor lives from year to year barely making ends

meet. To give vigorous moral leadership to the church is often to invite economic strangulation, so such leadership is withheld. But the evil thing is that *leadership withheld is in fact a kind of inverted leadership*. The man who will not lead his flock up the mountainside leads it down without knowing it.

3. *Ambition*. When Christ is not all in all to the minister he is tempted to seek place for himself, and pleasing the crowds is a time-proved way to get on in church circles. Instead of leading his people where they ought to go he skillfully leads them where he knows they *want* to go. In this way he gives the appearance of being a bold leader of men, but avoids offending anyone, and thus assures ecclesiastical preferment when the big church or the high office is open.

4. *Intellectual pride*. Unfortunately there is in religious circles a cult of the intelligentsia which, in my opinion, is merely beatnikism turned wrong side out. As the beatnik, in spite of his loud protestations of individualism, is in reality one of the most slavish of conformists, so the young intellectual in the pulpit shakes in his carefully polished Oxfords lest he be guilty of saying something trite or common. The people look to him to lead them into green pastures but instead he leads them in circles over a sandy desert.

5. *Absence of true spiritual experience*. No one can lead another farther than he himself has gone. For many ministers this explains their failure to lead. They simply do not know where to go.

6. *Inadequate preparation*. The churches are cluttered with religious amateurs culturally unfit

to minister at the altar, and the people suffer as a consequence. They are led astray and are not aware of it.

The rewards of godly leadership are so great and the responsibilities of the leader so heavy that no one can afford to take the matter lightly.

The Way of Christ Is Still Narrow

WE WHO FOLLOW Christ in these perilous times are engaged in a war that has many fronts.

Action ebbs in one sector only to flare up in another or two or ten others. The enemy is everywhere, assuming many forms and taking at any given time whatever shape best serves his evil purposes, and he is for that reason often mistaken for a friend.

Traditionally fighting men have proudly worn the uniform of their country, and could be identified as far as they could be seen. In World War II the Nazis sometimes donned the uniforms of Allied soldiers and thus managed to destroy some who would otherwise have been on the defensive against them. But this trick was no Nazi invention. It dates back to that hour when the devil in the guise of a friend won the confidence of Mother Eve and brought about the downfall of the race.

Deception has always been an effective weapon

and is deadliest when used in the field of religion. Our Lord warned against this when He said, "Beware of false prophets, which come to you in sheep's clothing, but inwardly they are ravening wolves." These words have been turned into a proverb known around the world, and still we continue to be taken in by the wolves.

There was a time, no longer ago than the twenties and thirties, when a Christian knew, or at least could know, where he stood. The words of Christ were taken seriously. A man either was or was not a believer in New Testament doctrine. Clear, sharp categories existed. Black stood in sharp contrast to white; light was separated from darkness; it was possible to distinguish right from wrong, truth from error, a true believer from an unbeliever. Christians knew that they must forsake the world, and there was for the most part remarkable agreement about what was meant by the world. It was that simple.

But over the last score of years a quiet revolution has taken place. The whole religious picture has changed. Without denying a single doctrine of the faith, multitudes of Christians have nevertheless forsaken the faith and are as far astray as the Modernists, who were at least honest enough to repudiate the Scriptures before they began to violate them.

Many of our best-known preachers and teachers have developed ventriloquial tongues and can now make their voices come from any direction. They have surrendered the traditional categories of religious thought. For them there is no black or white, there is only gray. Anyone who makes a claim to having "accepted Christ" is admitted at once into the goodly fellowship of the prophets and the glorious company of the apostles regardless of the worldliness of his life or the vagueness of his doctrinal beliefs.

I have listened to certain speakers and have recognized the ingredients that went to make up their teachings. A bit of Freud, a dash of Émile Coué, a lot of watered-down humanism, tender chunks of Emersonian transcendentalism, autosuggestion à la Dale Carnegie, plenty of hopefulness and religious sentimentality, but nothing hard and sharp and specific. Nothing of the either/or of Christ and Peter and Paul. None of the "Who is on the Lord's side" of Moses, or the "Choose you this day whom ye will serve" of Joshua: just tender pleading to "take Jesus and let Him solve your problems."

If such as I here describe were cultists or liberals of one stripe or another I would say nothing more about it, but many of them are professed evangelicals. Press them and they will insist that they believe the Scriptures and accept every tenet of the historic Christian faith, but listen to them teach and you are left wondering. They are building upon sand; the rock of sound theology is not under them.

The notion is now pretty well disseminated throughout the ranks of current evangelicalism that love is really all that matters and for that reason we ought to receive everyone whose intention is right, regardless of his doctrinal position, granted of course that he is ready to read the Scriptures, trust Jesus and pray. The unregenerate sympathies of the fallen human heart adopt this foggy creed eagerly. The trouble is that the Holy Scriptures teach nothing of the kind.

The apostle Paul warned against what he called "profane and vain babblings," as for instance that of Hymenaeus and Philetus, stating that their words would eat as doth a canker and overthrow the faith of some. And what was their error? They merely taught a spiritual resurrection instead of a physical one.

"If a man hath the mind to get the start of other sinners and be in hell before them," said an old divine, "he need do no more than open his sails to the winds of heretical doctrine, and he is like to make a short voyage to hell; for these bring upon their maintainers a swift destruction."

This is nearer to Paul's view than is that of the new evangelical latitudinarians. The way of the cross is still narrow.

The Best Things Come Hard

IN THIS TWISTED WORLD of ours the most important things are often the most difficult to learn; and conversely, the things that come easiest are mostly of little real value to us in the long haul.

This is seen clearly in the Christian life, where it often happens that the things we learn to do with the least trouble are the superficial and less important activities, and the really vital exercises tend to be avoided because of their difficulty.

It is seen still more clearly in our various forms of Christian service, particularly in the ministry. There the most difficult activities are the ones that produce the greatest fruit, and the less fruitful services are performed with the least effort. This constitutes a trap into which the wise minister will not fall, or if he should find that he is already caught in it he will assault heaven and earth in his determined fight to escape.

To pray successfully is the first lesson the preacher must learn if he is to preach fruitfully; yet prayer is the hardest thing he will ever be called upon to do and, being human, it is the one act he will be tempted to do less frequently than any other. He must set his heart to conquer by prayer, and that will mean that he must first conquer his own flesh, for it is the flesh that hinders prayer always.

Almost anything associated with the ministry may be learned with an average amount of intelligent application. It is not hard to preach or manage church affairs or pay a social call; weddings and funerals may be conducted smoothly with a little help from Emily Post and the Minister's Manual. Sermon making can be learned as easily as shoemaking—introduction, conclusion and all. And so with the whole work of the ministry as it is carried on in the average church today.

But prayer—that is another matter. There Mrs. Post is helpless and the Minister's Manual can offer no assistance. There the lonely man of God must wrestle it out alone, sometimes in fastings and tears and weariness untold. There every man must be an original, for true prayer cannot be imitated nor can it be learned from someone else. Everyone must pray as if he alone could pray, and his approach must be individual and independent; independent, that is, of everyone but the Holy Ghost.

Thomas à Kempis says that the man of God ought to be more at home in his prayer chamber than before the public. It is not too much to say that the preacher who loves to be before the public is hardly prepared spiritually to be before them. Right praying may easily make a man hesitant to appear before an audience. The man who is really at home in the presence of God will find himself caught in a kind of inward contradiction. He is likely to feel his responsibility so keenly that he would rather do almost anything than face an audience; and yet the pressure upon his spirit may be so great that wild horses could not drag him away from his pulpit.

No man should stand before an audience who has not first stood before God. Many hours of communion should precede one hour in the pulpit. The prayer chamber should be more familiar than the public platform. Prayer should be continuous, preaching but intermittent.

It is significant that the schools teach everything about preaching except the important part, praying. For this weakness the schools are not to be blamed, for the reason that prayer cannot be taught; it can only be done. The best any school or any book (or any article) can do is to recommend prayer and exhort to its practice. Praying itself must be the work of the individual. That it is the one religious work which gets done with the least enthusiasm cannot but be one of the tragedies of our times.

Honesty in Prayer

THE SAINTLY David M'Intyre, in his radiant little book, *The Hidden Life of Prayer,* deals frankly, if briefly, with a vital element of true prayer which in our artificial age is likely to be overlooked.

We mean just plain honesty.

"Honest dealing becomes us," says M'Intyre, "when we kneel in His pure presence."

"In our address to God," he continues, "we like to speak of Him as we think we ought to speak, and there are times when our words far outrun our feelings. But it is best that we should be perfectly frank before Him. He will allow us to say anything we will, so long as it is to Himself. 'I will say unto God, my rock,' exclaims the psalmist, 'why hast thou forgotten me?' If he had said, 'Lord, thou canst not forget. Thou hast graven my name on the palms of thy hands,' he would have spoken more worthily, but less truly.

"On one occasion Jeremiah failed to interpret God aright. He cried as if in anger, 'O Lord, thou hast deceived me, and I was deceived.' These are terrible words to utter before Him who is changeless truth. But the prophet spoke as he felt, and the Lord not only pardoned him, but met him and blessed him there.''

So far M'Intyre. Another spiritual writer of unusual penetration has advised frankness in prayer even to a degree that might appear to be downright rudeness. When you come to prayer, he says, and find that you have no taste for it, tell God so without mincing words. If God and spiritual things bore you, admit it frankly. This advice will shock some squeamish saints, but it is altogether sound nevertheless. God loves the guileless soul even when in his ignorance he is actually guilty of rashness in prayer. The Lord can soon cure his ignorance, but for insincerity no cure is known.

The basic artificiality of civilized human beings is hard to shake off. It gets into our very blood and conditions our thoughts, attitudes and relationships much more seriously than we imagine. A book on human relations has appeared within recent years whose underlying philosophy is deception and whose recommended technique is a skillful use of flattery to gain desired ends. It has had an unbelievably wide sale, actually running into the millions. Of course its popularity may be explained by the fact that it said what people wanted to hear.

The desire to make a good impression has become one of the most powerful of all the factors determining human conduct. That gracious (and scriptural) social lubricant called courtesy has in our times degenerated into a completely false and phony etiquette that hides the true man under a shimmery surface as thin as the oil slick on a quiet pond. The only time some persons expose their real self is when they get mad.

With this perverted courtesy determining almost everything men say and do in human society it is not surprising that it should be hard to be completely honest in our relations with God. It carries over as a kind of mental reflex and is present without our being aware of it. Nevertheless, it is extremely hateful to God. Christ detested it and condemned it without mercy when He found it among the Pharisees. The artless little child is still the divine model for all of us. Prayer will increase in power and reality as we repudiate all pretense and learn to be utterly honest before God as well as before men.

A great Christian of the past broke out all at once into a place of such radiance and victory as to excite wonder among his friends. Someone asked him what had happened to him. He replied simply that his new life of power began one day when he entered the presence of God and took a solemn vow never again to say anything to God in prayer that he did not mean. His transformation began with that vow and continued as he kept it.

We can learn something there if we will.

The Era of an Absentee God

"THERE ARE over many who have much knowledge and little virtue," said the blind saint, Malaval, "and who often speak of God while rarely speaking to Him."

These words were written a long time ago; whether they were true of Christians in Malaval's day I am not able to say; we have but his word for it. But I can testify that they describe vast numbers of Christians today.

The Bible teaches plainly enough the doctrine of the divine omnipresence, but for the masses of professed Christians this is the era of the Absentee God. Most Christians speak of God in the manner usually reserved for a departed loved one, rarely as of one present; but they do not often speak to Him.

Since errors are not equally harmful I suppose it is better to think of God as existing in some remote region of a lonely universe than not to think of Him at all or, worse, to deny outright that there is any such being as God. But truth is always better than error, and with the inspired Scriptures before us we need not think wrongly about such an important matter as this. We can know the truth if we will.

An Absentee God is among other things inadequate. He does not meet the needs of the being called man. As a baby is not satisfied away from its mother, and as life on earth is impossible without the sun, so human beings need a present God, and they can be neither healthy nor satisfied without Him. Surely God would not have created us to be satisfied with nothing less than His presence if He had intended that we should get on with nothing more than His absence. No. The Scriptures and moral reason agree that God is present.

Adam and his wife hid themselves from the presence of the Lord among the trees of the garden. Their fear and chagrin for the moment overcame their conscious need of God. Sin never feels comfortable in the divine presence. Jonah, in his determined refusal to obey God's command, rose up to flee to Tarshish from the presence of the Lord. Peter, with a sudden acute consciousness of personal guilt, sought not to flee from the Lord's presence but begged the Lord instead to depart from him. Men need God above everything else, yet are uncomfortable in His presence. This is the self-contradictory moral situation sin has brought us into.

A convinced atheist is more logical than a Christian who tries to worship an Absentee God. The atheist can ignore all moral and religious precepts without fear because he believes that there is no God to call him to account. His mental state is the same as that of a burglar who has talked himself into the belief that there are no policemen, no courts and no jails. Both may enjoy peace of mind for a while—till the truth catches up with them.

The notion that there is a God but that He is comfortably far away is not embodied in the doctrinal statement of any Christian church. Anyone who dared admit that he held such a creed would be considered a heretic and avoided by respectable religious people; but our actions, and especially our spontaneous utterances, reveal our true beliefs better than any conventional creed can do, and if we are to judge by these then I think it can hardly be denied that the average Christian thinks of God as being at a safe distance looking the other way.

One advantage gained from thinking of God as being absent is that we may assume that He is pleased with whatever we may be trying to do, as long as it is not downright wicked. There would seem to be no other way to account for the vast amount of religious nonsense being carried on these days in the name of the Lord. Ambitious persons burned up with desire to promote the kingdom hatch up religious schemes so moronic as to be altogether beyond credibility, and which would never be believed by serious-minded persons if they were not put on display in every city, town and hamlet throughout the country.

Since Protestants have no pope to keep them in line and since God is too far away to be consulted, the only limit to our modern religious folly is the amount the people will stand; and present indications are that they will stand plenty and pay for it, too. That the divine method and manner for evangelizing the world and conducting public services are set forth in the Holy Scriptures never seems to occur to the busy planners whom an Absentee God has left in charge of His affairs while He is away.

At the far end of the spectrum are the conventional churches. I think it is the deep-seated notion that God is absent that makes so many of our church services so insufferably dull. When true believers gather around a present Christ it is all but impossible to have a poor meeting. The drabbest sermon may be endured cheerfully when the sweet fragrance of Christ's presence fills the room. But nothing can save a meeting held in the name of an Absentee God.

Pragmatism Goes to Church

IT IS NOT by accident that the philosophy of pragmatism around the turn of the century achieved such wide popularity in the United States. The American temperament was perfect for it, and still is.

Pragmatism has a number of facets and can mean various things to various people, but basically it is the doctrine of the utility of truth. For the pragmatist there are no absolutes; nothing is absolutely good or absolutely true. Truth and morality float on a sea of human experience. If an exhausted swimmer can lay hold of a belief or an ethic, well and good; it may keep him afloat till he can get to shore; then it only encumbers him, so he tosses it away. He feels no responsibility to cherish truth for its own sake. It is there to serve him; he has no obligation to serve it.

Truth is to use. Whatever is useful is true for the user, though for someone else it may not be useful, so not true. The truth of any idea is its ability to produce desirable results. If it can show no such results it is false. That is pragmatism stripped of its jargon.

Now, since practicality is a marked characteristic of the American people they naturally lean strongly toward the philosophy of utility. Whatever will get things done immediately with a maximum of efficiency and a minimum of undesirable side effects must be good. The proof is that it succeeds; no one wants to argue with success.

It is useless to plead for the human soul, to insist that what a man can do is less important than what he is. When there are wars to be won, forests to be cleared, rivers to be harnessed, factories to be built, planets to be visited, the quieter claims of the human spirit are likely to go unregarded. The spectacular drama of successful deeds leaves the beholder breathless. Deeds you can see. Factories, cities, highways, rockets are there in plain sight, and they got there by the practical application of means to ends. So who cares about ideals and character and morals? These things are for poets, nice old ladies and philosophers. Let's get on with the job.

Now all this has been said, and said better, a few dozen times before, and I would not waste space on it here except that this philosophy of pragmatism has had and is having a powerful influence upon Christianity in the middle years of this century. And whatever touches the faith of Christ immediately becomes a matter of interest to me and, I hope, to my readers also.

The nervous compulsion to get things done is found everywhere among us. We are affected by a kind of religious tic, a deep inner necessity to accomplish something that can be seen and photographed and evaluated in terms of size, numbers, speed and distance. We travel a prodigious number of miles, talk to unbelievably large crowds, publish an astonishing amount of religious literature, collect huge sums of money, build vast numbers of churches and amass staggering debts for our children to pay. Christian leaders compete with each other in the field of impressive statistics, and in so doing often acquire peptic ulcers, have nervous breaks or die of heart attacks while still relatively young.

Right here is where the pragmatic philosophy comes into its own. It asks no embarrassing questions about the wisdom of what we are doing or even about the morality of it. It accepts our chosen ends as right and good and casts about for efficient means and ways to get them accomplished. When it discovers something that works it soon finds a text to justify it, "consecrates" it to the Lord and plunges ahead. Next a magazine article is written about it, then a book, and finally the inventor is granted an honorary degree. After that any question about the scripturalness of things or even the moral validity of them is completely swept away. You cannot argue with success. The method works; *ergo*, it must be good.

The weakness of all this is its tragic short-sightedness. It never takes the long view of religious activity, indeed it dare not do so, but goes cheerfully on believing that because it works it is both good and true. It is satisfied with present success and shakes off any suggestion that its works may go up in smoke in the day of Christ.

As one fairly familiar with the contemporary religious scene, I say without hesitation that a part, a very large part, of the activities carried on today in evangelical circles are not only influenced by pragmatism but almost completely controlled by it. Religious methodology is geared to it; it appears large in our youth meetings; magazines and books constantly glorify it; conventions are dominated by it; and the whole religious atmosphere is alive with it.

What shall we do to break its power over us? The answer is simple. *We must acknowledge the right of Jesus Christ to control the activities of His church.* The New Testament contains full instructions, not only about what we are to believe but what we are to do and how we are to go about doing it. *Any deviation from those instructions is a denial of the Lordship of Christ.*

I say the answer is simple, but it is not easy for it requires that we obey God rather than man, and that always brings down the wrath of the religious majority. It is not a question of knowing what to do; we can easily learn that from the Scriptures. It is a question of whether or not we have the courage to do it.

The Call to the Ministry

THE CHRISTIAN MINISTER, as someone has pointed out, is a descendant not of the Greek orator but of the Hebrew prophet.

The differences between the orator and the prophet are many and radical, the chief being that the orator speaks for himself while the prophet speaks for God. The orator originates his message and is responsible to himself for its content. The prophet originates nothing but delivers the message he has received from God who alone is responsible for it, the prophet being responsible to God for its delivery only. The prophet must hear the message clearly and deliver it faithfully, and that is indeed a grave responsibility; but it is to God alone, not to men.

It is a dubious compliment to a preacher to say that he is original. The very effort to be original has become a snare to many young men fresh out of seminary who feel that the old and tried ways are too dull for them. These reject the pure wheat of the Word and try to nourish their congregations on chaff of their own manufacture, golden chaff maybe, but chaff nevertheless that can never feed the soul.

I heard of one graduate of a theological school who determined to follow his old professor's advice and preach the Word only. His crowds were average. Then one day a cyclone hit the little town and he yielded to the temptation to preach on the topic "Why God Sent the Cyclone to Centerville." The church was packed. This shook the young preacher and he went back to ask his professor for further advice in the light of what had happened. Should he continue to preach the Word to smaller crowds or try to fill his church by preaching sermons a bit more sensational? The old man did not change his mind. "If you preach the Word," he told the inquirer, "you will always have a text. But if you wait for cyclones you will not have enough to go around."

The true preacher is a man of God speaking to men; he is a man of heaven giving God's witness on earth. Because he is a man of God he can speak from God. He can decode the message he receives from heaven and deliver it in the language of earth.

The response earth gives to the message of heaven at any given time varies with the moral conditions of those to whom it is addressed. The true messenger of God is not always successful as men judge success. The message delivered in power has sometimes returned to destroy the messenger, as witness the slain prophets of Israel in Old Testament times, and Stephen, the first Christian martyr.

The true minister is one not by his own choice but by the sovereign commission of God. From a study of the Scriptures one might conclude that the man God calls seldom or never surrenders to the call without considerable reluctance. The young man who rushes too eagerly into the pulpit at first glance seems to be unusually spiritual, but he may in fact only be revealing his lack of understanding of the sacred nature of the ministry.

The old rule, "Don't preach if you can get out of it," if correctly understood, is still a good one. The call of God comes with an insistence that will not be denied and can scarcely be resisted. Moses fought his call strenuously and lost to the compulsion of the Spirit within him; and the same may be said of many others in the Bible and since Bible times. Christian biography shows that many who later became great Christian leaders at first tried earnestly to avoid the burden of the ministry; but I cannot offhand recall one single instance of a prophet's having applied for the job. The true minister simply surrenders to the inward pressure and cries, "Woe is unto me, if I preach not the gospel!"

While there is only one way to become a true preacher, unfortunately there are many doors into the pulpit. One is to be endowed with what is sometimes called a "good pulpit presence." Many a tall Absalom whose commanding presence and sonorous voice mark him as a natural leader of men is attempting to speak for God when he has not been sent by God. His call is from the people instead of from the Spirit and the results cannot but be disastrous.

Others have become ministers from a genuine but altogether human love for mankind. These have a strong sense of social obligation which they feel they can best discharge by entering the ministry. Of all wrong reasons for becoming a preacher this would seem to be the most laudatory, but it is nevertheless not a spiritually valid reason, for it overlooks the sovereign right of the Holy Spirit to call whom He will.

Most surely the church has a service of compassion to render to the world, but her motives are not humanitarian. They are higher than this by as much as the new creation is higher than the old. It is inherent in the Christian spirit that the followers of Christ should wish to minister to the bodies as well as the souls of men. But the call to give God's prophetic message to the world is something apart.

The call to witness and serve comes to every Christian; the call to be a Voice to mankind comes only to the man who has the Spirit's gift and special enabling. We need not fewer men to show mercy, but we need more men who can hear the words of God and translate them into human speech.

Perils of the Preacher

SOME OCCUPATIONS have built-in hazards, such as that of the coal miner, the deep-sea diver and the steeple jack. Everyone knows that the men who follow these pursuits are in at least some degree of danger most of the time.

Contrasted with these the work of the ministry

would appear to carry with it no danger at all. For physical hazard the ministry stands just about at the bottom of the list and the minister is considered one of the best actuarial risks any insurance company can handle.

Yet the ministry is one of the most perilous of professions. The devil hates the Spirit-filled minister with an intensity second only to that which he feels for Christ Himself. The source of this hatred is not difficult to discover. An effective, Christlike minister is a constant embarrassment to the devil, a threat to his dominion, a rebuttal of his best arguments and a dogged reminder of his coming overthrow. No wonder he hates him.

Satan knows that the downfall of a prophet of God is a strategic victory for him, so he rests not day or night devising hidden snares and deadfalls for the ministry. Perhaps a better figure would be the poison dart that only paralyzes its victim, for I think that Satan has little interest in killing the preacher outright. An ineffective, half-alive minister is a better advertisement for hell than a good man dead. So the preacher's dangers are likely to be spiritual rather than physical, though sometimes the enemy works through bodily weaknesses to get to the preacher's soul.

There are indeed some very real dangers of the grosser sort which the minister must guard against, such as love of money and women; but the deadliest perils are far more subtle than these. So let's concentrate on them.

There is, for one, the danger that the minister shall come to think of himself as belonging to a privileged class. Our "Christian" society tends to increase this danger by granting the clergy discounts and other courtesies, and the church itself helps a bad job along by bestowing upon men of God various sonorous honorifics which are either comical or awe-inspiring, depending upon how you look at them.

Seeing whose name he bears, the unconscious acceptance of belonging to a privileged class is particularly incongruous for the minister. Christ came to give, to serve, to sacrifice and to die, and said to His disciples, "As my Father hath sent me, even so send I you." The preacher is a servant of the Lord and of the people. He is in great moral peril when he forgets this.

Another danger is that he may develop a perfunctory spirit in the performance of the work of the Lord. Familiarity may breed contempt even at the very altar of God. How frightful a thing it is for the preacher when he becomes accustomed to his work, when his sense of wonder departs, when he gets used to the unusual, when he loses his solemn fear in the presence of the High and Holy One; when, to put it bluntly, he gets a little bored with God and heavenly things.

If anyone should doubt that this can happen let him read the Old Testament and see how the priests of Jehovah sometimes lost their sense of divine mystery and became profane even as they performed their holy duties. And church history reveals that this tendency toward perfunctoriness did not die with the passing of the Old Testament order. Secular priests and pastors who keep the doors of God's house for bread are still among us. Satan will see to it that they are, for they do the cause of God more injury than a whole army of atheists would do.

There is the danger also that the preacher may suffer alienation of spirit from the plain people. This arises from the nature of institutionalized Christianity. The minister meets religious people almost exclusively. People are on their guard when they are with him. They tend to talk over their own heads and to be for the time the kind of persons they think he wants them to be rather than the kind of persons they are in fact. This creates a world of unreality where no one is quite himself, but the preacher has lived in it so long that he accepts it as real and never knows the difference.

The results of living in this artificial world are disastrous. There are no more casual conversations, there are only "conferences"; there are no more plain people such as our Lord loved so well, there are only "cases" and people with "problems." The simple, unaffected candor that should characterize all relationships between the Christian and his fellow men is lost and the church is turned into a religious clinic. The Holy Spirit cannot work in such an atmosphere, and this in the end is calamitous, for without Him the work of the ministry becomes wood, hay and stubble.

Then there is always the danger that the minister may suffer detachment of sympathy and his attitude become abstract and academic, so that he loves mankind without loving people. Christ was the exact opposite of this. He loved babies, publicans, harlots and sick people, and He loved them spontaneously and individually. The man who claims to follow Him cannot afford to do otherwise.

Another peril that confronts the minister is that he may come unconsciously to love religious and philosophic ideas rather than saints and sinners. It is altogether possible to feel for the world of lost men the same kind of detached affection that the naturalist Fabre, say, felt for a hive of bees or a hill of black ants. They are something to study, to learn from, possibly even to help, but nothing to weep over or die for.

Where this attitude prevails it soon leads to a stilted and pedantic kind of preaching. The minister assumes that his hearers are as familiar with history, philosophy and theology as he is, so he indulges in learned allusions, makes casual reference to books and writers wholly unknown to the majority of the people who listen to him, and mistakes the puzzled expression on the faces of his parishioners for admiration of his brilliance.

Why religious people continue to put up with this sort of thing, as well as to pay for it and support it, is beyond me. I can only add it to the long list of things I do not and probably never will understand.

Another trap into which the preacher is in danger of falling is that he may do what comes naturally and just take it easy. I know how ticklish this matter is and, while my writing this will not win me friends, I hope it may influence people in the right direction. It is easy for the minister to be turned into a privileged idler, a social parasite with an open palm and an expectant look. He has no boss within sight; he is not often required to keep regular hours, so he can work out a comfortable pattern of life that permits him to loaf, putter, play, doze and run about at his pleasure. And many do just that.

To avoid this danger the minister should voluntarily impose upon himself a life of labor as arduous as that of a farmer, a serious student or a scientist. No man has any right to a way of life less rugged than that of the workers who support him. No preacher has any right to die of old age if hard work will kill him.

Perhaps it should be said, however, that some men of God have learned to labor in the Holy Spirit and have thus escaped both idleness and death by exhaustion, and have lived to a great age. Such men were Moses and Samuel in olden times and men like John Wesley, Bishop Asbury, A. B. Simpson and Pastor Philpott of more recent times. These wrought mighty deeds without injuring their constitutions, but not every man has been able to find their secret. Charles Finney taught frankly that a man of God could hasten his end by carrying the burdens of a backslidden church, and he exonerated the preacher and blamed the church. Whether we agree with him or not, he is still a man whose convictions are not to be taken lightly.

Again, the usefulness of any minister may be greatly impaired by either of two opposite sins—too great flexibility or too great rigidity. Between these two rocks there is a deep, clear channel, and blessed is the man who finds it.

To bend to the wishes of an unspiritual congregation on matters of morals or doctrine is a dark evil; to modify the sermon to please a carnal deacon is a deep sin; but to refuse to compromise on trivial matters reveals a spirit altogether out of harmony with that described by James in the third chapter of his epistle: "But the wisdom that is from above is first pure, then peaceable, gentle, and easy to be intreated, full of mercy and good fruits, without partiality, and without hypocrisy."

The evil of too great rigidity was noted by Thomas à Kempis: "True it is that everyone willingly doeth that which agreeth with his own liking, and inclineth most to those that are of his own mind . . . but if God be among us we must sometimes cease for the sake of peace to adhere to our own opinion. Who is so wise that he can know all things? Be not therefore too confident in thine own opinion; but be willing to hear the judgment of others."

Two other perils to the man of God should be mentioned, and these also are opposites. One is to be elated by success and the other to be cast down by failure.

These may strike the reader as being trivial, but the history of the Christian ministry will not support this conclusion. They are critically dangerous and should be guarded against with great care. The disciples returned to Christ with brimming enthusiasm, saying, "Lord, even the devils are subject unto us through thy name," and He quickly reminded them of another being who had allowed success to go to his head. "I beheld Satan as lightning fall from heaven," He said. "In this rejoice not, that the spirits are subject unto you; but rather rejoice, because your names are written in heaven."

The second of these twin dangers need not be labored. Every minister of the gospel knows how hard it is to stay spiritual when his work appears to be fruitless. Yet he is required to rejoice in God as certainly when he is having a bad year as when he is seeing great success.

It is not my purpose here to accuse or belittle, but to point out dangers. We are all objects of the malicious hatred of the devil, and we are safe only as we are willing to humble ourselves and accept help from each other, possibly even from one who is as weak and who stands daily in as great peril as this writer.

Goodness and Greatness

WHEN THE MISTS have cleared away and all things appear in their proper light I think it will be revealed that goodness and greatness are synonymous. I do not see how it could be otherwise in a moral world.

In the meantime the two qualities are not the same but can be separated, and indeed are often contrary one to the other.

Judged by our tentative human standards mankind may be divided into four distinct classes: Those who are great but not good; those who are good but not great; those who are both great and good, and those who are neither good nor great. In the Bible they stand out with great clarity.

Among those who were *great and good* is Abraham the Hebrew. By goodness here I mean moral soundness within the framework of the individual's understanding of it. Abraham was not perfect according to Christian standards, but his moral character nevertheless rose above that of his contemporaries like a mountain peak above the hills below.

For the greatness of the man no brief need be submitted here. He was a big man, a giant in a field of utmost importance, the field of religion. As the father of the faithful and founder of the nation of Israel his place has been long established.

In secular history it is not difficult to identify men who were *great but not good*. Three men of more recent times come at once to mind—Napoleon, Hitler and Stalin. However grudgingly we admit it, they were great men and must be acknowledged as such if we would be completely honest. A man who can forge out an empire, change radically the course of world history or hold in his iron control nearly a third of the human race must be called a great man, even a prodigy, regardless of what kind of personal character he may possess. And these men did these things. They were great but not good.

Then there are the men who are *good but not great,* and we may thank God that there are so many of them, being grateful not that they failed to achieve greatness but that by the grace of God they managed to acquire plain goodness.

These men move quietly enough across the pages of the Bible, but where they walk there is pleasant weather and good companionship. Such was Isaac, who was the son of a great father and the father of a great son, but who himself never rose above mediocrity. Such were Boaz the ancestor of King David, Joseph the husband of Mary, and Barnabas the son of consolation.

Every pastor knows this kind—the plain people who have nothing to recommend them but their deep devotion to their Lord and the fruit of the Spirit which they all unconsciously display. Without these the churches as we know them in city, town and country could not carry on. These are the first to come forward when there is work to be done and the last to go home when there is prayer to be made. They are not known beyond the borders of their own parish because there is nothing dramatic in faithfulness or newsworthy in goodness, but their presence is a benediction wherever they go. They have no greatness to draw to them the admiring eyes of carnal men but are content to be good men and full of the Holy Ghost, waiting in faith for the day that their true worth shall be known. When they die they leave behind them a fragrance of Christ that lingers long after the cheap celebrities of the day are forgotten.

The fourth class consists of persons who are *neither great nor good*. Into this class fall the majority of men.

A Bible example of this kind of man was Ahab, the king of Israel. True he had the external trappings of greatness; he was a king. But the very contrast between what he should have been and was serves but to accent the shabby, contemptible character of the man. Beneath his royal robes beats the heart of a weakling. This whimpering, sulking fellow was the craven tool of a strong but vicious wife who corrupted him and ruined his people. He has not one lonely virtue to commend him. He was neither good nor great.

At the other extreme are the millions of common people who can claim neither goodness nor greatness. Thomas Gray in his exquisite *Elegy* describes those who have been overlooked by the world.

> *"Far from the madding crowd's ignoble strife*
> *Their sober wishes never learned to stray;*
> *Along the cool sequestered vale of life*
> *They kept the noiseless tenor of their way."*

Beautiful as this thought is it yet represents what we want things to be rather than what they are. It raises tender feelings within us to dream of the noble masses of mankind living their hidden lives as pure as undiscovered gems and as fragrant as unseen flowers, but the hard facts are quite otherwise.

The masses of men are not great, but his does not argue them good. The truth is that they are almost without exception selfish, lustful, egotistical, opinionated, vain and afraid. If this appears a harsh judgment on my fellow men, please know that I claim for myself no inspiration, and commend my readers to an inspired apostle. Read Paul's words in Romans 3:9-19 and Ephesians 2:1-3.

It remains only to be said that not all men can be great, but all men are called to be good by the blood of the Lamb and the power of the Holy Ghost.

The Prayer of a Minor Prophet*
The covenant and prayer of a preacher

THIS IS THE PRAYER of a man called to be a witness to the nations. This is what he said to his Lord on the day of his ordination. After the elders and ministers had prayed and laid their hands on him he withdrew to meet his Saviour in the secret place and in the silence, farther in than his well-meaning brethren could take him.

And he said: O Lord, I have heard Thy voice and was afraid. Thou hast called me to an awesome task in a grave and perilous hour. Thou art about to shake all nations and the earth and also heaven, that the things that cannot be shaken may remain. O Lord, my Lord, Thou hast stooped to honor me to be Thy servant. No man taketh this honor upon himself save he that is called of God as was Aaron. Thou hast ordained me Thy messenger to them that are stubborn of heart and hard of hearing. They have rejected Thee, the Master, and it is not to be expected that they will receive me, the servant.

---

* Written in 1950, this chapter has been reprinted many times and widely circulated.

THE PRAYER OF A MINOR PROPHET

My God, I shall not waste time deploring my weakness nor my unfittedness for the work. The responsibility is not mine, but Thine. Thou hast said, "I knew thee—I ordained thee—I sanctified thee," and Thou hast also said, "Thou shalt go to all that I shall send thee, and whatsoever I command thee thou shalt speak." Who am I to argue with Thee or to call into question Thy sovereign choice? The decision is not mine but Thine. So be it, Lord. Thy will, not mine, be done.

Well do I know, Thou God of the prophets and the apostles, that as long as I honor Thee Thou wilt honor me. Help me therefore to take this solemn vow to honor Thee in all my future life and labors, whether by gain or by loss, by life or by death, and then to keep that vow unbroken while I live.

It is time, O God, for Thee to work, for the enemy has entered into Thy pastures and the sheep are torn and scattered. And false shepherds abound who deny the danger and laugh at the perils which surround Thy flock. The sheep are deceived by these hirelings and follow them with touching loyalty while the wolf closes in to kill and destroy. I beseech Thee, give me sharp eyes to detect the presence of the enemy; give me understanding to see and courage to report what I see faithfully. Make my voice so like Thine own that even the sick sheep will recognize it and follow Thee.

Lord Jesus, I come to Thee for spiritual preparation. Lay Thy hand upon me. Anoint me with the oil of the New Testament prophet. Forbid that I should become a religious scribe and thus lose my prophetic calling. Save me from the curse that lies dark across the face of the modern clergy, the curse of compromise, of imitation, of professionalism. Save me from the error of judging a church by its size, its popularity or the amount of its yearly offering. Help me to remember that I am a prophet—not a promoter, not a religious manager, but a prophet. Let me never become a slave to crowds. Heal my soul of carnal ambitions and deliver me from the itch for publicity. Save me from bondage to things. Let me not waste my days puttering around the house. Lay Thy terror upon me, O God, and drive me to the place of prayer where I may wrestle with principalities and powers and the rulers of the darkness of this world. Deliver me from overeating and late sleeping. Teach me self-discipline that I may be a good soldier of Jesus Christ.

I accept hard work and small rewards in this life. I ask for no easy place. I shall try to be blind to the little ways that could make life easier. If others seek the smoother path I shall try to take the hard way without judging them too harshly. I shall expect opposition and try to take it quietly when it comes. Or if, as sometimes it falleth out to Thy servants, I should have grateful gifts pressed upon me by Thy kindly people, stand by me then and save me from the blight that often follows. Teach me to use whatever I receive in such manner that will not injure my soul nor diminish my spiritual power. And if in Thy permissive providence honor should come to me from Thy church, let me not forget in that hour that I am unworthy of the least of Thy mercies, and that if men knew me as intimately as I know myself they would withhold their honors or bestow them upon others more worthy to receive them.

And now, O Lord of heaven and earth, I consecrate my remaining days to Thee; let them be many or few, as Thou wilt. Let me stand before the great or minister to the poor and lowly; that choice is not mine, and I would not influence it if I could. I am Thy servant to do Thy will, and that will is sweeter to me than position or riches or fame and I choose it above all things on earth or in heaven.

Though I am chosen of Thee and honored by a high and holy calling, let me never forget that I am but a man of dust and ashes, a man with all the natural faults and passions that plague the race of men. I pray Thee, therefore, my Lord and Redeemer, save me from myself and from all the injuries I may do myself while trying to be a blessing to others. Fill me with Thy power by the Holy Spirit, and I will go in Thy strength and tell of Thy righteousness, even Thine only. I will spread abroad the message of redeeming love while my normal powers endure.

Then, dear Lord, when I am old and weary and too tired to go on, have a place ready for me above, and make me to be numbered with Thy saints in glory everlasting. *Amen.* AMEN.

The Holy Spirit Is Indispensable

THE CONTINUED NEGLECT of the Holy Spirit by evangelical Christians is too evident to deny and impossible to justify.

Evangelical Christianity is Trinitarian: "Praise Father, Son and Holy Ghost" is sung in almost every church every Sunday of the year; and whether the singer realizes it or not he is acknowledging that the Holy Spirit is God indeed with equal claim to be worshiped along with the Father and the Son. Yet after this claim is sung at or near the beginning of the service little or nothing is heard of the Spirit again until the benediction. Why?

There is no single answer to this question. The historic church has not as a rule done much better than we. The Apostles' Creed dismisses the Holy Spirit with the words, "I believe in the Holy Ghost." Various other ancient creeds follow this one-sentence acknowledgment. The Nicene Creed goes a bit further, saying, "And in the Holy Spirit, the Lord and Life-giver, that proceedeth from the Father, who with Father and Son is worshipped together and glorified together, who spake through the prophets."

The Athanasian Creed, the fullest and most explicit of them all, attributes full deity to the Spirit, but while the right truth about the Father and the Son is set forth at considerable length in the document, the most that is said of the Spirit is this: "The Holy Ghost is of the Father and the Son: not made, nor created, nor begotten, but proceeding." The *Te Deum Laudamus*, that most famous and most beautiful of ancient Christian hymns, praises at great length the Father and the Son, but of the Spirit it says only, "Also, the Holy Ghost, the Comforter."

Is it not strange that so much is made of the Holy Spirit in the New Testament and so little in Christian writings supposed to be based upon the New Testament? One of the church fathers, in a treatise on the Trinity written in the third century, devotes to the Holy Spirit but six pages of a book 140 pages in length. While defending the deity of the Spirit he yet says twenty times as much about the Father and the Son as about the Spirit.

I think it would be only fair to admit that there is more in the New Testament about the Son than about the Spirit, but the disproportion is surely not so great as in the writings referred to above, and certainly the all but total neglect of the Spirit in contemporary Christianity cannot be justified by the Scriptures. The Spirit appears in the second verse of the first book of the Bible and in the last chapter of the last book of the Bible, as well as hundreds of times between the first and the last.

It is not, however, the frequency of the Spirit's mention in the Bible or in other writings that matters most, but the importance attached to Him when He is mentioned. And there can be no doubt that there is a huge disparity between the place given to the Spirit in the Holy Scriptures and the place He occupies in popular evangelical Christianity. In the Scriptures the Holy Spirit is necessary. There He works powerfully, creatively; here He is little more than a poetic yearning or at most a benign influence. There He moves in majesty, with all the attributes of the Godhead; here He is a mood, a tender feeling of good will.

According to the Scriptures everything God did in creation and redemption He did by His Spirit. The Spirit was found brooding over the world at the moment God called it into being. His presence there was necessary. The life-giving work of the Spirit is seen throughout the entire Bible; and it is precisely because He is the Lord and giver of life that the mystery of the Incarnation could occur. "The Holy Ghost shall come upon thee, and the power of the Highest shall overshadow thee: therefore also that holy thing which shall be born of thee shall be called the Son of God."

It is highly significant that our Lord, though He was very God of very God, did not work until He had been anointed with the Holy Spirit (Acts 10:38). The Son did His work of love as a Spirit-anointed Man; His power derived from the Spirit of power.

It has been wisely suggested that a more revealing title for The Acts of the Apostles would be The Acts of the Holy Spirit. The men whose mighty deeds are recorded there could have done not one lone act of power if they had not been filled with the Spirit. Indeed the Lord specifically forbade them to try to do anything in their own strength. "But tarry ye in the city of Jerusalem," He told them, "until ye be endued with power from on high."

The only power God recognizes in His church is the power of His Spirit whereas the only power actually recognized today by the majority of evangelicals is the power of man. God does His work by the operation of the Spirit, while Christian leaders attempt to do theirs by the power of trained and devoted intellect. Bright personality has taken the place of the divine afflatus.

Everything that men do in their own strength and by means of their own abilities is done for time alone; the quality of eternity is not in it. Only what is done through the Eternal Spirit will abide eternally; all else is wood, hay, stubble.

It is a solemn thought that some of us who fancy ourselves to be important evangelical leaders may find at last we have been but busy harvesters of stubble.

Religion Can Be a Front or a Fount

IF WE THINK of the Christian religion as faith in Christ, love toward God and loving service toward men we can readily see how it may be a fountain of sweet water springing up unto eternal life. And such it is surely meant to be.

On the other hand, if we think of religion as the outward profession of inward grace (and it must be that to some extent), then we can see how it may become a mere facade behind which there is no reality, a showcase containing everything in the store, the shelves inside being completely bare. The passerby never dreams how empty the interior is until he goes inside and takes a look around; then he will understand that the window display has been a front to hide the poverty of the owner.

If these remarks should seem unpleasantly realistic, remember that the burden of the Old Testament was the disparity between the external and the internal life of Israel, and much of the preaching of Christ was directed against the Jews for their failure to be inwardly what their outward profession proclaimed them to be. Paul, too, warned of those who had but a form of godliness without the corresponding substance, and the history of the church provides all the proof we need that the temptation to make a front of religion is very real and very strong. Our wisest course will be not timidly to skirt this subject, but to face up to it and deal with it courageously.

The tendency to make a mere front of religion is strongest among persons engaged in professional Christian service, such as pastors, evangelists, teachers, Sunday school workers and those who write, edit, publish and promote religion generally. The Christian worker must be always ready to lead in public prayer or to offer a "word of prayer" under all sorts of circumstances and in almost every imaginable situation. He must be ready with a spiritual epigram for all occasions and on a moment's notice must be able to come up with wise and devotional counsel for anyone who might ask for it. The necessity to say the godly thing at all times often forces him to display an enthusiasm he does not feel and to settle for others questions about which he is not too sure himself. His profession compels him to *seem* spiritual whether he is or not. Human nature being what it is, the man of God may soon adopt an air of constant piety and try to appear what the public thinks he is. The fixed smile and hollow tones of the professional cleric are too well known to require further mention.

All this show of godliness, by the squeeze of circumstances and through no fault of the man himself, may become a front behind which the man hides, a plaintive, secretly discouraged and lonely soul. Here is no hypocrisy, no intentional double living, no actual desire to deceive. The man has been mastered by the circumstances. He has been made the keeper of other people's vineyards but his own vineyard has not been kept. So many demands have been made upon him that they have long ago exhausted his supply. He has been compelled to minister to others while he himself is in desperate need of a physician.

While this condition prevails more widely than we like to admit, it must not be accepted as inevitable. There is a better, a truer, a happier way, and it is not hard to find. We need only be bold and frank about the whole thing and the remedy will soon be discovered.

Briefly, the way to escape religion as a front is to make it a fount. See to it that we pray more than we preach and we will never preach ourselves out. Stay with God in the secret place longer than we are with men in the public place and the fountain of our wisdom will never dry up. Keep our hearts open to the inflowing Spirit and we will not become exhausted by the outflow. Cultivate the acquaintance of God more than the friendship of men and we will always have abundance of bread to give to the hungry.

Our first responsibility is not to the public but to God and our own souls. Moses came down from the mount to speak to the people. Christ told His disciples to *tarry* before they *went*. Nicolas Grou refused to write a line until his heart was in a state of glowing worship. George Mueller would not step into the pulpit until he had first bathed his soul in prayer and was feeling within the stirrings of divine grace.

These men show us the way. It is by humility, simplicity and constant trustful communion with

God that we keep the fountain open within our hearts.

We Need Sanctified Thinkers

I

THE CHURCH TODAY is languishing for men who can bring to the problems of religion reverent, courageous minds intent upon a solution.

Unfortunately fundamentalism has never produced a great thinker. One may examine the output of the religious press since the turn of the century and not find a single book written by a fundamentalist Christian that gives evidence of any real independent thought. And as for those Christian scholars who, while thoroughly orthodox, yet do not care to be classed with the fundamentalists, they have done little better.

Let it be understood by everyone that I am now and have always been an evangelical. I accept the Bible as the very Word of God and believe with complete and restful confidence that it contains all things necessary to life and godliness. I embrace the tenets of the historical Christian faith without reservation and am conscious of no spiritual sympathy with liberalism in any of its manifestations. Yet it is my painful duty to record not only that I have not been challenged by the intellectual output of the evangelicals of this generation, but that I have found evidence of genuine religious thinking almost exclusively on the side of those who for one or another reason are in revolt against fundamentalism. We of the gospel churches have sat quietly by and allowed those on the other side to do all the thinking. We have been content to echo the words of other men and to repeat religious clichés *ad nauseam*.

By this I do not mean to assert that there have been no good or useful books produced in gospel circles in the last fifty years. Undoubtedly there have been. Many good doctrinal books have appeared, mainly expositions of the Pauline Epistles. Some excellent devotional works have also been written, as well as some good Christian biographies and a number of fine books on foreign missions, not to mention a whole raft of books on revival, written usually by persons who never saw a revival of more than local proportions. All these books have served some good end, no doubt, and we may in all sincerity be grateful for them; but the trouble with them is that they are no more than rehashes of other works that have appeared before them. They carry no evidence that they are in any sense original. They were put together out of pieces borrowed from others rather than born out of the anguish and joy of personal experience. They cost the authors nothing beyond the mechanical labor of writing them.

After committing myself to the foregoing sweeping statements I suppose I should provide myself with an escape hatch in case someone drops a depth charge in my vicinity. I admit that I am forced to speak within the framework of my own limited experience, and it could be that some great evangelical thinker has appeared unknown to me and written a masterpiece of which I have not yet heard. If this is so, then I am in error.

Again, if some of my readers should consider such a man as C. S. Lewis an original thinker, I might explain that I would classify Mr. Lewis as an apologist rather than as a creative religious writer. He brings to the defense of historic Christianity a mind as clear as sunlight and an amazing ability to make the faith of our fathers appear reasonable. His weakness, or rather the weakness of his books, lies in an almost total absence of moral urgency. One may read his arguments, admit their soundness and remain completely unmoved by the whole thing. In short, his books persuade the intellect but never get the conscience in trouble. For this reason C. S. Lewis must remain an apologist; he can never be a reformer.

While I am in my spiritual sympathies wholly on the side of the orthodox Christian faith, I am nevertheless forced to acknowledge that evangelicalism as it has been held and taught over the last half century has tended to paralyze the critical faculties and discourage vigorous thinking. Modern gospel Christians are parrots, not eagles, and rather than sail out and up to explore the illimitable ranges of the kingdom of God they are content to sit safe on their familiar perches and repeat in a bright falsetto religious words and phrases the meaning of which they scarcely understand at all. Another generation or two of this and what is now evangelicalism will be liberalism. No living thing can subsist for long on its yesterdays.

The Christians of this generation must see and hear something for themselves if they are to escape religious stultification. Effete catchwords cannot save them. Meanings are expressed in words, but it is one of the misfortunes of life that words tend to persist long after their meanings have departed, with the result that thoughtless men and women believe they have the reality because they have the word for it. That's where we are now.

II

The creative religious thinker is not a daydreamer, not an ivory tower intellectual carrying on his lofty cogitations remote from the rough world. He is more likely to be a troubled, burdened man weighed down by the woes of existence, occupied not with matters academic or theoretical but the practical and personal.

The great religious thinkers of the past were rarely men of leisure; mostly they were men of affairs, close to and very much a part of the troubled world. Neither will the sanctified thinker of our times be a poet gazing at a sunset from some quiet secluded spot, but one who feels himself a traveler lost in a wilderness who must find his way to safety. That others will later follow the path he makes will not be primary in his thinking. Later he will understand this, but for the time being he will be all engaged hunting the way out for himself.

WE NEED SANCTIFIED THINKERS

To think well and usefully a man must be endowed with certain indispensable qualifications. He must, for one thing, be completely honest and transparently sincere. The trifler is automatically eliminated. He is weighed in the balance and found too light to be entrusted with the thoughts of God. Let but a breath of levity enter the mind and the power to do creative thinking instantly goes out. And by levity I do not mean wit or even humor; I do mean insincerity, sham, the absence of moral seriousness. Great thoughts require a grace attitude toward life and mankind and God.

Another qualification is courage. The timid man dare not think lest he discover himself, an experience to him as shocking as the discovery that he has cancer. The sincere thinker comes to his task with the abandonment of a Saul of Tarsus, crying, "Lord, what wilt thou have me to do?" Thinking carries a moral imperative. The searcher for truth must be ready to obey truth without reservation or it will elude him. Let him refuse to follow the light and he dooms himself to darkness. The coward may be shrewd or clever but he can never be a wise thinker, for wisdom is at bottom a moral thing and will have no truck with evil.

Again, the effective religious thinker must possess some degree of knowledge. A Chinese saying has it, "Learning without thought is a snare; thought without learning is a danger." I have met Christians with sharp minds but limited outlook who saw one truth and, being unable to relate it to other truths, became narrow extremists, devoutly cultivating their tiny plot, naïvely believing that their little fence enclosed the whole earth.

An acquaintance with or at least a perception

of the significance of what Kant called "the starry heavens above and the moral law within" is necessary to right thinking. Add to this a thorough knowledge of the Scriptures, a good historic sense and some intimate contact with the Christian religion as it is practiced currently and you have the raw material for creative thought. Still, this is not enough to make a thinker.

Man is a worshiper and only in the spirit of worship does he find release for all the powers of his amazing intellect. A religious writer has warned us that it may be fatal to "trust to the squirrel-work of the industrious brain rather than to the piercing vision of the desirous heart." The Greek church father, Nicephorus, taught that we should learn to think with our heart. "Force your mind to descend into the heart," he says, "and to remain there . . . When you thus enter into the place of the heart give thanks to God and, praising His mercy, keep always to this doing, and it will teach you things which in no other way will you ever learn."

It is itself a cliché that the Christian faith is full of apparent self-contradictions commonly called paradoxes. One such paradox is the necessity to repudiate self and depend wholly upon God while at the same time having complete confidence in our own ability to receive and know and understand with the faculties God Himself has given us. That brand of humility which causes a man to distrust his own mentality to the point of moral diffidence and chronic irresolution is but a weak parody on the real thing. It is a serious reflection upon the wisdom and goodness of God to question

His handiwork. "Shall the clay say to him that fashioned it, What makest thou?"

A religious mentality characterized by timidity and lack of moral courage has given us today a flabby Christianity, intellectually impoverished, dull, repetitious and, to a great many persons, just plain boresome. This is peddled as the very faith of our fathers in direct lineal descent from Christ and the apostles. We spoon-feed this insipid pabulum to our inquiring youth and, to make it palatable, spice it up with carnal amusements filched from the unbelieving world. It is easier to entertain than to instruct, it is easier to follow degenerate public taste than to think for oneself, so too many of our evangelical leaders let their minds atrophy while they keep their fingers nimble operating religious gimmicks to bring in the curious crowds.

Well, I dare to risk a prophecy: The sheep are soon going to become weary both of the wilted clover we are giving them and the artificial color we are spraying over it to make it look fresh. And when they get sick enough to leave our pastures, the Pope, Father Divine, Mrs. Eddy and their kind will find them easy victims.

Christianity must embrace the total personality and command every atom of the redeemed being. We cannot withhold our intellects from the blazing altar and still hope to preserve the true faith of Christ.

The Wasp and the Church Member

ONCE WHILE WALKING among the hills of a southeastern state I noticed a piece of white paper lying by the roadside.

Its presence there was, under the circumstances, so unexpected that it aroused my curiosity. I picked it up and found written on it in a clear, legible hand these words: "In all the world there are only two creatures that are larger when they are born than when they get their growth; one is a wasp and the other is a church member."

Whether this was a lost gem taken from a sermon delivered in a church somewhere among the hills or in the nearby town, or whether it had been placed there by some friendly philosopher who had observed my approach and dropped it there for my edification I will probably never know, but I found it more than a little interesting.

Not being an apiarist I am unable to judge the truth of the statement that a baby wasp is larger than an adult one; but that part about the church member I find too true to be amusing or even comfortable.

Knowing the good people of the hills as I do, and being familiar with their religious terminology, I am sure that the writer of the epigram meant the term "church member" to be understood as synonymous with Christian, and intended to say that his experience had taught him that the average Christian lost "size" and became less a Christian later on than when he was first converted.

Why do so many enthusiastic new converts later run out of steam and settle down to a life of dull religious routine? Why do they lose their first zeal and accept the dead average of subnormal spirituality they see about them as the best they can hope to maintain in this present world? Why are they often "smaller" after they have been on the way for several years than they were when they first started on their journey toward the Celestial City?

Now I do not insist that my description applies to all Christians. In fact I think our epigrammatist was covering too much territory when he gave the impression that *all* church members get smaller as they get older. I do not think they all do, but the fact that *some* do is enough to disturb one who loves the church and carries the welfare of the saints on his heart; and the fact that *any* do calls for prayer and careful investigation.

Could it be that after a joyful conversion many have without knowing it become enamored of their experience instead of fixing their eyes upon the Lord? Then when the novelty wears off their experience the joy and enthusiasm go out of their lives. What they should be taught is that a true Christian is converted to Christ, not to peace or rest or joy. These things will come in their time, but they will go again unless the gaze is fixed upon Christ who is the source and fountain of all spiritual delights.

Every emotion has its reaction and every pleasurable experience will dim after a while. The human organism is built that way and there is nothing we can do about it. It is well known that the second year of marriage is often the most critical, for then the first excitement has worn off the relation and the young couple has not had time to acquire a new set of common interests and to learn to accept a more stable if less emotional kind of life.

Only engrossment with God can maintain perpetual spiritual enthusiasm because only God can supply everlasting novelty. In God every moment is new and nothing ever gets old. Of things religious we may become tired; even prayer may weary us; but God never. He can show a new aspect of His glory to us each day for all the days of eternity and still we shall have but begun to explore the depths of the riches of His infinite being.

If we offer our converts something beside Christ or something in addition to Christ we should not be disappointed if they do not run well or long. Novelty soon wears off everything, no matter how precious. When the interest begins to flag we try to recapture it by fiery exhortations. I for one admit that I am weary of the familiar religious pep talk. I am tired of being whipped into line, of being urged to work harder, to pray more, to give more generously, when the speaker does not show me Christ. This is sure to lead to a point of diminishing return and leave us exhausted and a little bored with it all. And from there we may easily grow backwards and become smaller and less fervent than when we were first converted.

I have spent many uncomfortable hours in prayer meetings listening to my brethren begging for blessings, but all prayer is comfortable when the heart is having fellowship with God and the inner eyes are looking upon His blessed face. I have suffered through many a dull and tedious sermon, but no sermon is poor or long when the preacher is showing me the beauty of Jesus. A sight of His face will inspire love and zeal and a longing to grow in grace and in the knowledge of God.

The sum of all this is that nothing can preserve the sweet savor of our first experience except to be preoccupied with God Himself. Our little rill is sure to run dry unless we keep it replenished from the fountain. Let the new convert know that if he would grow instead of shrink he must spend his nights and his days in communion with the Triune God.

Artificiality Is a Disease of the Soul

WHEN I WAS A YOUNG LAD and first beginning to observe the human scene one thing that struck me forcibly was the artificiality of preachers. The world they inhabited was, it seemed to me, always once removed from reality.

I was not brought up in a Christian home and so was not accustomed to the conventional language of religion, and when I chanced occasionally to hear a sermon I listened with an ear undulled by familiarity. How strange the preachers sounded to me, how artificial their tones and how unnatural their demeanor.

They were men, obviously, but they lacked completely the candor and downrightness I knew so well in other men. The bold, man-to-man approach was missing. They seemed to be afraid of something, though I could not tell what, for certainly the tame, patient, almost indifferent persons who listened to them were harmless enough. No one paid much attention to what they said anyway. I am sure that if one of them had slyly interspersed into his sermon stray bits of the Gettysburg Address repeated backwards few of those present would have noticed or cared. Yet they spoke so gingerly and apologetically that one got the impression that they would rather remain silent forever than to offend anyone. After listening to some of them now and again I knew the meaning of the French saying (though I did not hear it till many years later), "There are three sexes: men, women and preachers."

Now I am all for preachers and I do not expect them to be perfect, but I am all for downrightness, too. I think it highly improbable that anyone who speaks cautiously can speak effectively. His timidity will deactivate his effort and render it impotent.

ARTIFICIALITY IS A DISEASE OF THE SOUL

It is true that the church has suffered from pugnacious men who would rather fight than pray, but she has suffered more from timid preachers who would rather be nice than be right. The latter have done more harm if for no other reason than that there are so many more of them. I do not think, however, that we must make our choice between the two. It is altogether possible to have love and courage at the same time, to be both true and faithful. "Let your speech be alway with grace, seasoned with salt." It is the absence of salt that makes so much of our preaching vapid and dull. "Can that which is unsavoury be eaten without salt? or is there any taste in the white of an egg?"

Our theological schools may be at fault here. They strive to turn out preachers who will be all things to all men in a sense Paul never had in mind. They want their students to be cultured if it kills them and they begin by draining off all salt and leaving only a sweetness and light that appears to some of us to be neither sweet nor light. Everything natural is as far as possible refined away. All tang is eliminated from the speech, all angularity carefully filed off the language. The young man is trained to gesture gracefully, smile faintly and sound scholarly. The direct language that men naturally use when speaking to each other is edited out and a vague, stilted jargon is substituted for it. The total result is artificiality and ineffectiveness.

But back to my own experience: it was by the mercy of God that I was later permitted to hear an evangelist who was completely human and paid his hearers the compliment of assuming they were human too. He knew what he wanted to say and said it fearlessly; and the people knew what he meant and either took it or left it. Thank God a good number of them took it.

Every man who stands to proclaim the Word should speak with something of the bold authority of the Word itself. The Bible is the book of supreme love, but it is at the same time altogether frank and downright. Its writers are never rude or unkind, but they are invariably honest and entirely sincere. A great sense of urgency is upon everything they write. They are deeply concerned with moral decisions. Protocol is of less interest to them than the glory of God and the welfare of the people.

One is tempted to offer advice to the young preacher to prevent him from becoming a mere purveyor of artificial religious platitudes, but further consideration shows how useless that would be. One might urge him to study the best writers and speakers, to strive to be original, to look at and through things before speaking of them, to avoid cliches, to speak in the vernacular; but this is to miss the point entirely. Religious artificiality is not a technical thing but a deeply human and spiritual one. It is a disease of the soul and can only be healed by the Physician of souls.

To escape the snare of artificiality it is necessary that a man enjoy a satisfying personal experience with God. He must be totally committed to Christ and deeply anointed with the Holy Spirit. Further, he must be delivered from the fear of man. The focus of his attention must be God and not men. He must let everything dear to him ride out on each sermon. He must so preach as to jeopardize his future, his ministry, even his life itself. He must make God responsible for the consequences and speak as one who will not have long to speak before he is called to judgment. Then the people will know they are hearing a voice instead of a mere echo.

Wanted: Courage with Moderation*

SIN HAS DONE a pretty complete job of ruining us and the process of restoration is long and slow.

The works of grace in the individual life may be never so clear and definite, but it is indeed the labor of a God to bring the once fallen heart back into the divine likeness again. In nothing is this seen more plainly than in the great difficulty we experience in achieving spiritual symmetry in our lives. The inability of even the most devout souls to show forth the Christian virtues in equal proportion and without admixture of unChristlike qualities has been the source of heartache to how many of God's believing people.

The virtues before us, courage and moderation, when held in correct proportion, make for a well-balanced life and one of great usefulness in the kingdom of God. Where one is missing or present

_____

* This chapter appeared in *The Alliance Witness* (then *Weekly*) in July, 1946.

only in minute degree, the result is a life out of balance and powers wasted.

Almost any sincere writing, if examined closely, will be found to be autobiographic. We know best what we have ourselves experienced. This article is not an exception. I may as well admit frankly that it is autobiographic, for the discerning reader will discover the truth no matter how hard I may try to conceal it.

Briefly, I have seldom been called a coward, even by my most cordial enemies, but my want of moderation has sometimes caused grief to my dearest friends. An extreme disposition is not easy to tame, and the temptation to bring severe, immoderate methods to the aid of the Lord is one not easily resisted. The temptation is further strengthened by the knowledge that it is next to impossible to pin a preacher down and make him eat his words. There is a ministerial immunity accorded a man of God which may lead Boanerges into extravagant and irresponsible language unless he uses heroic measures to bring his nature under the sway of the Spirit of love. This I have sometimes failed to do, and always to my own real sorrow.

Here again the contrast between the ways of God and the ways of man is seen. Apart from such wisdom as painful experience may give, we are prone to try to secure our ends by direct attack, to rush the field and win by assault. That was Samson's way, and it worked well except for one minor oversight: it slew the victor along with the vanquished! There is a wisdom in the flank attack, but a wisdom which the rash spirit is likely to reject.

Of Christ it was said, "He shall not strive, nor cry; neither shall any man hear his voice in the streets. A bruised reed shall he not break, and smoking flax shall he not quench, till he send forth judgment into victory." He achieved His tremendous purposes without undue physical exertion and altogether without violence. His whole life was marked by moderation; yet He was of all men the most utterly courageous. He could send back word to Herod who had threatened Him, "Go ye, and tell that fox, Behold, I cast out devils, and I do cures today and tomorrow, and the third day I shall be perfected." There is consummate courage here, but no defiance, no sign of contempt, no extravagance of word or act. He had courage with moderation.

The failure to achieve balance between these virtues has caused much evil in the church through the years, and the injury is all the greater when church leaders are involved. Lack of courage is a grave fault and may be a real sin when it leads to compromise in doctrine or practice. To sit back for the sake of peace and allow the enemy to carry off the sacred vessels from the temple is never the part of a true man of God. Moderation to the point of surrender where holy things are concerned is certainly not a virtue; but pugnacity never yet won when the battle was a heavenly one. The fury of man never furthered the glory of God. There is a right way to do things, and it is never the violent way. The Greeks had a famous saying: "Moderation is best"; and the homely proverb of the American farmer, "Easy does it," has in it a wealth of profound philosophy.

God has used, and undoubtedly will yet use

men in spite of their failure to hold these qualities in proper balance. Elijah was a man of courage; no one could doubt that, but neither would anyone be so rash as to claim that he was a man of patience or moderation. He carried the day by assault, by challenge, and was not above satire and abuse when he thought it would help things; but when the enemy was confounded he went into a tailspin and sank into the depths of despair. That is the way of the extreme nature, of the man of courage without moderation.

Eli, on the other hand, was a man of moderation. He could not say "no" even to his own family. He loved a weak peace, and stark tragedy was the price he paid for his cowardice. Both these men were good men, but they could not find the happy mean. Of the two, the fiery Elijah was certainly the greater man. It is painful to think what Eli would have done in Elijah's circumstances. And I could pity even Hophni and Phinehas if Elijah had been their father!

This leads us logically to think of Paul, the apostle. Here is a man whom we need never take at a discount. He seems to have had an almost perfect courage along with a patient disposition and a forbearance truly Godlike. What he might have been apart from grace is seen in the brief description given of him before his conversion. After he had helped to stone Stephen to death, he went out Christian hunting, "breathing out threatenings and slaughter." Even after his conversion he was capable of summary judgments when he felt strongly on a question. His curt rejection of Mark after he had gone back from the work was an example of his short way of dealing with men in whom he had lost confidence. But time and suffering and an increasing intimacy with the patient Saviour seems to have cured this fault in the man of God. His later days were sweet with love and fragrant with forbearance and charity. So should it be with all of us.

It is a significant thing that the Bible gives no record of a coward ever being cured of his malady. No "timid soul" ever grew into a man of courage. Peter is sometimes cited as an exception, but there is nothing in his record that would mark him as a timid man either before or after Pentecost. He did touch the borderline once or twice, it is true, but for the most part he was a man of such explosive courage that he was forever in trouble by his boldness.

How desperately the church at this moment needs men of courage is too well known to need repetition. Fear broods over the church like some ancient curse. Fear for our living, fear of our jobs, fear of losing popularity, fear of each other: these are the ghosts that haunt the men who stand today in places of church leadership. Many of them, however, win a reputation for courage by repeating safe and expected things with comical daring.

Yet self-conscious courage is not the cure. To cultivate the habit of "calling a spade a spade" may merely result in our making a nuisance of ourselves and doing a lot of damage in the process. The ideal seems to be a quiet courage that is not aware of its own presence. It draws its strength each moment from the indwelling Spirit and is hardly aware of *self* at all. Such a courage will be patient also and well-balanced and safe

115

from extremes. May God send a baptism of such courage upon us.

We All Think in Circles

MINISTERS and religious writers are often blamed for repeating themselves. The implication is that an idea, once it has been annunciated, should be left behind and mentioned no more forever, the notion being, apparently, that ideas are like birthdays: nobody can have the same one twice, or if he does, there is something wrong with his memory or his honesty.

The truth is that we all think in circles. It is totally impossible for anyone to take off on a train of thought and move away in a straight line from the point of departure. We are all compelled by the structure of our minds to move around a circle, passing every so often the same ideas, which appear to us as loved and familiar landmarks.

There are accessible to mankind only a relatively few ideas, and these make up the whole fabric of human thought possible to anyone from a schoolboy to Plato. New *facts* may be added to the sum of our knowledge day by day to the end of our lives, but these can do no more than enlarge the tapestry somewhat; they cannot change the color or alter the pattern appreciably. Greatness lies in the ability to combine and recombine the old and familiar ideas to form new and "original" beauties.

This is not to assert that all men are equal in their acquisition of ideas. Certainly they are not. Some try to weave with but a small fraction of the number of ideas they could possess if they would but take advantage of the opportunities life affords; consequently their tapestries are dull and monotonous. But the most learned scholar or the profoundest thinker has never more than a *relatively* few major ideas to work with.

If the mere statement of this fact should tend to discourage anyone, let us remember that the greatest artists of the centuries were compelled to paint their famous masterpieces with only seven basic colors. Their genius enabled them to create innumerable combinations and shades, but never to find any new colors. And the mighty works of a Beethoven or a Donizetti are but a handful of musical tones skillfully combined.

So the creative art of the genius as well as the humbler thoughts of the less endowed minister must move around the familiar circle. And this is true in every field of human thought, including Christian theology. There are, for instance, 150 psalms in our Bible, every one of which is a treasure in itself and inestimably precious to the worshiping heart. Yet if we were to eliminate all repetition we could reduce the whole collection to a mere half dozen or less. The same shining thoughts occur over and over again, as the colors in a painting or the notes in a symphony; but they never tire the mind that is aflame with the love of God; each old sweet thought seems as new and as fresh as if we had discovered it only a moment before.

In the New Testament the same thing is true. Were some critic to decide arbitrarily that he would not permit Paul to express the same idea twice, his thirteen epistles could be shortened from the eighty pages they now occupy in the average English Bible to a surprising few. Yet no Christian would think of permitting such an outrage. We want all the Pauline Epistles left just as they are. The ideas they contain are not many but they are like the pillars that uphold the universe, and up out of them rises the mighty soaring temple of Christian doctrine in whose shadow men have for centuries lived their joyous lives and for whose sake they have gladly laid their lives down when necessary.

Again, the hymnal reveals the same wealth of beauty growing up in wild profusion out of a few root ideas. Look at the index of any well-edited hymnal and you will see that the hymns found there cover a relatively few topics: God, Christ, the Holy Spirit, the cross, the resurrection, etcetera. Examine any hymn, or ten hymns or one hundred, for actual theological ideas, and you will find only a few; but when combined and applied to human needs or offered as a lyric expression of loving worship these few ideas are all we need for this world and the next. So we sing in happy circles, and the recurrence of the familiar instead of boring us actually serves to delight us like the sight of home after a short time away.

Some preachers have such a phobia for repetition and such an unnatural fear of the familiar that they are forever straining after the odd and the startling. The church page of the newspaper almost any Saturday will be sure to announce at least one or two sermon topics so far astray as to be positively grotesque; only by the most daring flight of uncontrolled imagination can any relation be established between the topic and the religion of Christ. We dare not impugn the honesty or the sincerity of the men who thus flap their short wings so rapidly in an effort to take off into the wild blue yonder, but we do deplore their attitudes. No one should try to be more original than an apostle.

Evangelical Snobbery

WE ARE A bad lot, we sons of Adam.

One convincing proof of our inherent badness is the way we manage to turn good into evil and make our very blessings a curse to us. Indeed I think a strong case can be made for the belief that sin is merely righteousness in reverse and evil but perverted good. Sin is at bottom the abuse of things in themselves innocent, an illegitimate use of legitimate gifts.

We Christians are cut from the same bolt as the rest of mankind, and while we have been made partakers of a new nature we have not yet been entirely divested of the old. For this reason we are under constant temptation to lapse into the flesh and manifest the old nature rather than the new. I know the arguments against this, but they have never seemed very convincing to me, especially when those who advance them are as likely as not to reveal pretty plain evidences of the old nature before the argument is ended.

Because we are so very human there is real danger that we may inadvertently do the human thing and turn our blessings upside down. Unless we watch and pray in dead earnest we may turn our good into evil and make the grace of God a trap instead of a benefit.

Among the purest gifts we have received from God is truth. Another gift almost as precious, and without which the first would be meaningless, is our ability to grasp truth and appreciate it. For these priceless treasures we should be profoundly grateful; for them our thanks should rise to the Giver of all good gifts throughout the day and in the night seasons. And because these and all other blessings flow to us by grace without merit or worth on our part we should be very humble and watch with care lest such undeserved favors, if unappreciated, be taken from us.

Men are notoriously lacking in gratitude. Bible history reveals that Israel often took God's gifts too casually and so turned their blessings into a curse. This human fault appears also in the New Testament, and the activities of Christians through the centuries show that as Christ was followed by Satan in the wilderness so truth is often accompanied by a strong temptation to pride. The very truth that makes men free may be and often is fashioned into chains to keep them in bondage. And never forget it: there is no pride so insidious and yet so powerful as the pride of orthodoxy.

Snobbery is the child of pride. Pride at first may be eager and ambitious as it tries to make a place for itself or to prove that it has already attained that place. Later it loses its eager quality and becomes defensive. Finally it ceases to struggle or defend and accepts its own image of itself as something too well established for discussion and too beautiful to improve. When it reaches that stage it has produced a snob, and no snob is ever aware that he is one.

The snob whose claim to superiority is her material possessions is a comical figure, but because she is so pathetic she may with some effort be tolerated. The snob whose glory lies in her ancestors is less easy to endure, but she may be dismissed with the remark that since all she has to be proud of is her forebears the best part of her is under ground. But what shall we say of the intellectual snob? He is unbearable, a man difficult to love and impossible to like.

A new school of evangelical Christianity has come up of late which appears to me to be in grave danger of producing a prime crop of intellectual snobs. The disciples of this school are orthodox in creed, if by that we mean that they hold the fundamental tenets of the historic faith; but right there the similarity of their school to New Testament Christianity ends. Their spirit is quite other than the spirit of the Early Church.

This new breed of Christian may be identified by certain field marks. One is the habit of puffing out the chest and uttering a noise that sounds suspiciously like crowing. Another is the habit of nesting so high that ordinary Christians have difficulty in locating the aerie, and when they do they are unable to climb to it. Then, the song is also quite noticeable in that it consists almost wholly of imitations. Rarely does one of them manage to give forth an original note, but each one waits to hear what Barth or Brunner or Bultmann or Tillich has to say and then imitates it as nearly as possible, only transposing it into the orthodox key. Their mating call is a shrill "Me too! Me too!" which may be heard any time between September and June ringing through the halls of various institutions of evangelical higher learning.

What is overlooked by this new school is that truth is not mental only but moral. The Apostles' Creed quoted in pride, though true, is not true for the one who thus quotes it; one indispensable quality is missing—humility. A theological fact becomes a spiritual truth only when it is received by a humble mind. The proud mind, however orthodox, can never know spiritual truth. Light means nothing to a blind man.

In the Christian life we know most when we know that we do not know, and we understand best when we know that we understand little and that there is much that we will never understand. In the Scriptures knowledge is a kind of experience and wisdom has a moral content. Knowledge without humility is vanity. The religious snob is devoid of truth. Snobbery and truth are irreconcilable.

I Believe in the Brotherhood of Man

CENTURIES before the present highly self-conscious and, in some quarters, legally enforced love feast between the races began, the apostle Paul, a Jew, was saying to the Greeks at Athens, "God . . . hath made of one blood all nations of men for to dwell on all the face of the earth."

That modern sociological discovery, the unity and equality of all men, is therefore very old hat indeed and not, as claimed, a new, advanced concept and a proof of human progress.

By teaching that all men have a common origin the Bible, as usual, anticipated by several thousand years every sound thing that is being said today about human brotherhood. The Book of Genesis lays down as a historical fact that the human race began with the original pair, Adam and Eve. All that now live or that have ever lived descended from those first parents. According to the Bible, there has not been introduced into the human organism any non-Adamic strain that might have made for basic differences between men and men. Before the Flood of Noah God lumped the human inhabitants of the earth to-

123

gether under the generic title *man*. "And God saw
that the wickedness of man was great in the
earth." After the Flood He again referred to all
peoples as *man*. "Whoso sheddeth man's blood,
by man shall his blood be shed: for in the image
of God made he man."

The subsequent separation of Israel from the
rest of mankind to fulfill the high purposes of God
did not and could not make any biological difference between Jew and Gentile. All men sprang
from the loins of Adam and are born after the
human pattern. While Israel received the adoption
and the glory and the covenants, the giving of
the Law and the service of God and the promises,
and while it was through Israel that the Redeemer
came, yet Israel is biologically one with all the
rest of mankind. Christ recognized this and called
Himself the Son of Man. He came *through* Israel
but He came *to* the race of man.

Fundamentally all men are one. They are all
members of the same order of created life and
can never escape the vital unity that exists between them. No matter how they may war on one
another they are still closer to each other than
they can ever be to any other order of created
life. They are brothers in Adam.

This knowledge does not by any means clear
up the problem of differences that exist between
individuals, races and nations. These differences
are incidental only and lie on the surface of our
common life. Physiologically they have to do with
size, body shape, skull structure and especially
skin color. To these have been added over the
centuries such further differences as political
groupings, languages and social customs. Trifling

as these may be they appear important enough to cause no end of misery among men. Cain still slays Abel and Jacob cheats Esau out of his birthright. So it has always been and so it will always be, let the social dreamers say what they will.

And why must it always be so? Because the human race is morally and spiritually fallen. The much-talked-of human brotherhood is a brotherhood of fallen men. Should the hope expressed in the sticky little song be realized and "the world become one through a prayer" it would still be a lost world. Were the United Nations truly united they would still be but a confederation of nations in rebellion against God.

The very idea of human brotherhood, about which large numbers of pseudo philosophers bleat so plaintively these days, rather than bringing us comfort should throw the fear of God into us, for the apostle Paul was long ago inspired to write: "By one man sin entered into the world, and death by sin; and so death passed upon all men, for that all have sinned." The unity of mankind with itself means universal condemnation for all its members.

Strange as it may seem, hope for all of us lies not in huddling up to the human race but in renouncing allegiance to the world altogether. To put our trust in a brotherhood of condemned men is but to die with them at last.

Highly significant among the words of the Christian message are the little prepositions "from" and "out" and "unto." The first call of the New Testament evangel is to repentance from sin, the next is to separation from the world. Not until the lost man has transferred his hope from human "togetherness" and fixed it upon Christ will he know the joy of sins forgiven and the deep, deep assurance that he has been reconciled to God. He must come out to come unto.

The brotherhood of man is a fact, but it carries with it no hope for the race. Out from this old condemned brotherhood Christ is calling unto Himself a people for His own possession. These are redeemed and regenerated men and women and they are saved by renouncing the original Adamic fellowship, not by cultivating it. Taken together they form a new human race, a brotherhood of ransomed men who are related to and yet separated from the fallen world as the ark of Noah was related to and yet separated from the waters of the Flood.

Midsummer Madness*

AS THE SUN makes its annual climb up from the south a strange restlessness comes over those of our citizens who live north of the Mason-Dixon Line, and by the time summer has finally arrived

---

* This chapter first appeared in *The Alliance Witness* in 1937. Twenty-three years later (1960) it was reprinted because, said Dr. Tozer, "apparently it had little or no effect, for the

this has increased into a pathological condition which turns the country into one vast cage of waltzing mice. A kind of madness grips the populace, and then begins that four-month frenzied effort on everybody's part to get somewhere other than where he is. No one stops to ask what it is all about, but practically everyone who is not in the hospital or in jail joins the general stampede from everywhere to anywhere and return.

An irresistible impulse picks most of us up like grains of dust caught by the wind, and spins and churns us about dizzily and dangerously till the first frost comes to ripen the pumpkin and drive home the trailers.

The sturdy old deacon who spent his entire life in the same county where he was born has passed and gone forever. He existed before the days of the modern nomad. Changing times have eliminated him as surely as the buggy shed and the hitching post. His chief use now is to decorate a museum along with the three-toed horse and the dinosaur.

His basic error was that he failed to take a vacation. He needed a change and a rest, also a bit of recreation; but not having heard of these wonderful aids to health and longevity, he kept his nose to the grindstone, raised ten healthy children, worked his own farm, attended the Baptist Church four times a week, and managed also to read one or two good books a month. Though he had failed to relax properly at yearly intervals,

conditions it describes have grown increasingly worse year by year. And to make matters still more serious, crippled churches have now been accepted as normal.... When will this abuse end?" The article has been widely circulated during the past ten years, and still bears repeating.

he could still shoot a squirrel out of a chestnut tree at a hundred yards without glasses and chin himself a dozen times running when he was eighty-seven. When he finally died he was mourned sincerely by his family and a host of real neighbors who had learned to appreciate his sterling worth by living beside him for a lifetime.

How anyone can claim that his grandson, who changes apartments every two years and spends his summers roaring through the landscape in a cloud of fumes, is his equal in manly character is beyond comprehension. Goldsmith's famous lines come back to trouble the serious-minded:

"Ill fares the land, to hastening ills a prey,
Where wealth accumulates, and men decay."

Now we believe in liberty as guaranteed by the Constitution and the inalienable right of every man to do as he likes as long as he stays within the law. If most of the population choose to forsake their homes and spend all their spare time scudding between filling stations, there is nothing we can do about it. To protest it is to blow against the wind or shout against the tide. However, some of us old-fashioned throwbacks to a saner if slower age may be forgiven if we indulge in a few honest tears for the havoc this midsummer madness works among the churches of this hectic day.

Even though the vacation habit is a craze and a curse, even though millions each season take long and expensive vacations from nothing more strenuous than loafing, we are still willing to concede that there might be some therapeutic value in a vacation trip where and when needed. I would surely not begrudge the hard-working man or woman a rest from the daily grind.

But the sad truth is that the vacation habit, plus the habit of making weekend trips throughout the summer season, has worked practically to paralyze the church of God for several months out of the year. Some churches close altogether, some are forced to give up evening services for the duration of the summer and many are compelled to join with several other churches in union services in order to have an attendance large enough to justify a meeting. Even full-gospel churches and tabernacles are seriously crippled, the finances go into the red, the morale suffers and faith burns down to a gray ash.

It is hard to understand how a follower of Christ can justify himself in laying down his cross so frequently and so shamelessly in this day of the world's judgment. The army of the Lord is the only army on earth where the soldiers expect a four-month furlough in time of war. It is an ironic fact that in the very months of the year when Satan is the busiest the children of God are the laziest. Hell reaps her harvest during the summer season, while the poor overburdened heirs of the ages crisscross the continent at eighty miles an hour in a grim effort to relax.

If someone should remind me that it is during the summer that the great conventions and camp meetings are held, I would reply that a ten-day period of fun at a camp meeting is a poor substitute for a summer of faithful service back at the home church.

It is a pitiful thing to see on any summer Sunday morning a discouraged Sunday school superintendent standing before the tattered remnant of his school, trying to appear cheerful with half of his teachers missing. And it is a tragicomic sight

129

to see a peripatetic playboy of the church getting down on his knees on a Saturday afternoon to thank God for that prosperity which enables him to desert the house of God more frequently than he was able to do in his leaner years, and pray for "journeying mercies" as he speeds away from his post of duty to commune with nature among sardine cans.

That the church of Christ should so completely succumb to this mid-summer madness is proof enough of our low spiritual condition. It is little wonder that the people of the world smile cynically when we come back and go to work on them after the cool weather sets in. They do not take us seriously, and we have ourselves to thank for their attitude.

We need a revival! We need a revival of consecration to death, a revival of happy abandonment to the will of God that will laugh at sacrifice and count it a privilege to bear the cross through the heat and burden of the day. We are too much influenced by the world and too little controlled by the Spirit. We of the deeper life persuasion are not immune to the temptations of ease and we are in grave danger of becoming a generation of pleasure lovers.

Any who disagree with these conclusions are within their rights, and I would be the last to deny them the privilege. But in the name of a thousand struggling churches and disheartened pastors, may I not plead for a little more loyalty to the local church during this season of difficulty?

May God raise up a people who will consult their pleasures less and the great need more. I know of one successful layman who refuses again and again to take perfectly legitimate pleasure trips because he cannot bring himself to leave his class of adolescent Sunday school boys. May God multiply such men and women among us till the reproach of Egypt is rolled away and man's confidence in us restored.

All Truths Agree in Christ

ALL TRUTH is one and the many truths revealed in the Holy Scriptures are but various facets of the one truth.

The follower of Christ is called upon to embrace all truths and every truth. That is, he must open his heart to God's truth, and having done so he must be prepared to accept all truths and reject none. Where one truth seems to contradict another the wise Christian will not make his choice between them but will believe both and wait for the day of Christ to resolve what appears to be their differences.

Wherever men think and try to express their thoughts two types of mind are clearly revealed, the scientific and the poetic. I do not mean that all men are either poets or scientists; I mean rather that the cast of mind that makes a poet is marked in some men while others have a bent distinctly scientific. The one may never write poetry nor the other engage in scientific pursuits, but the bent is there.

The scientist is concerned with differences, the poet with likenesses. The poet may see the world in a grain of sand; the scientist is more concerned with the number and composition of the grains of sand in the world. I believe not only that this difference is among men, but within each man. In every one of us there is somewhat of both scientist and poet until one gains the ascendancy and crowds the other out. Then we have a man bent only on analysis or a man incapable of analysis, a man altogether scientist or altogether poet—that is, only half a man.

Unfortunately this controversy between the poet and the scientist among men and within each man is found also in the field of religion. The Church of Christ has not escaped the conflict but has been pulled and torn by the play of these contrary forces. Strong leaders have risen to stamp their images upon whole denominations for centuries, and the body of believers has divided where the leaders differed. In one group certain truths have been ignored or suppressed to make greater room for other truths that were felt to be more important; in another the same thing has taken place with an opposite set of truths. Serious cleavage has been the result.

Those who insist upon seeing the world in a grain of sand have their slavish, unthinking followers, and those who go doggedly about the task of counting the grains of sand in the world have theirs. The moral texture and spiritual complexion of the two groups are so completely different from each other that an uninformed but intelligent person who might chance to spend some time with each group could be forgiven for concluding that they drew their beliefs from different Bibles or perhaps even worshiped different gods.

There fell into my hands some time ago a new hymnbook. It came from a far country and looked inviting. I opened it eagerly with the hope of finding some rare psalm or hymn or spiritual song that I had not known before, but my hope was short-lived. The book was published by a Christian group of the sand-counting school of doctrine and I soon discovered that each hymn was a prosaic lesson intended to indoctrinate the user in a narrow, one-eyed view of Christianity. The breath of sacred poesy was absent from the book. It did not mount up on wings as an eagle but walked solemnly and awkwardly along the ground. What original songs it contained were stuffy, joyless, unlovely and weighed down heavily with the half-dozen doctrines this particular group has chosen for constant and monotonous emphasis. Worst of all, many of the old favorite hymns were there but so mangled and emasculated as to be almost unrecognizable. The editors did not play on David's harp; rather they used it as a sledge to hammer hard, angular doctrines into the heads of their followers. They did not intend that the hymns should give the singer joy, only that they should bring him into line and make him correct in his doctrinal position.

I believe the uninspired view of the Christian faith set forth in such a book to be a real tragedy for everyone concerned, but we cannot help things by going to the opposite extreme. We dare not turn our undisciplined imagination loose in the holy place. We dare not bring strange fire to the altar of God. We dare not trust the uninstructed religious teacher who finds equal inspiration in the sunrise and the Book of Romans, who gives to Homer and Shakespeare the same authority that he gives to the prophets and apostles of the Holy Scriptures.

It is necessary that we escape both the shackles of textualism and the irresponsible liberty of soulish emotionalism; that is, the scientist and the poet. To do this we must learn a few simple things:

Words are not truth, but caskets in which the gem of truth is carried. God will hold us responsible for meanings, not for texts only. If God is hard to satisfy He is also easy to please. Love is more important than correct doctrine, though there is no incompatibility between the two: love without right doctrine is sentimentality and right doctrine without love is dead. Our spirits are vaster than our intellects and can penetrate behind the veil where our conscious thoughts cannot come. We may believe all that God has revealed, however self-contradictory it may appear to be, because all truths meet and harmonize in the truth, and the truth makes free.

Faith Without Expectation Is Dead

EXPECTATION AND FAITH, though alike, are not identical. An instructed Christian will not confuse the two.

True faith is never found alone; it is always

accompanied by expectation. The man who believes the promises of God expects to see them fulfilled. Where there is no expectation there is no faith.

It is, however, quite possible for expectation to be present where no faith is. The mind is quite capable of mistaking strong desire for faith. Indeed faith, as commonly understood, is little more than desire compounded with cheerful optimism. Certain writers make a comfortable living promoting that kind of so-called faith which is supposed to create the "positive" as opposed to the negative mind. Their effusions are dear to the hearts of those in the population who are afflicted with a psychological compulsion to believe, and who manage to live with facts only by the simple expedient of ignoring them.

Real faith is not the stuff dreams are made of; rather it is tough, practical and altogether realistic. Faith sees the invisible but it does not see the nonexistent. Faith engages God, the one great Reality, who gave and gives existence to all things. God's promises conform to reality, and whoever trusts them enters a world not of fiction but of fact.

In common experience we arrive at truth by observation. Whatever can be verified by experiment is accepted as true. Men believe the report of their senses. If it walks like a duck, looks like a duck and quacks like a duck it is probably a duck. And if its eggs hatch into little ducks the test is about complete. Probability gives way to certainty; it is a duck. This is a valid way to deal with our environment. No one dare complain about it for everyone does it. It is the way we manage to get on in this world.

But faith introduces another and radically different element into our lives. "By faith we know" is the word that lifts our knowing onto a higher level. Faith engages facts that have been revealed from heaven and by their nature they do not respond to scientific tests. The Christian knows a thing to be true, not because he has verified it in experience but because God has said it. His expectations spring from his confidence in the character of God.

Expectation has always been present in the church in the times of her greatest power. When she believed, she expected, and her Lord never disappointed her. "And blessed is she that believed: for there shall be a performance of those things which were told her from the Lord."

Every great movement of God in history, every unusual advance in the church, every revival, has been preceded by a sense of keen anticipation. Expectation accompanied the operations of the Spirit always. His bestowals hardly surprised His people because they were gazing expectantly toward the risen Lord and looking confidently for His word to be fulfilled. His blessings accorded with their expectations.

One characteristic that marks the average church today is lack of anticipation. Christians when they meet do not expect anything unusual to happen; consequently only the usual happens, and that usual is as predictable as the setting of the sun. A psychology of nonexpectation pervades the assembly, a mood of quiet ennui which the minister by various means tries to dispel, the means depending upon the cultural level of the congregation and particularly of the minister.

One will resort to humor, another will latch on to some topic currently dividing the public, such as fluoridation, capital punishment or Sunday sports. Another who may have a modest opinion of his gifts as a humorist and who is not sure which side of a controversy he may safely support will seek to arouse expectation by outlining enthusiastically the shape of things to come: the Men's Banquet to be held at the Chicken-in-a-Basket Tea Room next Thursday evening; or the picnic with its thrilling game to be played between the Married Men and the Single Men, the outcome of which the jocular minister coyly refuses to predict; or the coming premier of the new religious film, full of sex, violence and false philosophy but candied over with vapid moralizings and gentle suggestions that the enraptured viewers should be born again.

The activities of the saints are thus laid out for them by those who are supposed to know what they need better than they do. And this planned play is made acceptable to the more pious-minded by tagging on a few words of devotion at the close. This is called "fellowship," though it bears scant resemblance to the activities of those Christians to which the word was first applied.

Christian expectation in the average church follows the program, not the promises. Prevailing spiritual conditions, however low, are accepted as inevitable. What will be is what has been. The weary slaves of the dull routine find it impossible to hope for anything better.

We need today a fresh spirit of anticipation that springs out of the promises of God. We must declare war on the mood of nonexpectation, and come together with childlike faith. Only then can we know again the beauty and wonder of the Lord's presence among us.

Humility, True and False

FOR THE CHRISTIAN, humility is absolutely indispensable. Without it there can be no self-knowledge, no repentance, no faith and no salvation.

The promises of God are made to the humble: the proud man by his pride forfeits every blessing promised to the lowly in heart, and from the hand of God he need expect only justice.

We should not forget, however, that there is pseudo humility which can scarcely be distinguished from the real thing and which passes commonly among Christians without their being aware that it is false.

True humility is a healthy thing. The humble man accepts the truth about himself. He believes that in his fallen nature dwells no good thing. He acknowledges that apart from God he is nothing, has nothing, knows nothing and can do nothing. But this knowledge does not discourage him, for he knows also that in Christ he is somebody. He knows that he is dearer to God than the apple of His eye and that he can do all things through Christ who strengthens him; that is, he can do all that lies within the will of God for him to do.

Pseudo humility is in truth only pride with a different face. It is evident in the prayer of the man who condemns himself roundly before God as weak, sinful and foolish but who would angrily resent the same thing being said about him by his wife.

Nor is such a man necessarily hypocritical. The prayer of self-condemnation may be completely sincere, and the defense of self as well, though the two appear to contradict each other. Where they are alike is in their being born of the same parents, self-love being the father and self-trust the mother.

The man filled with high self-regard naturally expects great things of himself and is bitterly disappointed when he fails. The self-regarding Christian has the loftiest moral ideals: he will be the holiest man in his church, if not the saintliest one in his generation. He may talk of total depravity, grace and faith, while all the time he is unconsciously trusting self, promoting self and living for self.

Because he has such noble aspirations, any failure to reach his ideals fills him with disappointment and disgust. Then comes the attack of conscience which he mistakenly believes to be evidence of humility but which is in fact no more than a sour refusal to forgive himself for falling below his own high opinion of himself. A parallel is sometimes found in the person of the proud, ambitious father who hopes to see in his son the kind of man he himself had hoped to be and is not, and who when the son fails to live up to his expectation will not forgive him. The father's grief springs not from his love for his son but from love of self.

The truly humble man does not expect to find virtue in himself, and when he finds none he is not disappointed. He knows that any good deed he may do is the result of God's working in him, and if it is his own work he knows that it is not good, however good it may appear to be.

When this belief becomes so much a part of a man that it operates as a kind of unconscious reflex he is released from the burden of trying to live up to his own opinion of himself. He can relax and count upon the Spirit to fulfill the moral law within him. The emphasis of his life shifts from self to Christ, where it should have been in the first place, and he is thus set free to serve his generation by the will of God without the thousand hindrances he knew before.

Should such a man fail God in any way he will be sorry and repent, but he will not spend his days castigating himself for his failure. He will say with Brother Lawrence: "I shall never do otherwise if You leave me to myself; it is You who must hinder my falling and mend what is amiss," and after that "give himself no further uneasiness about it."

It is when we read the lives and writings of the saints that false humility becomes particularly active. We read Augustine and know that we have not his intellect; we read Bernard of Clairvaux and feel a heat in his spirit which is not in our own in anything like equal degree; we read the journal of George Whitefield and are forced to confess that compared with him we are mere beginners, spiritual tyros, and that for all our supposed "busy lives" we get little or nothing accomplished. We read the letters of Samuel Rutherford and feel that his love for Christ so far outstrips our own that it would be folly to mention the two in the same breath.

It is then that pseudo humility goes to work in the name of true humility and brings us to the dust in a welter of self-pity and self-condemnation. Our self-love turns on us angrily and reproaches us in great bitterness for our lack of godliness. Let us be careful here. What we believe to be penitence may easily be a perverted form of envy and nothing more. We may simply envy these mighty men and despair of ever equaling them and imagine we are very saintly for feeling cast down and discouraged.

I have met two classes of Christians: the proud who imagine they are humble and the humble who are afraid they are proud. There should be another class: the self-forgetful who leave the whole thing in the hands of Christ and refuse to waste any time trying to make themselves good. They will reach the goal far ahead of the rest.

Let's Break That "Guilty Silence"

ONE OF THE GREAT SAINTS of the past, in a well-known hymn, calls on his tongue to break its "guilty silence" and praise the Lord.

The logic behind the stanza is that if it is right

to praise God it is wrong not to praise Him and for that reason the tongue that is silent is sinful. Dr. R. A. Torrey taught that, since the greatest commandment is to love God, the greatest sin is failure to love Him. Such sins as not praising and not loving are called "sins of omission" because no positive act has been committed. The guilt lies in what is *not* done and might be designated as passive guilt rather than active. But though passive, it is nonetheless real.

Under the Law of Moses a man could incur guilt by keeping still about some evil he knew was present in the camp of the Lord, and in the New Testament James tells us bluntly, "Therefore to him that knoweth to do good, and doeth it not, to him it is sin." Is it not a serious thought that many clean-living, decent persons, against whom no overt act of wrongdoing can be charged, may yet be deeply guilty and inwardly stained with the sin that does not show, the sin of silence and inaction? There are moral situations where it is immoral to say nothing and basely immoral to do nothing.

The Bible has much to say in praise of prudence and circumspection, but it has nothing but condemnation for the coward. It is plainly taught in the New Testament that the soul that is too timid to own Christ before men on earth will be denied before the Father who is in heaven. And in the Book of the Revelation the fearful are classed with the unbelievers, the murderers, the whoremongers, the sorcerers, the liars, and all are relegated to the lake which burneth with fire and brimstone. Obviously moral cowardice is a sin, a grave and deeply injurious sin.

The fear that keeps us quiet when faith and

love and loyalty cry out for us to speak is surely evil and must be judged as evil before the bar of eternal justice. The fear that prevents us from acting when the honor of God and the good of mankind call for bold action is unalloyed iniquity. God will not overlook it and, if it is persisted in, He will not forgive it.

The sinfulness of silence and inaction is more than academic; it is sharply practical and may impinge upon the soul of any one of us at anytime. Let a moral situation shape itself so that righteousness demands speech and action, and theory becomes practical fact instantly. We have but to keep still and sit tight to become guilty of real sin.

The world situation today is such that sin by silence may be more widespread than at any other time in the history of the world. For the first time in human history a shockingly wicked ideology has been organized into a world conspiracy, shrewd, cruel, inhuman and fanatically determined. Of course, I mean international Communism, the devil's most cunning and most effective imitation of Christianity to date. It is as if the boiling cauldrons of Gehenna had sprung a leak and the noxious vapors had entered the brains of men and turned them into moral cave men without any conscience or any sense of common decency. They appear to be possessed and morally demented to a degree known nowhere else on earth. These men, though numerically few, yet constitute a threat to the world so grave, so deadly, that nothing else on earth can be compared to it.

Standing as we do under the shadow of such a mighty evil, how can any informed person be still? How can any member of the non-Communist world be indifferent as he sees every value that differentiates man from the beasts being destroyed and every spiritual quality that makes life worth the living being extinguished? The statesman who refuses to take sides has already taken sides. His tolerance has made him a traitor to his own country and to the human race.

Serious as all this may be, there is something more serious still. It is the failure to take sides and to speak up when the enemy stalks into the very sanctuary and pollutes the holy place. Precious as human values may be, such values as freedom and decency and the dignity of the individual, divine values, are infinitely more precious. As high as is the heaven above the earth so great are the spiritual treasures revealed to us by the inspiration of the Spirit and secured to us by the blood of the everlasting covenant. The wisdom of God contained in the message and practice of the redemptive revelation is above a king's ransom. "For the merchandise of it is better than the merchandise of silver, and the gain thereof than fine gold. She is more precious than rubies: and all the things thou canst desire are not to be compared unto her. Length of days is in her right hand; and in her left riches and honour. Her ways are ways of pleasantness, and all her paths are peace" (Prov. 3:14-17).

At this hour in world history the state of religion is such that the church is in grave danger of losing this priceless treasure. Her gold is being turned to copper and her diamonds to glass. The religion of Cain is now in the ascendancy—and marching under the banner of the cross. Even among those who make a great noise about believing the Bible, that Bible has virtually no practical influence left. Fiction, films, fun, frolic, religious entertainment, Hollywood ideals, big business techniques and cheap, worldly philosophies now overrun the sanctuary. The grieved Holy Spirit broods over the chaos but no light breaks forth. "Revivals" come without rousing the hostility of organized sin and pass without raising the moral level of the community or purifying the lives of professing Christians. Why?

Could it be that too many of God's true children, and especially the preachers, are sinning against God by guilty silence? When those whose eyes are opened by the touch of Christ become vocal and active God may begin to fight again on the side of truth. I for one am waiting to hear the loud voices of the prophets and reformers sounding once more over a sluggish and drowsy church.

They'll pay a price for their boldness, but the results will be worth it.

A Christian and His Money

THE WHOLE QUESTION of the believer and his money is so involved and so intimate that one hesitates to approach a consideration of it. Yet it is of such grave importance that one who desires to qualify as a good servant of Christ dare not avoid it lest he be found wanting in the day of reckoning. Someone should tackle the problem in the light of Scripture. God's people will have reason to thank the man who has the courage to deal with it.

Four considerations should govern our Christian giving. They are: (1) That we give systematically; (2) that we give from a right motive; (3) that we give enough in proportion to what we possess, and (4) that we give to the right place or places.

First, we should see to it that we give of our substance to the Lord with regularity. It is so very easy to fall into the habit of forgetting to do this. We tell ourselves that we are not able to give at the moment, but that when we are better fixed financially we shall catch up on our giving. Or we assure ourselves that while we do not give systematically we no doubt give far beyond our tenth, if the truth were known. These are sure ways to deceive ourselves. Spotty, unsystematic giving has a way of appearing far greater than it is. We would likely be quite shocked if we took the trouble to find out just how little we really give that way.

Then we must give from a right motive. Money paid to a church or missionary society may be for the giver money wasted unless he first makes sure that his heart is in his gift. Gifts that do not carry the heart with them may do the receiver some good, but it is certain that they will bring the giver no reward. "Though I bestow all my goods to feed the poor . . . and have not charity (love), it profiteth me nothing."

Then it is also important that we give enough in proportion to what we possess. The story of the widow and her two mites makes this very clear. The widow gave out of her "poverty," and though her gift was small it was in the sight of God a far greater treasure than all the huge sums donated by the rich "out of their abundance." This is a solemn warning and we shall do well to heed it.

We humans judge "after the sight of our eyes" and so are prone to make a great deal over a large donation and pass over the small ones without comment. By so doing we are letting ourselves in for a fearful shock in the day of Christ. The safest rule to appraise our giving and determine our expectations in the day of rewards is this: Remember, *my giving will be rewarded not by how much I gave but by how much I had left.* Ministers are sometimes tempted to shy away from such doctrine as this lest they offend the important givers in their congregation. But it is better to offend men than to grieve the blessed Spirit of God which dwells in the church. No man ever yet killed a true church by withdrawing his gifts from it because of a personal pique. The Church of the Firstborn is not dependent upon the patronage of men. No man has ever been able really to harm a church by boycotting it financially. The moment we admit that we fear the displeasure of the carnal givers in our congregations we admit also that our congregations are not of heaven but of the earth. A heavenly church will enjoy a heavenly and supernatural prosperity. She cannot be starved out. The Lord will supply her needs.

147

That we place our gifts intelligently is also of vital importance if we would please our Heavenly Father and save those gifts from the fate of "wood, hay and stubble" at the coming of our Lord.

The matter of where to give is a large one, and one that we had all better settle while we can. Careless, unintelligent and prejudiced giving is wasting millions of consecrated dollars among evangelical Christians. Many believers toss their gifts around as if they did not expect to give an account of them to the Lord. They have not found the mind of the Lord on the question of their own giving, so they become the prey of anyone who happens along with an interesting story. In this way innumerable religious rackets are enabled to flourish which should never receive one cent from serious-minded and God-honoring people.

Now, we are quite aware that the reply to the above could be a polite request that we stay in our own back yard and let people put their own money where they please; after all it is theirs, and what they do with it is their own affair. But it is not that simple. If we must give account of every idle word, surely we must also give account of every idle dollar. Spotty, prayerless and whimsical giving will come under the just scrutiny of God in the day when He judges every work of men. We can do something about this whole thing now. Very soon it will be too late.

The Dangers of Too Much Liberty

FREEDOM IS PRICELESS. Where it is present almost any kind of life is enjoyable. When it is absent life can never be enjoyed; it can only be endured.

Though millions have died in freedom's defense and though her praise is in everyone's mouth, yet she has been tragically misunderstood by her advocates and sorely wounded in the house of her friends. I think the difficulty lies with our failure to distinguish freedom from liberty, which are indeed sisters but not identical twins.

Freedom is liberty within bounds: liberty to obey holy laws, liberty to keep the commandments of Christ, to serve mankind, to develop to the full all the latent possibilities within our redeemed natures. True Christian liberty never sets us free to indulge our lusts or to follow our fallen impulses.

The desire for unqualified freedom caused the fall of Lucifer and wrought the destruction of the angels that sinned. These sought freedom to do as they willed, and to get it they threw away the beautiful liberty that meant freedom to do the will of God. And the human race followed them in their tragic moral blunder.

To anyone who bothers to think a bit it should be evident that there is in the universe no such thing as absolute freedom. Only God is free. It is inherent in creaturehood that its freedom must be limited by the will of the Creator and the nature of the thing created. The glory of heaven lies in the character of the freedom enjoyed by those who dwell therein. That innumerable company of angels, the general assembly and Church of the First-born and the spirits of just men made perfect are at liberty to fulfill all the broad purposes of God, and this liberty secures for them an infinitely greater degree of happiness than unqualified freedom could do.

Unqualified freedom in any area of human life is deadly. In government it is anarchy, in domestic life free love, and in religion antinomianism. The freest cells in the body are cancer cells, but they kill the organism where they grow. A healthy society requires that its members accept a limited freedom. Each must curtail his own liberty that all may be free, and this law runs throughout all the created universe, including the kingdom of God.

Too much liberty weakens whatever it touches. The corn of wheat can bring forth fruit only as it waives its freedom and surrenders itself to the laws of nature. The robin may fly about all summer enjoying her freedom, but if she wants a nest full of fledglings she must sit for weeks a voluntary captive while the mystery of life gestates beneath her soft feathers. She has her choice: be free and barren or curtail her freedom and bring forth young.

Every man in a free society must decide

whether he will exploit his liberty or curtail it for intelligent and moral ends. He may take upon him the responsibility of a business and a family and thus be useful to the race, or he may shun all obligations and end on Skid Row. The tramp is freer than president or king, but his freedom is his undoing. While he lives he remains socially sterile and when he dies he leaves behind him nothing to make the world glad he lived.

The Christian cannot escape the peril of too much liberty. He is indeed free, but his very freedom may prove a source of real temptation to him. He is free from the chains of sin, free from the moral consequences of evil acts now forgiven, free from the curse of the law and the displeasure of God. Grace has opened the prison door for him, and like Barabbas of old he walks at liberty because Another died in his stead.

All this the instructed Christian knows and he refuses to let false teachers and misguided religionists rivet a yoke of bondage upon his neck. But now what shall he do with his freedom? Two possibilities offer themselves. He may accept his blood-won freedom as a cloak for the flesh, as the New Testament declares that some have done, or he may kneel like the camel to receive his voluntary burden. And what is this burden? The woes of his fellowmen which he must do what he can to assuage; the debt which he along with Paul owes to the lost world; the sound of hungry children crying in the night; the church in Babylonian captivity; the swift onrush of evil doctrines and the success of false prophets; the slow decay of the moral foundations of the so-called Christian nations, and whatever else demands self-sacrifice, cross-carrying, long prayer vigils and courageous witness to alleviate and correct.

Christianity is the religion of freedom and democracy is freedom in organized society, but if we continue to misunderstand this freedom we may soon have neither Christianity nor democracy. To protect political liberty free men must lay a voluntary obligation upon themselves; to preserve the religion of salvation by free grace a great many Christians must waive their right to be free and take upon themselves a load greater than they have ever carried before.

When in danger the state can conscript men to fight for her freedom, but there are no conscripts in the army of the Lord. To bear a cross the Christian must take it up of his own free will. No authority can compel us to feed the hungry or evangelize the lost or pray for revival or sacrifice ourselves for Christ's sake and the sake of suffering humanity.

The ideal Christian is one who knows he is free to do as he will and *wills* to be a servant. This is the path Christ took; blessed is the man who follows Him.

This World: Playground or Battleground?

THINGS ARE FOR US not only what they are; they are what we hold them to be. Which is to say that our attitude toward things is likely in the long run to be more important than the things themselves.

This is a common coin of knowledge, like an old dime, worn smooth by use. Yet it bears upon it the stamp of truth and must not be rejected because it is familiar.

It is strange how a fact may remain fixed, while our interpretation of the fact changes with the generations and the years.

One such fact is the world in which we live. It is here, and has been here through the centuries. It is a stable fact, quite unchanged by the passing of time, but how different is modern man's view of it from the view our fathers held. Here we see plainly how great is the power of interpretation. The world is for all of us not only what it is; it is what we believe it to be. And a tremendous load of woe or weal rides on the soundness of our interpretation.

Going no further back than the times of the founding and early development of our country we are able to see the wide gulf between our modern attitudes and those of our fathers. In the early days, when Christianity exercised a dominant influence over American thinking, men conceived the world to be a battleground. Our fathers believed in sin and the devil and hell as constituting one force; and they believed in God and righteousness and heaven as the other. These were opposed to each other in the nature of them forever in deep, grave, irreconcilable hostility. Man, so our fathers held, had to choose sides; he could not be neutral. For him it must be life or death, heaven or hell, and if he chose to come out on

God's side he could expect open war with God's enemies. The fight would be real and deadly and would last as long as life continued here below. Men looked forward to heaven as a return from the wars, a laying down of the sword to enjoy in peace the home prepared for them.

Sermons and songs in those days often had a martial quality about them, or perhaps a trace of homesickness. The Christian soldier thought of home and rest and reunion, and his voice grew plaintive as he sang of battle ended and victory won. But whether he was charging into enemy guns or dreaming of war's end and the Father's welcome home, he never forgot what kind of world he lived in. It was a battleground, and many were the wounded and the slain.

That view of things is unquestionably the scriptural one. Allowing for the figures and metaphors with which the Scriptures abound, it still is a solid Bible doctrine that tremendous spiritual forces are present in the world, and man, because of his spiritual nature, is caught in the middle. The evil powers are bent upon destroying him, while Christ is present to save him through the power of the gospel. To obtain deliverance he must come out on God's side in faith and obedience. That in brief is what our fathers thought; and that, we believe, is what the Bible teaches.

How different today: the fact remains the same but the interpretation has changed completely. Men think of the world, not as a battleground but as a playground. We are not here to fight, we are here to frolic. We are not in a foreign land, we are at home. We are not getting ready to live, we are already living, and the best we can do is to rid ourselves of our inhibitions and our frustrations and live this life to the full. This, we believe, is a fair summary of the religious philosophy of modern man, openly professed by millions and tacitly held by more multiplied millions who live out that philosophy without having given verbal expression to it.

This changed attitude toward the world has had and is having its effect upon Christians, even gospel Christians who profess the faith of the Bible. By a curious juggling of the figures they manage to add up the column wrong and yet claim to have the right answer. It sounds fantastic but it is true.

That this world is a playground instead of a battleground has now been accepted in practice by the vast majority of evangelical Christians. They might hedge around the question if they were asked bluntly to declare their position, but their conduct gives them away. They are facing both ways, enjoying Christ and the world too, and gleefully telling everyone that accepting Jesus does not require them to give up their fun, and that Christianity is just the jolliest thing imaginable.

The "worship" growing out of such a view of life is as far off center as the view itself, a sort of sanctified night clubbing without the champagne and the dressed-up drunks.

This whole thing has grown to be so serious of late that it now becomes the bounden duty of every Christian to reexamine his spiritual philosophy in the light of the Bible, and having discovered the scriptural way to follow it, even if to do so he must separate himself from much that he formerly accepted as real but which now in the light of truth he knows to be false.

A right view of God and the world to come requires that we have also a right view of the world in which we live and our relation to it. So much depends upon this that we cannot afford to be careless about it.

We Are Becoming What We Love*

"To be another than I am I must abandon that I am."—Chrysostom.

WE ARE ALL in process of becoming. We have already moved from what we were to what we are, and we are now moving toward what we shall be.

That our character is not solid but fluid is not in itself a disturbing thought. Indeed, the man who knows himself may take great comfort in the realization that he is not fixed in his present state, that he may cease to be what he is ashamed that he has ever been and go on to be "remolded nearer to the heart's desire."

The perturbing thought is not that we are becoming, but *what* we are becoming; not that we are moving, but *toward what* we are moving. For it is not in human nature to move on a horizontal plane; we are either ascending or descending, mounting up or sinking down. When a

---

* This chapter was written for *Eternity* Magazine and is included here with the kind permission of the editors of that magazine.

moral being travels from one to another position it must always be toward the worse or toward the better. This corresponds to a spiritual law revealed in the Revelation: "Let the evil-doer do worse and worse, let the base grow baser and baser, let the upright man be more and more upright, and the man who is holy be more and more holy" (22:11, Goodspeed).

Not only are we all in process of becoming; *we are becoming what we love.* We are to a large degree the sum of our loves and we will of moral necessity grow into the image of what we love most; for love is among other things a creative affinity; it changes and molds and shapes and transforms. It is without doubt the most powerful agent affecting human nature next to the direct action of the Holy Spirit of God within the soul.

What we love is therefore not a small matter to be lightly shrugged off; rather it is of present, critical and everlasting importance. It is prophetic of our future. It tells us what we shall be, and so predicts accurately our eternal destiny.

Loving wrong objects is fatal to spiritual growth; it twists and deforms the life and makes impossible the appearing of the image of Christ in the soul. It is only as we love right objects that we become right, and only as we go on loving them that we continue to experience a slow but continuous transmutation toward the objects of our purified affection.

This furnishes in part (but only in part) a rational explanation for the first and greatest commandment: "Thou shalt love the Lord thy God with all thy heart, and with all thy soul, and with all thy mind."

To become like God is and must be the supreme goal of all moral creatures. This is the reason for their creation, the end apart from which no excuse can be found for their existence. Leaving out of consideration for the moment those strange and beautiful heavenly beings of which we have hints in the Bible but about which we know so little, we concentrate upon the fallen race of mankind. Once made in the image of God we kept not our first estate, but left our proper habitation, consorted with Satan and walked according to the course of this world, according to the prince of the power of the air, the spirit that now worketh in the children of disobedience. But God who is rich in mercy, for His great love wherewith He loved us even when we were dead in sins, provided atonement for us. The supreme work of Christ in redemption is not to save us from hell but to restore us to Godlikeness again, the purpose being stated in Romans 8: "Whom he did foreknow, he also did predestinate to be conformed to the image of his Son" (verse 29).

While perfect restoration to the divine image awaits the day of Christ's appearing, the work of restoration is now going on. There is a slow but steady transmutation of the base metal of human nature into the gold of Godlikeness effected by the faith-filled gaze of the soul at the glory of God in the face of Jesus Christ (2 Cor. 3:18).

Right here we might do well to anticipate a difficulty and try to clear it away, a difficulty that arises from an erroneous conception of love. The problem may be stated this way: Love is whimsical, unpredictable and almost wholly beyond our control. It springs up and burns on or dies of itself. How then can we control our love? How can we direct it toward worthy objects? And particularly, how can we force it to rest on God as the proper and permanent object of its devotion?

Were love indeed unpredictable and beyond our control, these questions could have no satisfactory answers and our outlook would be hopeless. The simple truth is, however, that spiritual love is not the capricious and irresponsible emotion men mistakenly believe it to be. It is the servant of the will and must ever go where it is sent and do what it is told. The romantic phrase "fall in love" has given people the notion that we are perforce victims of the arrows of Cupid and can have no control over our affections. The average young person these days expects to fall in love after the love-in-idleness pattern of Oberon and Titania and be swept away by a tempest of delightful emotions. Unconsciously we extend this concept of love to our relation to our Creator and ask, How can we make ourselves love God supremely?

The answer to this and all related questions is that the love we have for God is not the love of *feeling*, but the love of *willing*. Love is within our power of choice, otherwise we would not be commanded to love God nor be held accountable for not loving Him.

The taking over of the romantic love ideal into our relation to God has been extremely injurious to our Christian lives. The idea that we should "fall in love" with God is ignoble, unscriptural, unworthy of us and certainly does no honor to the Most High God. We do not come to love God by a sudden emotional visitation. Love for God results from repentance, amendment of life and a fixed determination to love Him. As God moves more perfectly into the focus of our hearts our love for Him may indeed rise and swell within us till like a flood it sweeps everything before it.

But we should not wait for this intensity of feeling. We are not responsible to *feel* but we *are* responsible to love, and true spiritual love begins in the will. We should set our hearts to love God supremely, however cold or hard they may seem to be, and go on to confirm our love by careful and happy obedience to His Word. Enjoyable emotions are sure to follow. Bird song and blossoms do not make the spring, but when the spring comes they come with it.

Now I would hasten to disclaim all sympathy with the popular salvation-by-willpower cult. I am in radical disagreement with all forms of quasi-Christianity that depend upon the "latent power within us" or trust to "creative thinking" instead of to the power of God. All these paper-thin religious philosophies break down at the same place—in the erroneous assumption that the stream of human nature can be made to run backward up over the falls. This it can never do. "Salvation is of the Lord."

To be saved a lost man must be picked up bodily by the power of God and raised to a higher level. There must be an impartation of divine life in the wonder of the second birth before the words of the apostle apply to him: "But we all, with open face beholding as in a glass the glory of the Lord, are changed into the same image from glory to glory, even as by the Spirit of the Lord" (2 Cor. 3:18).

It has been established here, I hope, that human nature is in a formative state and that it is being changed into the image of the thing it loves. Men and women are being molded by their affinities, shaped by their affections and powerfully transformed by the artistry of their loves. In the unregenerate world of Adam this produces day-by-day tragedies of cosmic proportions. Think of the power that turned an innocent pink-cheeked boy into a Nero or a Himmler. And was Jezebel always the "cursed woman" whose head and hands the very dogs, with poetic justice, refused to eat? No; once she dreamed her pure girlish dreams and blushed at the thoughts of womanly love; but soon she became interested in evil things, admired them and went on at last to love them. There the law of moral affinity took over and Jezebel, like clay in the hand of the potter, was turned to the deformed and hateful thing the chamberlains threw down from the window.

For His own children our Heavenly Father has provided right moral objects for admiration and love. These are to God as the colors in the rainbow round about the throne. They are not God but they are nearest to God; we cannot love Him without loving them and as we love them we are enabled to love Him more. What are they?

The first is *righteousness*. Our Lord Jesus loved righteousness and hated iniquity (Heb. 1:9), and for this reason God anointed Him with the oil of gladness above His fellows. Here the pattern is fixed. To love is also to hate. The heart that is drawn to righteousness will be repulsed by iniquity in the same degree, and this moral repulsion is hate. The holiest man is the one who

161

loves righteousness most and hates evil with the most perfect hatred.

The next is *wisdom.* From the Greeks we take the word "philosophy," the love of wisdom, but before the Greek philosophers were the Hebrew prophets and their concept of wisdom was loftier and more spiritual than anything known in Greece. The wisdom literature of the Old Testament—Proverbs, Ecclesiastes (and to some degree the Psalms)—breathes with a love of wisdom unknown even to Plato.

So high do the Old Testament writers place wisdom that sometimes we can scarcely distinguish the wisdom that comes from God from the wisdom that is God. The Hebrews anticipated by some centuries the Greek idea of God as essential wisdom, though their concept of wisdom was less intellectual than moral. To them the wise man was the good man, the godly man, and wisdom at its noblest reaches was to love God and keep His commandments. The Hebrew thinker could not divorce wisdom from righteousness. Two of the greatest of the apocryphal books, *Wisdom of Solomon* and *Ecclesiasticus,* celebrate the wisdom that consorts with righteousness with an eloquence that is sometimes equal to that of the canonical Scriptures.

Another object for Christian love to fix upon is *truth,* and again we have difficulty separating the truth of God from God Himself. Christ said, "I am the truth," and in so saying joined truth and the Deity in inseparable union. To love God is to love truth, and to love truth with steadfast ardor is to grow toward the image of truth and away from the lie and the error.

It is unnecessary to name or try to name all the other good and holy things God has approved as our models. The Bible sets them before us— mercy, kindness, purity, humility and many more, and the Spirit-taught souls will know what to do about them.

The sum of it all seems to be that we should cultivate interest in and love for the morally beautiful. Was that why Paul wrote to the Philippians (4:8): "Finally, brethren, whatsoever things are true, whatsoever things are honest, whatsoever things are just, whatsoever things are pure, whatsoever things are lovely, whatsoever things are of good report; if there be any virtue, and if there be any praise, think on these things"?

The Waning Authority of Christ in the Churches*

HERE IS THE BURDEN of my heart; and while I claim for myself no special inspiration I yet feel that this is also the burden of the Spirit.

If I know my own heart it is love alone that

---

* This article appeared in *The Alliance Witness* May 15, 1963, just two days after the death of Dr. Tozer. In a sense it was his valedictory, for it expressed the concern of his heart. Because of its wide acceptance it has been included in this selection.

moves me to write this. What I write here is not the sour ferment of a mind agitated by contentions with my fellow Christians. There have been no such contentions. I have not been abused, mistreated or attacked by anyone. Nor have these observations grown out of any unpleasant experiences that I have had in my association with others. My relations with my own church as well as with Christians of other denominations have been friendly, courteous and pleasant. My grief is simply the result of a condition which I believe to be almost universally prevalent among the churches.

I think also that I should acknowledge that I am myself very much involved in the situation I here deplore. As Ezra in his mighty prayer of intercession included himself among the wrongdoers, so do I. "O my God, I am ashamed and blush to lift up my face to thee, my God: for our iniquities are increased over our head, and our trespass is grown up unto the heavens." Any hard word spoken here against others must in simple honesty return upon my own head. I too have been guilty. This is written with the hope that we all may turn unto the Lord our God and sin no more against Him.

Let me state the cause of my burden. It is this: *Jesus Christ has today almost no authority at all among the groups that call themselves by His name.* By these I mean not the Roman Catholics nor the liberals, nor the various quasi-Christian cults. I do mean Protestant churches generally, and I include those that protest the loudest that they are in spiritual descent from our Lord and His apostles, namely, the evangelicals.

It is a basic doctrine of the New Testament that after His resurrection the Man Jesus was declared by God to be both Lord and Christ, and that He was invested by the Father with absolute Lordship over the church which is His Body. All authority is His in heaven and in earth. In His own proper time He will exert it to the full, but during this period in history He allows this authority to be challenged or ignored. And just now it is being challenged by the world and ignored by the church.

The present position of Christ in the gospel churches may be likened to that of a king in a limited, constitutional monarchy. The king (sometimes depersonalized by the term "the Crown") is in such a country no more than a traditional rallying point, a pleasant symbol of unity and loyalty much like a flag or a national anthem. He is lauded, feted and supported, but his real authority is small. Nominally he is head over all, but in every crisis someone else makes the decisions. On formal occasions he appears in his royal attire to deliver the tame, colorless speech put into his mouth by the real rulers of the country. The whole thing may be no more than good-natured make-believe, but it is rooted in antiquity, it is a lot of fun and no one wants to give it up.

Among the gospel churches Christ is now in fact little more than a beloved symbol. "All Hail the Power of Jesus' Name" is the church's national anthem and the cross is her official flag, but in the week-by-week services of the church and the day-by-day conduct of her members someone else, not Christ, makes the decisions. Under proper circumstances Christ is allowed to say "Come unto me, all ye that labour and are heavy laden" or "Let not your heart be troubled," but when the speech is finished someone else takes over. Those in actual authority decide the moral standards of the church, as well as all objectives and all methods employed to achieve them. Because of long and meticulous organization it is now possible for the youngest pastor just out of seminary to have more actual authority in a church than Jesus Christ has.

Not only does Christ have little or no authority; His influence also is becoming less and less. I would not say that He has none, only that it is small and diminishing. A fair parallel would be the influence of Abraham Lincoln over the American people. Honest Abe is still the idol of the country. The likeness of his kind, rugged face, so homely that it is beautiful, appears everywhere. It is easy to grow misty-eyed over him. Children are brought up on stories of his love, his honesty and his humility.

But after we have gotten control over our tender emotions what have we left? No more than a good example which, as it recedes into the past, becomes more and more unreal and exercises less and less real influence. Every scoundrel is ready to wrap Lincoln's long black coat around him. In the cold light of political facts in the United States the constant appeal to Lincoln by the politicians is a cynical joke.

The Lordship of Jesus is not quite forgotten among Christians, but it has been relegated to the hymnal where all responsibility toward it may be comfortably discharged in a glow of pleasant religious emotion. Or if it is taught as a theory in the classroom it is rarely applied to practical living. The idea that the Man Christ Jesus has absolute and final authority over the whole church and over all of its members in every detail of their lives is simply not now accepted as true by the rank and file of evangelical Christians.

What we do is this: We accept the Christianity of our group as being identical with that of Christ and His apostles. The beliefs, the practices, the ethics, the activities of our group are equated with the Christianity of the New Testament. Whatever the group thinks or says or does is scriptural, no questions asked. It is assumed that all our Lord expects of us is that we busy ourselves with the activities of the group. In so doing we are keeping the commandments of Christ.

To avoid the hard necessity of either obeying or rejecting the plain instructions of our Lord in the New Testament we take refuge in a liberal interpretation of them. Casuistry is not the possession of Roman Catholic theologians alone. We evangelicals also know how to avoid the sharp point of obedience by means of fine and intricate explanations. These are tailor-made for the flesh. They excuse disobedience, comfort carnality and make the words of Christ of none effect. And the essence of it all is that Christ simply could not have meant what He said. His teachings are accepted even theoretically only after they have been weakened by interpretation.

Yet Christ is consulted by increasing numbers of persons with "problems" and sought after by those who long for peace of mind. He is widely recommended as a kind of spiritual psychiatrist with remarkable powers to straighten people out. He is able to deliver them from their guilt complexes and to help them to avoid serious psychic traumas by making a smooth and easy adjustment to society and to their own ids. Of course this strange Christ has no relation whatever to the Christ of the New Testament. The true Christ is also Lord, but this accommodating Christ is little more than the servant of the people.

But I suppose I should offer some concrete proof to support my charge that Christ has little or no authority today among the churches. Well, let me put a few questions and let the answers be the evidence.

What church board consults our Lord's words to decide matters under discussion? Let anyone reading this who has had experience on a church board try to recall the times or time when any board member read from the Scriptures to make a point, or when any chairman suggested that the brethren should see what instructions the Lord had for them on a particular question. Board meetings are habitually opened with a formal prayer or "a season of prayer"; after that the Head of the Church is respectfully silent while the real rulers take over. Let anyone who denies this bring forth evidence to refute it. I for one will be glad to hear it.

What Sunday school committee goes to the Word for directions? Do not the members invariably assume that they already know what they are supposed to do and that their only problem is to find effective means to get it done? Plans, rules, "operations" and new methodological techniques absorb all their time and attention. The prayer before the meeting is for divine help to carry out their plans. Apparently the idea that the Lord might have some instructions for them never so much as enters their heads.

Who remembers when a conference chairman brought his Bible to the table with him for the purpose of using it? Minutes, regulations, rules of order, yes. The sacred commandments of the Lord, no. An absolute dichotomy exists between the devotional period and the business session. The first has no relation to the second.

What foreign mission board actually seeks to follow the guidance of the Lord as provided by His Word and His Spirit? They all think they do, but what they do in fact is to assume the scripturalness of their ends and then ask for help to find ways to achieve them. They may pray all night for God to give success to their enterprises, but Christ is desired as their helper, not as their Lord. Human means are devised to achieve ends assumed to be divine. These harden into policy, and thereafter the Lord doesn't even have a vote.

In the conduct of our public worship where is the authority of Christ to be found? The truth is that today the Lord rarely controls a service, and the influence He exerts is very small. We sing of Him and preach about Him, but He must not interfere; we worship our way, and it must be right because we have always done it that way, as have the other churches in our group.

What Christian when faced with a moral problem goes straight to the Sermon on the Mount or other New Testament Scripture for the authoritative answer? Who lets the words of Christ be final on giving, birth control, the bringing up of a family, personal habits, tithing, entertainment, buying, selling and other such important matters?

What theological school, from the lowly Bible institute up, could continue to operate if it were to make Christ Lord of its every policy? There may be some, and I hope there are, but I believe I am right when I say that most such schools to stay in business are forced to adopt procedures which find no justification in the Bible they profess to teach. So we have this strange anomaly: the authority of Christ is ignored in order to maintain a school to teach among other things the authority of Christ.

The causes back of the decline in our Lord's authority are many. I name only two.

One is the power of custom, precedent and tradition within the older religious groups. These like gravitation affect every particle of religious practice within the group, exerting a steady and constant pressure in one direction. Of course that direction is toward conformity to the status quo. Not Christ but custom is lord in this situation. And the same thing has passed over (possibly to a slightly lesser degree) into the other groups such as the full gospel tabernacles, the holiness churches, the pentecostal and fundamental churches and the many independent and undenominational churches found everywhere throughout the North American continent.

The second cause is the revival of intellectualism among the evangelicals. This, if I sense the situation correctly, is not so much a thirst for learning as a desire for a reputation of being learned. Because of it good men who ought to know better are being put in the position of collaborating with the enemy. I'll explain.

Our evangelical faith (which I believe to be the

true faith of Christ and His apostles) is being attacked these days from many different directions. In the Western world the enemy has forsworn violence. He comes against us no more with sword and fagot; he now comes smiling, bearing gifts. He raises his eyes to heaven and swears that he too believes in the faith of our fathers, but his real purpose is to destroy that faith, or at least to modify it to such an extent that it is no longer the supernatural thing it once was. He comes in the name of philosophy or psychology or anthropology, and with sweet reasonableness urges us to rethink our historic position, to be less rigid, more tolerant, more broadly understanding.

He speaks in the sacred jargon of the schools, and many of our half-educated evangelicals run to fawn on him. He tosses academic degrees to the scrambling sons of the prophets as Rockefeller used to toss dimes to the children of the peasants. The evangelicals who, with some justification, have been accused of lacking true scholarship, now grab for these status symbols with shining eyes, and when they get them they are scarcely able to believe their eyes. They walk about in a kind of ecstatic unbelief, much as the soloist of the neighborhood church choir might were she to be invited to sing at La Scala.

For the true Christian the one supreme test for the present soundness and ultimate worth of everything religious must be the place our Lord occupies in it. Is He Lord or symbol? Is He in charge of the project or merely one of the crew? Does He decide things or only help to carry out the plans of others? All religious activities, from the simplest act of an individual Christian to the ponderous and expensive operations of a whole denomination, may be proved by the answer to the question, Is Jesus Christ Lord in this act? Whether our works prove to be wood, hay and stubble or gold and silver and precious stones in that great day will depend upon the right answer to that question.

What, then, are we to do? Each one of us must decide, and there are at least three possible choices. One is to rise up in shocked indignation and accuse me of irresponsible reporting. Another is to nod general agreement with what is written here but take comfort in the fact that there are exceptions and we are among the exceptions. The other is to go down in meek humility and confess that we have grieved the Spirit and dishonored our Lord in failing to give Him the place His Father has given Him as Head and Lord of the Church.

Either the first or the second will but confirm the wrong. The third if carried out to its conclusion can remove the curse. The decision lies with us.